The Cheeky Guide to Student Life
Written and researched by David Bramwell, Brian Mitchell, Dave Mounfield, Joseph Nixon and Steve Law.
Edited by David Bramwell
Designed by Jeremy Plotnikoff

Business enquiries: jeremy@cheekyguides.com
For comments or editorial enquiries: david@cheekyguides.com

ISBN 0 9536110 35

Published in 2003 by Cheekyguides Ltd
72 Buckingham Road Brighton BN1 3RJ
www.cheekyguides.com

Acknowledgements:
Thanks to the students of Nottingham Trent University, Portsmouth University, Sheffield University and Sussex University for all their help, particularly:
Nikki and Tom, Anick Landau, Hannah Cooper, Vicci Stratton and Jen Warren. Thanks also to the Student Union team at Sussex University for answering umpteen questions and allowing us to photograph them all in the nude.

Thanks to the following contributors:
Kirsty Gascoin, Polly Tuckett, Joanna Neary, Gwyn Williams, Katie Clarke, Martin Johnson, Dave Robinson, Dr Alex Berardi and Daniel Menhinnitt. And special thanks to Nadya Kassam from the NUS for helping with data.

Illustrations
Enormous thanks again to Lisa Holdcroft for the front and back cover and countless illustrations inside this book. Not only is Lisa able to draw misshapen penises, severed ears and doctors performing anal examinations, but she is pretty good on the Penny Whistle too. She is available for freelance work and can be contacted on: (01273) 705658 lj.holdcroft@virgin.net

'Halls of Residence Parts 1-3', 'Student Experience' and 'Irony Free Zone' were drawn by Brighton University Arts Graduate and award-winning illustrator Richard Cowdry. He can be contacted at richardcowdry@hotmail.com or rmcowdry@aol.com and would love to hear from anyone who is interested in comics or wants to use his work.

Proof-Reading
Ably supplied by coffee house aficionado and lounge-lizard Michael Keane.

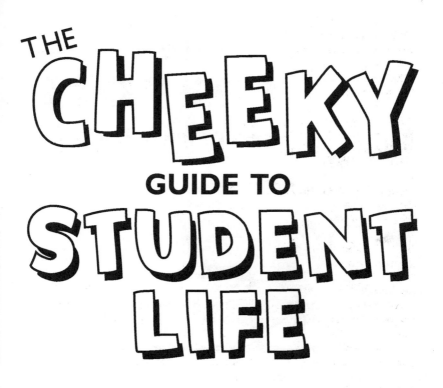

THE CHEEKY GUIDE TO STUDENT LIFE

Written and researched by David Bramwell, Brian Mitchell,
Dave Mounfield, Joseph Nixon and Steve Law.

Edited by David Bramwell

About the Creators of this Book

Richard Hadfield
The Chief

Jeremy Plotnikoff
Financial Director

Picture Researcher
Ciggy Machine

David Bramwell
Words, editing and photography

Cheeky History

Cheekyguides Ltd are a small independent publishing company set up in 1999 by three friends. Our aim has always been to produce honest, humorous and informative guidebooks, free from censorship and corporate sponsors. This book was written and researched based on our travels and discussions with countless students from various universities around the UK, together with recollections of our own experiences and hugely subjective vision of how to make the best of your time at university. We welcome all comments, ideas, and tales of your own university experiences and, wherever possible, will endeavour to include them in the second edition of this book. E-mail *david@cheekyguides.com*

The Authors are:

David Bramwell

David studied Geography at Coventry University on the grounds that it was the only thing he could find through clearing. His most memorable incident was getting a part-time job behind the bar at a local strip club and feeling strangely inadequate whenever 'Donkey Dick from Jamaica' was on stage. While at university he devoted all of his time to playing in bands and even wangled a record deal in the States soon after he left, though as he has to make his living editing this rubbish, you can guess how many records he sold. He has never found any use whatsoever for his Geography Degree and still doesn't know what the capital of Paraguay is.
He got a 2:2

Joseph Nixon

Joseph attended The University of Essex the only university that would take him with his lamentable A level results – where he studied American Literature. He managed to get through his entire university career without joining any clubs, societies or groups but did develop his interest in scriptwriting, which lead to him (along with Brian) to write for 'Live and Kicking' (just before it went down the pan). He and Brian are probably the only two people in the world to have written for both Basil Brush and Jerry Sadowitz.
He got a 2:2.

Brian Mitchell

Brian attended Sussex University where he studied music. His most memorable incident was embezzling The Poetry Society's entire budget to put out a collection of his own verse, 'Nice Poems' (of which there are still several thousand copies left). At university he became

interested in writing and performing and in 2001 Brian co-wrote and starred in his own ITV sketch show 'Slightly Filthy' (but would like to add that the name wasn't his idea). The only thing his degree did for him was to give him a grounding in music that allowed him to write a musical about biscuits that toured the South-East. No, really.
He got a 2:2.

David Mounfield

David studied English literature at Sussex University. While at uni David developed a passion for acting and comedy, which has subsequently ruined his life. Despite having been a regular on the Jerry Sadowitz vs the People show on Channel 5 and having appeared on stage alongside the lovely Felicity Kendall in the West End, he is still only ever recognised on the street as 'that bloke from the Iceland ad'.
He got a 2:1 (by mistake, and would like to thank the person who got his third for not complaining).

Stephen Law

Steve attended Sussex University, spending his time dabbling in mysticism and the occult when he really should have been reading up on Sociology.
In his first year, he distinguished himself in the halls of residence by driving a female student to within an inch of madness by constantly leaving his tonenail clippings in the soap dish. Now a computer whizz-kid and married man, Steve's indulgences in the Dark Arts are still tolerated by his wife, but only after he's done the washing-up and swept the patio.
He got a 2:1 (after threatening to turn his personal tutor into a newt).

CONTENTS

ACCOMMODATION 115

Finding housing in the first year • Furnishings • Decorating your first room • Getting a place in the second year • Contracts • Terminology • Choosing who to live with • Flatmate crimes • House meetings • Shabitat's new range of student furniture • Wildlife spotter's guide • House parties • House horror stories • Safety and repairs

MONEY & JOBS 143

Coping with the bank • Credit cards • Cheating money out of the cash dispenser • Getting blacklisted • Extra funding • Money saving scams • Charity shopping • Budgeting • Student jobs • Strange and seedy jobs • Jobs to avoid

FOOD 167

Your local supermarket • Shopping tips • Fridge rules • A crash course in nutrition • Recipes from the authors • Dinner parties • Food horror stories • Cookbooks & websites • Vegetarianism

ALCOHOL 189

Drinking games • Strange brew • Lost weekends • Getting drunk on the cheap • Hangovers and hangover cures

SMOKING 207

Different brands • The ashtray shimmy • The Marlboro conspiracy • Styles of smoking • Concealing your smoking habit from your parents • Giving up

DRUGS 221

Cannabis • Rolling your first joint • Hash brownies • Cocaine • Ecstasy • Speed • Heroin • Ketamine • The U.F.O experience • Poppers • Types of drug dealers • A brief history of psychedelics • Tripping tips • LSD • Magic mushrooms • Drug myths and household highs • Herbal highs • Books and comedy

SEX, LOVE & RELATIONSHIPS 263

Good and bad societies for sex • Faking a sexual C.V. • Ditching your childhood sweetheart • Types of student couples • Unrequited love • International relationships • Sex horror stories • Coming out

7

CONTENTS

HOW TO USE THIS BOOK

Where appropriate, the chapters of this book each finish with a brief section
entitled – 'Don't Suffer in Silence.' These have been included as your first port of
call, should you find yourself needing immediate practical no-nonsense advice, with
regard to problems concerning, for example, your finances, health, accommodation
etc. This is not to suggest that the rest of the book's content is a load of rambling,
useless nonsense (though some would disagree) but owing to its sheer bulk and
exhaustive information, these sections will point you in the right direction for finding
the help you need, without having to plough through endless crap about how to
make a vegetarian pie or the natural habitat of the hyaena.

In contrast the back of the book includes a pretty comprehensive index, in case you
do immediately need to know, more fascinating facts about this scavenging mammal.

'This place is the devil, or at least his principle residence, they call it the university but any other appellation would have suited it much better, for study is the last pursuit of the Society: the Master eats, drinks and sleeps, the fellows drink, dispute and pun, the employment of the undergraduates you will probably conjecture without my description…'
Lord Byron

'A lecture is a process by which the notes of the professor become the notes of the students without passing through the minds of either.'
R. K. Rathbun

'If you feel that you have both feet planted on level ground, then the university has failed you.'
Robert Goheen (*Time Magazine*, 23 June 1961)

'A professor is someone who talks in someone else's sleep.'
W. H. Auden

'The aim of education should be to teach us rather how to think, than what to think – rather to improve our minds, so as to enable us to think for ourselves, than to load the memory with thoughts of others.'
Bill Beattie

'You want either a first or third. There is no value in anything between. Time spent on a good second is time thrown away…'
Evelyn Waugh (from *Brideshead Revisited*)

'Education is an admirable thing, but it is well to remember from time to time that nothing worth knowing can be taught.'
Oscar Wilde

'Be who you are and say what you feel, because those who mind don't matter and those who matter don't mind.'
Dr. Seuss

THEY HERD 'EM IN AND THEY HERD 'EM OUT. AS ONE GROUP STUMBLES WINCING INTO THE HARSH LIGHT OF THE "REAL" WORLD, ANOTHER ARE PACKING THEIR CD COLLECTIONS AND PREPARING TO LEAVE THE NEST... THE LATEST IN A LONG LINE TO ENJOY (OR ENDURE) THE...

STUDENT EXPERIENCE

© RICHARD COWDRY 2002

YOUR FIRST WEEK

Leaving home and coming away to university for the first time is very likely to be one of the biggest transformations in your life, somewhat akin to your first day at school. In fact, the two still have much in common; you don't know anybody, you don't know where anything is and you've got a Button Moon poster on your bedroom wall. And though, by now, you should be more in control of your bladder and no longer burst into tears when someone borrows a pen from your pencil case, like that first week at school, you are bound to experience feelings of uncertainty until you find your feet. But rest assured, once you're over that initial hurdle, you'll never look back. In fact, those first few weeks are actually rather a special time in your life. With everyone eager to get to know each other, no work pressures (as of yet), and all the social events on offer, you shall, undoubtedly, forge friendships at this time, which could last the rest of your life. Or at least for a week.

11

THINGS YOU SHOULDN'T FORGET TO PACK

(IN ORDER OF IMPORTANCE)

1) **Your mobile phone**
2) **Condoms**
3) **A Computer/dad's laptop/an abacus**
4) **200 Marlboro Lights**
   (only if you smoke, that is — we're not trying to cajole non-smokers)
5) **A bottle of whisky**
   (lifted from your parents' drinks cabinet)
6) **Filofax/palm pilot**
   (or tatty bit of paper with your friends' phone numbers on it)
7) **TV/Playstation**
8) **Your hi-fi and favourite vinyl/CDs**
9) **Enormous supply of sticky labels for your food**
   (which will be nicked regardless)
10) **A photo-collage of your mates from Sixth Form**
11) **Board games: eg. Twister, Outburst, Pictionary**
12) **Alarm Clock**
13) **A pen**

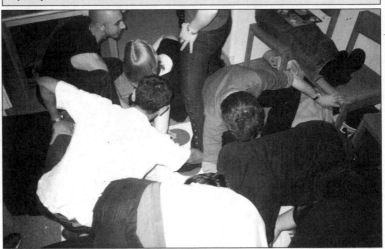

THINGS YOUR PARENTS MIGHT TRY AND GIVE YOU

(to be read in the style of the bloke who announces the conveyor belt prizes on the Generation Game)

...a travel iron ... a Breville sandwich maker ... a pair of carpet slippers ... a cuddly toy ...Tupperware ... tea-towels ... rubber-gloves ... cleaning-products ... hot water bottle ... a briefcase....

When we asked a bunch of students at Sussex University 'what did your parents give you in the first week that you didn't want?', the most common answer was 'crap advice' the most disturbing was 'crabs' and the silliest was 'a perm'.

HIDING YOUR PARENTS ON THE FIRST DAY

One of the problems with your first day at university is that you will, almost inevitably, have to bring your parents with you. After all, who else is going to be kind enough to drive you and your junk on a 500-mile journey to Aberystwyth University, say? But, despite their good intentions, you can, of course, rely on your parents to be *extremely* embarrassing within minutes of your arrival.

Whether you're in halls or shared accommodation, your dad will doubtless, spend the first hour standing around wringing his hands and looking awkward, until your new flat-mates arrive, with whom to your shame, he will try and appear hip by making small-talk about his collection of Dire Straits records, before asking if any of them are 'courting'.

Meanwhile, to your horror, your mum will have produced 17 gallons of bleach from nowhere, and started cleaning your room, the toilet, the kitchen, the stairs and your neighbours' rooms, before moving onto the outside of the building and the pavement.

Forgive them; they are expressing their love in the best way they know. But still, if you can avoid this scenario, all the better. Here are a few suggestions:

1) Tell your parents it is vitally important you arrive at 7am on your first day, as you want to be in your room studying by no later than 9am. This will not only impress them, but allow enough time for your mum to disinfect half of London before any of your room-mates show up.

2) On arrival announce, with a huge exclamation of horror, that you're positive you left the gas on at home **and** the bath-water running.

3) Break the news to them that you're gay. Even if it's not true. Chances are they'll bugger off sharpish to a Little Chef somewhere for a spot of soul-searching.

Just remember, your first day is vital in throwing off that old stuffy image you've been carrying around for the past 18 years, and time to slip into a newer, sexier you. But if, in front of your new flatmates, your mum unexpectedly whips out her hankie, licks it, and wipes a bit of dried banana off your face with the comment – *'Who's a messy Lambikins?'*, you can kiss all that goodbye.

YOUR FIRST FRIEND

In the scary, alienating chaos of your first day, you will be, figuratively speaking, clutching at straws and will therefore, befriend the first person to spare you a kind word, or even a smile. Like two condemned prisoners waiting to die, the two of you will bond instantly, exchanging hopes, fears and secrets. You will sup ale long into the night and part, determined to seek each other out the next day. What happens to such putative friendships can be best expressed as a pie-chart.

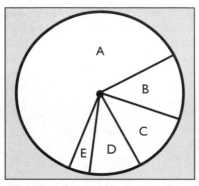

A) 65% – Never see the person again

B) 15% – Meet the next morning, and realize, to your horror, that you have absolutely nothing in common. Leave each other with a few half-hearted avowals to 'get together for a drink sometime.', and then avoid each other like the plague for the rest of the year.

C) 11% – Carry on seeing the person for the next couple of months, gradually recognizing the full extent of your mutual animosity, before the relationship finally withers and dies.

D) 8% – Don't see hide nor hair of them for two years, but a chance encounter through a mutual acquaintance (whom neither of you thought knew the other) resurrects the friendship, which may even outlast university.

E) 1% – Becomes friend for life, with them ending up Best Man/Matron of Honour at your wedding.

"I made my first friend at university while wandering from room to room saying hello to all and sundry. He was called Nadav. For the first week, we shared everything. It was as if I had met my soul brother. Then, he disappeared. The only other time I saw him was two years later, when he wandered into the library with tales of dropping out, drug frenzies and bumming round America. He had changed from a fresh-faced lad to a hard-bitten world travelled lunatic. I never saw him again."

Sheffield University Graduate

TV NOSTALGIA QUIZ

In your first year, knowledge about old Eighties TV shows will prove invaluable in your group bonding sessions with relative strangers. Awkward conversations down the local bar about what you're studying and where you come from can be transformed into bawdy, drunken and passionate discussions about the programmes you remember loving as a kid, with everyone taking it in turns trying to remember theme tunes, quotes and the names of characters. It's great fun and breaks the ice with strangers, but how well do you really know your subject? We challenge your years of wasted youth with the following quiz. Answers on page 373

1. A-Team
No matter how many armoured cars they blew up, Hannibal Smith and team never ever seemed to ever kill anyone, though they did have to drug BA every time they needed to get him on a plane (which was every episode). Can you recall Hannibal's annoying catch-phrase and do you remember which gender-bending Eighties pop star famously appeared in this naff Eighties series?

2. Buffy the Vampire Slayer
This compelling American supernatural high-school drama is still going strong after six years. But can you cast your mind back far enough to remember which character was turned into a rat in season 2, only to briefly re-appear as a human in series 4?

3. Bananaman
Cool theme tune, can you still whistle it? And can you name the Seventies comedy trio who provided the voices?

4. Blackadder
'Baldrick, you are madder than Mad Jack McMad, a mad-man eight times winner of Britain's maddest man competition'. This excellent BBC sitcom ran for 5 series and was, arguably, Rowan Atkinson's finest hour. But think back to series two and see if you can remember what Edmund discovers to be lacking in Tom Baker's trouser department after he is told — *'You have a woman's bottom my lord.'*

5. Button Moon
'Let's put plates on our heads and spoons up our sleeves, we could even visit Button Moon'. What were they on about? In fact, what were they on? This kids programme pushed the boundaries of cheap TV, as everything seemed to be made of washing up bottles, loo rolls and anything they could find in a skip. But, do you know which Doctor Who narrated it?

6. Captain Pugwash
Those stories about Seaman Stains, Roger the Cabin Boy and Master Bates were, unfortunately, only stories, but can you recall who his arch-rival was and what, according to the **rumour**, was Pugwash actually meant to mean??

15

7. Cheers

Hugely popular Boston comedy based in the bar where 'everybody knows your name', and it made Friday nights bearable if you were too baby-faced to get in the pub. But can you remember what unfortunate affliction prevented Cliff from ever going on a date?

Favourite quote — *'What are you up to Norm?'*
'My ideal weight if I was 9 feet tall.'

8. The Crystal Maze

Did you, like us, waste an hour every week of your teenage years watching middle-aged accountants dressed in green dungarees running around in blind panic in a stone cell shouting 'I can't see what to do'? Basically, this show was a huge televised corporate training day aimed at creating team bonding, which it abjectly failed to do. Hosted by faux-sinister baldy Richard O'Brien, can you name the cult film and stage show he penned?

9. Dangermouse

Every university seems to have a student that resembles Penfold, but what links the affable hamster to Edina's mother in 'Absolutely Fabulous'?

10. He-Man

Badly animated, badly dubbed and badly scripted. If you loved it as much as we did you'll remember the cheeky catchphrase that gave He-Man his powers and the name of his mortal enemy.

11. Inspector Gadget

Anyone with extending arms and a helicopter hat naturally deserves having a live-action big-budget film of great emotional intensity and depth made about him. And speaking of great acting, who bared his soul in playing the role of the bandy-legged Cyborg copper?

12. Knightrider

Big-hair, gay car. But which rap act sampled the theme tune?

13. Only Fools and Horses

'By this time next year Rodney we'll be millionaires,' said Del- Boy every year for fifteen years. And then they were. And then it wasn't funny any more. In the theme tune what did God bless and can you name the four things that it didn't have????*

14. Pob

What was his trademark offensive habit?

15. Rainbow

According to the creator of the voices of George and Zippy, the two most common questions he still gets asked are: 'What is Zippy?', and, 'Is George gay?' Perhaps we'll never find out, but do you know what Zippy's nickname for Bungle was?

a) Bunglebonce
b) Hairy trousers
c) Spunk bubble

16. Red Dwarf

Erratically funny but with occasionally brilliant plots, ranging from the one where Rimmer creates a race entirely of himself and becomes emperor, to the one with the polymorph that disguises itself as a kebab and tries to kill Lister. Any real fans of the series should also remember that there were, in fact, two particular episodes where the computer was not called Holly. What were his/her aliases?

17. Star Trek
(the original series)

A masterpiece of high camp, surreal plots and polystyrene planets. And no matter which galaxy they were travelling through, Kirk would always find some planet where he would get his oats with some buxom Sixties chick, before committing genocide and buggering off back to the Enterprise.

Now, you should remember the green dancing woman in the credits, but what was her very unique status in the episode in which she appears???

18. SuperTed

A cruelly discarded teddy bear is visited by Spottyman, a benevolent alien, and given super powers. But who was his arch-enemy?

19. Transformers

Why did robots need to be disguised as sheds and fork-lift trucks anyway? The start of a long road that leads to Pokemon and insidious product placement targeting kids. Which of these items did a transformer actually turn into?

a) Scooter b) Penny Farthing c) Wheelchair d) Plough e) Helicopter f) Sieve

20. Trev and Simon
on 'Going Live'

The duo who coined the phrase 'swing your pants' were the only good reason for watching 'Going Live' on Saturday mornings (unless you were a lonely teenage boy who fancied Zoë Ball). Well-loved and fondly remembered they may be but did you ever actually know which was Trev and which was Simon??

FRESHERS' FAIR

'Freshers' fortnight is two days of collecting leaflets and free pens, followed by two weeks of solid work and heaps of coursework'.

First Year Portsmouth University Student

Held every year at the beginning of term, this long-standing institution is not only a golden opportunity to meet some like-minded people who share your passions, hobbies and perversions, but also a chance for you to discover a few new ones. Usually held in a big space in the Students' Union (invariably called either the Mandela or Robbie Williams Hall), Freshers' Fair is a large noisy affair in which every university society sets up a stall of some kind in the aim of persuading you to part with a few quid and join their club. Beware though; for the uninitiated, visiting Freshers' Fair can be somewhat akin to Luke Skywalker's experiences in the bar in Star Wars. Society members will try every trick in the book to get you to part with your parents' hard-earned money. Many will try and bribe you with sweets, some will flirt (Drama Society), a few will plead (the Engineering Society), some will try and hypnotise you (Hypnotist Society), plenty will bore you into submission (Socialist/ Marxist Society), while others might simply resort to violence (Women's Rugby Society).

The Golden rule is: eat all the sweets, grab all the freebies, flirt with all the people you fancy but don't commit to more than a couple of societies on the day; 65% of students drop out of their societies after the first term. So unless you desperately want to join 10 clubs, all of which have limited numbers of places (like Scuba-Diving or Five-a-side Kerr-Plunk) you can be secure in the knowledge that you can join the others at any time of the year.

The Obligatory Silly Society

A particular favourite of Oxbridge, and other universities with large public school intakes, these 'specialist' societies have been around since the dawn of time, and never seem to have changed their identity. Notable for their 'zany' name (which could be anything from the 'Shaved Hedgehog' to the 'Pickled Carrot Society') they will try to draw you in with the false notion that in joining you will be meeting a subversive collective of anarchic misfits who thrive on absurdity and indulge in the extremities of life.

Don't be fooled. Instead they will, almost unfailingly, consist of groups of nerdy ex-public schoolboys who hang around together drinking real ale, regurgitating verbatim, every single Monty Python and League of Gentlemen sketch, and occasionally blowing raspberries. An example of the dangers of inter-breeding amongst the upper classes they may be, but nature, in her infinite wisdom, has closed the doors to any further reproductive mishaps by making them utterly unattractive to the opposite sex.

Men that join can expect chastity to welcome them with open arms for the entire duration of their college years. Women who join should seek psychiatric help.

THE TRADE FAIR

Usually falling on the same day as (or the day after) Freshers' Fair, the trade fair is, by contrast, a ghastly event where mobile phone companies, newspapers, local nightclubs and other desperados turn up for a spot of whoring. Expect to leave with 4,000 useless fliers, a copy of the Guardian and more sweets. Despite this cynicism, you still ought to pay it a visit, in case there are any genuinely useful freebies being dished out, like loo roll, clean socks and long-life milk. But don't say we didn't warn you.

COMPARING EXAM RESULTS

In your first week it is hard to avoid the fact that, having little in common yet with your new neighbours and acquaintances, after the first few minutes of exchanging pleasantries your conversation may well fall into an abyss. After asking their name and where they come from, your mind will turn to rice pudding, followed by an awkward silence in which, despite yourself, you find yourself uttering those ghastly words – 'so.............*what A level results did you get?*'

This is, of course, understandable and nothing to be ashamed of, unless you are still doing it by your third year. These embarrassing incidents will soon be forgotten, as within just a few days, you and these strangers will be constantly in and out of each other's rooms, day and night, sharing tales of clubbing, all-nighters and wild orgies. Either that, or you will hate the sight of each other by then.

This largely fictitious tradition is kept alive in myth, by Rugger-Buggers and writers of Rag Mags, who entertain the notion that showing a fresher where to catch the nightbus will mean access to their private parts in the first week. To believe that Freshers are gagging to jump into bed with any oily second year who comes prowling round at the bar, and buys them a drink is, primarily, the fantasy of a few select desperate men. Sure, plenty of drunken snogging and one-night stands do take place in the first week, but mostly amongst the lecturers.

Of course, if the opportunity for a steamy one-night stand with a stranger is reciprocated then that's something else entirely. We're sure we can speak for at least some of our fellow men by proclaiming that, as freshers once ourselves, the thought of being corrupted by a sassy and worldy-wise third year drama student was enough to put a rosy glow on our complexions. But there's a difference between a bit of mutual drunken passion, and being taken advantage of, which, ultimately, is something only you can determine.

CHANGING YOUR IDENTITY

C.V.

Name: Jeremy Dickson
Background: Vicar's son from Sevenoaks
Hobbies: Singing in church choir, stamp collecting, watercolours, birdwatching
Favourite Book: Wind in the Willows
Favourite Record: Pirates of Penzance – Gilbert & Sullivan
Favourite Article Of Clothing: Marks and Spencer's cardigan
Drink: Shandy
Favourite Food: Steak and kidney pie
Likes: His parents, country walks, the queen
Dislikes: Scruffy people, left-wingers, loud music
Belongs To: Venture scouts, R.S.P.B., Dennis the Menace fan club, Sealed Knot Society
Friends: Crispin, Toby and Jonathon from the choir
Love Of Life: His mum
Ambition: To spot a great-crested grebe

C.V.

Name: D.J. Jazzy Jez
Background: Claims to be orphan from slums of Manchester
Hobbies: Smoking skunk, magic mushrooms, ley lines
Favourite Book: Fear and Loathing in Las Vegas – Hunter S. Thompson
Favourite Record: Rare white-label pressing of 'Hitler Kiss' by Skin Metallurgy
Favourite Article Of Clothing: Cock ring
Drink: Jack Daniels
Favourite Food: Lentil curry
Likes: Scruffy people, left-wingers, loud music
Dislikes: His parents, country walks, the Queen
Belongs To: Scooby Doo Appreciation Society, Socialist Worker Alliance and Legalize Pot Society
Friends: Rizla Dave, Dodgy Martin, Mr. Natural, Spod, Gandalf
Love Of Life: His turntable and collection of empty beer cans
Ambition: To roll a 24-skinner

Let's face facts, while Oxfam and Dr Barnado's were once de rigueur as student fashion houses, nowadays international high street chains like Gap and H&M, seem to be the primary source of fashion-wear for many.

But, against the tide of increasingly homogeneity there will always be a small band of adventurous souls, for whom university marks a chance for pastures new, and therefore an opportunity for some serious experiments in dress and attitude.

For fledgling bohemians and countless first year art students, it's out with the boring old jeans, t-shirt and spiky haircut of youth, and in with the shaved head, tattoos, genital piercings and obligatory sex change. Last year, one art student at Brighton even went so far as to have his bottom teeth filed into the New York skyline, just to be different. But while experimenting with your look is certainly not something to be ashamed of, beware taking it too far and becoming something you're not…

C.V.

Name: Florence Warner
Background: Both parents are lecturers at Warwick University
Hobbies: Horse-riding, ballet, playing viola, making photo-collages of her mates.
Favourite Book: Bridget Jones' Diary
Favourite Record: The Best of Enya
Favourite Article Of Clothing: Hard rock Café T Shirt
Drink: Pimms
Favourite Food: Vegetarian Lasagne
Likes: Foxhunting, Hugh Grant, Jamie Oliver, cuddly toys
Dislikes: Vulgar women, scruffy men, drugs
Belongs To: Elton John Fan Club, Young Conservatives, Christian Youth Club
Friends: Cecily, Sarah and Catherine from Young Conservatives
Love Of Life: Christopher (boyfriend since primary school)
Ambition: To live in little cottage in the country

C.V.

Name: Crazy Flo
Background: Claims to come from a broken home
Hobbies: Clubbing, group sex, ecstasy, cocaine, Tarot
Favourite Book: The Prophet
Favourite Record: Radiohead – Kid A
Favourite Article Of Clothing: Rubber nurse's uniform
Drink: Pimms
Favourite Food: Kebab and chips
Likes: Vulgar women, scruffy men, drugs
Dislikes: Foxhunting, Hugh Grant, Jamie Oliver, Cuddly toys
Belongs To: Lesbian Society (currently experimenting with her sexuality)
Friends: Rizla Dave, Dodgy Martin, Mr. Natural, Spod, Gandalf, D.J. Jazzy Jez
Love Of Life: Rizla Dave, Dodgy Martin, Mr. Natural, Spod, Gandalf, D.J. Jazzy Jez
Ambition: To get three up her

HOMESICKNESS

Chances are, in the mayhem and excitement of your first term of college, you'll probably forget you ever had a family (until you run out of money, that is). This is perfectly normal. The move to university marks the first real time away from home, and this newfound freedom can bring its fair share of excitement and debauchery. But, for some, there is another side to the coin.

In the first few weeks, some new students experience pangs of apprehension, isolation and loneliness. What if you are missing your family and friends? Well you'd have to be a bit heartless if you didn't. So listen, we're only going to say this once:

IT'S ALL RIGHT TO MISS YOUR MUM

To be frank though, there's no magical cure to homesickness other than weathering the storm and entering wholeheartedly into your new situation. Here are a few pointers though, to help you through this potentially difficult time:

1. DON'T BROOD

Sitting alone in your room for days on end with the curtains closed, smoking, listening to Radiohead, chalking the days on the wall and eating nothing but dead flies doesn't do anyone any good, and will gain you a reputation as a psychopath, or worse, a Philosophy Student. Go out. Meet your neighbours. Be sociable. And stop eating insects.

2. TRY TO LIMIT THE NUMBER OF TIMES YOU CALL HOME

It's no use picking at the scab. Apart from anything else, you don't want to worry your parents, which you surely will if you're calling home sixteen times a day, sobbing into the phone and asking for teddy.

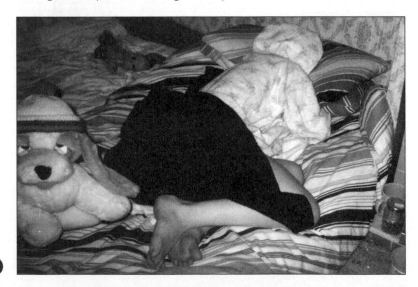

Juggling – a sure sign that something is 'wrong'

3. TALK TO SOMEONE

There's an enormous support network at university for the depressed or homesick – counsellors, personal tutors, chaplains, Samaritans. Try at least one of these should you actually come to feel desperately low.

4. REMIND YOURSELF OF THE ADVANTAGES OF YOUR NEW SITUATION

Remember – you can now stay up as late as you like, drink as much as you like, sleep with whomever you like, dress as you like, etc. Sounds bloody great, doesn't it?

5. DON'T GIVE UP

At least give it a fair try. If the worst comes to the worst, pop home for a few days in your first term. After a few days of your mum's moaning and your dad's incessant farting, this will probably remind you of why you wanted to get away so badly in the first place.

And if things haven't improved after the first couple of terms, it could well be the fault of the place. There are many towns in Britain, which will remain nameless, where it's impossible to have any fun; oh, go on then – Stoke-on-Trent, Scunthorpe and Grimsby, for starters. So if you really don't like where you are, try transferring to another university and giving it a go there. Lots of students do this and find, to their surprise, that a change of scenery works wonders*.

*A note of caution. If your original choice of university in your first year was a windswept and inhospitable hellhole, miles from anywhere, it's best not to transfer to Lancaster University.

URBAN MYTHS

University has always had its fair share of tall tales that do the rounds every year, particularly amongst first years in halls. The following academic urban myths, though disturbing and macabre, are totally genuine, and were shared with us by Freshers from 3 separate universities. What they say about the collective psyche of new students is, perhaps a little worrying, but should these gruesome tales have not made it to your particular uni, it is of course your duty to start spreading them around...

BLOW-UP

"In the summer there was this Post-Grad Engineering student doing some kind of research in the labs and staying in one of the rooms on this floor. But he was depressed and suicidal, and he killed himself one night. What he did was – he got a canister of compressed air from the engineering lab and sneaked it back to his room. Then he wrote a note, stuck the valve of the canister into his mouth and quickly opened the valve to wide open, blowing his head off and his chest cavity wide open. Blood and guts everywhere. One of the porters was saying that apparently they had to go in with gloves and plastic bags and pick all the pieces up. They were really pissed off about it. There were brains dripping off the lampshade and one of his lungs on top of the wardrobe. It was one of these rooms along here apparently, I heard someone say that it was actually yours..."
(If you're in halls, try this one out on whoever's just moved in next door...)

UP THE JUNCTION

"A couple of years ago this bloke started here and was given one of the shared rooms with another guy he didn't know. This other bloke seemed all right but was a bit weird. Anyway, after about a week the first bloke has to go to the doctor because he's got this really sore arse. He just woke up with it really hurting a couple of mornings before. The doctor has a look at it and just says, "Are you a practising homosexual?" and the guy goes "No" and the doctor just looks at him and says, "I think you're lying to me because it certainly looks as if you are". So he goes back to the room he shares with the other guy and searches his stuff when he's out and finds a bottle of chloroform. Turns out the other bloke was chloroforming him in the middle of the night and then buggering him, and he never knew a thing about it."*

THE GREEN MAN

"There was this first year student who blew his entire year's money in the first week on hi-fi equipment. In an effort to minimise his debts over the oncoming year, he bought a giant sack of oats and locked himself away in his room night after night, listening to music and eating nothing but porridge. By the end of the second term his neighbour realised that she hadn't seen him for a couple of weeks and got worried. His door was kicked down and he was found on his bed, emaciated, foaming at the mouth and barely able to move. It was the first recorded case of scurvy in England for over 80 years..."

*What does this tell us about latent homophobia in male students??

HOME ALONE 2

"A group of students, sharing a house, pop out to the local pub for a drink, leaving behind one of their flatmates. Halfway into the night, one of them, realizing she has forgotten her cigarettes, nips home to get them. Entering the house, she walks into the darkened living room, and, just as she's fumbling for the light switch, suddenly remembers she's left them in her coat pocket hanging by the front door and so re-traces her steps, grabs the cigarettes and returns to the pub. Returning home a few hours later the students enter the house and go into the living room to discover the mutilated body of their flat-mate lying on the floor, but it isn't the sight of this that makes the girl who forgot her cigarettes scream. It is the message written in blood on the living room mirror: 'good job you didn't turn the light on'..."

CULTS

"Steer clear of all the religious groups; they do nothing but harm…."
(Brideshead Revisited)

"In my first weekend at university, I was stopped in the street by a young woman, who asked if I would care to take part in a survey. Delighted by this opportunity to talk about myself, I entered wholeheartedly into the spirit of the thing – and was not disappointed. The questionnaire was designed to appeal peculiarly to the egomania of an eighteen-year-old. Eventually, my answers having proved me the highly intelligent, gifted, and spiritual sort of chap they were looking for, I was led to a dingy backroom behind McDonald's, where the purpose of the survey was to be revealed. At this point I started to smell a rat. There then ensued a half-hour long sales pitch, in which the surveyor tried to sell me a copy of "Dianetics", while I tried to convince her that I'd already seen a copy in the university library and that if I were interested I could have a look at that one, thank you very much.

At long last I managed to wriggle free, and although nothing very sinister had occurred, I felt like a chump. I didn't mention the incident to anyone, but soon learnt that several Freshers I knew had similarly fallen for this ploy, sitting IQ tests, and all manner of psychometric grilling. In comparison, mine had been a narrow escape, but no-one, as far as I could tell, had actually signed up."

Student's own account

Although far from being a common occurrence, student-targeting by cults is in on the increase, and their methods of recruitment can often be manipulative and insidious. Graham Baldwin, the director of 'Catalyst', a support group for people trying to leave cults, says: *'Cult recruiters use well-documented psychological techniques to break down and remould the victim's personality, securing total dependence.'*

One institution worth mentioning is the Church of Scientology. This huge and powerful cult boasts vast wealth and is even endorsed by such celebrities as insecure short-arse Tom Cruise. While we are not at liberty to criticise them (they notoriously sue anyone who gives them a funny look) we can at least suggest that should they take an interest in you, for goodness' sake do a bit of independent research into them and their founder L. Ron Hubbard, before handing your life over.

TEN DEAD GIVEAWAYS THAT
A CULT MIGHT BE DODGY

1) It has a charismatic leader who owns more than twelve Rolls Royces.
2) It advertises in the 'Friday Ad'.
3) There is a large portrait of Hitler in the leader's office.
4) Attractive blonde female disciples are summoned to the leader's room three times a day for 'sermons'.
5) Its founding father is a paranoid racist, the author of 87 lousy science-fiction novels, and was raised in Iowa.
6) Its teachings are based on a mixture of The Bible, The Koran, The Prophet, The Naked Chef, Lord of the Rings and Chitty Chitty Bang Bang.
7) It has a large complement of celebrity followers consisting of shallow Hollywood actors and actresses (all curiously short), alcoholic footballers and ex-soap stars.
8) Cult members mysteriously vanish and are assumed to have left the order, but there are meat pies for dinner that evening.
9) The altar has a credit card-checking machine on it.
10) There is a large jar of cyanide next to a catering pack of diet coke in the pantry.

Although some universities have banned cults altogether, it still pays to be vigilant. University can be, for some, a lonely and confusing time, but any group which seems to offer unqualified love and a solution to nearly everything must be treated with caution, especially if it's the Rugby Society. **www.cultinformation.org.uk**

DON'T SUFFER IN SILENCE

The first week for many students can be a lonely and trying time. Not everyone can play the confident socialite and if you are suffering from homesickness or loneliness it's nothing to be ashamed of, as you certainly won't be alone with these feelings. A surprisingly large number of students drop out in the first term for a whole variety of reasons, but to be fair to yourself and your new surroundings, give university life a real try before jacking it all in. It can help enormously by talking to someone about your concerns and the university should have a good system set up for this. You could approach your personal tutor for advice, or if you don't feel that you can relate to them, try your student welfare officer, or approach the health centre for counselling.

Above all, don't feel ashamed. Literally thousands of new students go through some sort of crisis in their first term and far too many simply pack their bags and flee. Whatever problems you have in your first few weeks, get help to see them through, give university a fair go, and the chances are you will stick it out, grow to love it and end up remembering these as some of the best years of your life.

CHOICES, COURSES & STATISTICS

If you only take away one useful piece of advice from this book, make it this one:

Never willingly choose any university that may be in, or close to, your hometown.

In the USA there is a tradition for students to attend their local university. What inevitably happens, of course, is that a fair proportion of them end up staying with their parents. Choose a university near your home, and, in all likelihood, you too will continue to live with your mum.

On first appearance, this might not seem too bad – you'll save on the rent, have your meals cooked for you, have your bed made every day, never have to pay bills or shop for food, and never be woken up by four drunken strangers wandering into your room at 3am to invite you to a party. But, of course, these are the things that make university such a life-changing experience.

Academic duties are merely a formal requirement that supplement a higher reason for being at university: your self-development as a responsible adult and a chance to fully explore your desires, ambitions, sexuality and beliefs. This is not going to happen if you've still got mum making you soldiers for breakfast and tucking you up in bed every night.

In a nutshell; stay at home and you are going to miss out on perhaps the most important, entertaining and life-shaping elements of university life that will create countless anecdotes for years to come and help transform you into an outstanding, independent and sophisticated man/woman about town.

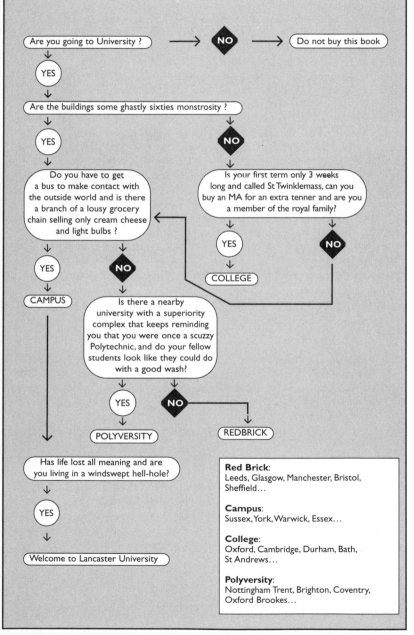

UNIVERSITY IDENTIFICATION CHART

Are you going to University? → NO → Do not buy this book

YES ↓

Are the buildings some ghastly sixties monstrosity?

YES ↓ / NO ↓

Do you have to get a bus to make contact with the outside world and is there a branch of a lousy grocery chain selling only cream cheese and light bulbs?

Is your first term only 3 weeks long and called St Twinklemass, can you buy an MA for an extra tenner and are you a member of the royal family?

YES ↓ / NO ↓

YES → COLLEGE / NO →

CAMPUS

Is there a nearby university with a superiority complex that keeps reminding you that you were once a scuzzy Polytechnic, and do your fellow students look like they could do with a good wash?

YES ↓ / NO →

POLYVERSITY

REDBRICK

Has life lost all meaning and are you living in a windswept hell-hole?

↓

YES

↓

Welcome to Lancaster University

Red Brick:
Leeds, Glasgow, Manchester, Bristol, Sheffield...

Campus:
Sussex, York, Warwick, Essex...

College:
Oxford, Cambridge, Durham, Bath, St Andrews...

Polyversity:
Nottingham Trent, Brighton, Coventry, Oxford Brookes...

STAYING AT HOME: A CASE STUDY.

Meet Gary, a real life 'stay at homer'. Gary is 34, single, and lives in a small soulless commuter town near Reading. He has a dependency on Prozac, daytime quiz shows and cheap lager. Gary is one of life's losers. But where did it all go wrong?

1. Our story begins in 1986, when, like the foolish King Lear, Gary made a fatal error of judgment. To save money and to get his washing and cooking done, Gary decided to stay at home and attend his local University.

2. All went well for a while, he was saving cash, he had no need to worry about the complexities of using a launderette and he was getting free meals to boot. Apart from the odd essay, and learning how to dress like Morrissey, he hadn't a care in the world.

3. By the end of the first year however, Gary realised that something was wrong. He felt strangely disassociated from the university's cultural and social life. He'd never woken up hung-over to find a girl/ boy/ police cone in his bed. In fact he hadn't dreamt of inviting anyone back to his house ever, partly out of embarrassment for living with his parents, and partly out of even more embarrassment because he still had Thomas the Tank wallpaper in his bedroom.

4. In his second year, out of desperation, Gary got a flat. Sadly though, he had no one to share with, having made no house buddy deals in the first year, so he moved in on his own.

5. It wasn't long before Gary realised that he didn't know how to cook, wash, clean or pay his bills. As a result he spent four miserable months wearing the same pair of underpants and socks, and phoning for pizzas every night. One fateful day with his money having run out, his phone and electricity cut off and his underpants rotted away to little more than a string of elastic round his waist, Gary returned to his parents.

6. Gary is still there today, fifteen years on, with his parents (now incontinent), a dog (also incontinent) and a bald patch. Despite achieving a 2:2 in English Literature, he never found a use for it in the 3-mile radius around his home that he rarely ventures beyond, and instead accepted a job stacking shelves at his local supermarket until something better came along. Nothing ever did.

7. With growing ill-health and agoraphobia, Gary recently accepted early retirement at the age of 33. He spends his days now sitting at home listening to Cradle of Filth, watching Kilroy and drinking heavily. He has still never washed his own pants, boiled an egg or cleaned a saucepan. He is also still a virgin.

If the grizzly tale of Gary isn't enough to encourage you to venture to pastures new, let's not also forget that the other important issues here are: taking the opportunity to live in a new area of the country, meeting types of people you otherwise wouldn't have met, and – most importantly of all – finally having the chance to start to undo the psychological damage that your parents have exerted over you for the past 18 years.

If you live in Oxford go to Cambridge; if you live in Liverpool go to Bath; if you live in Coventry, go anywhere – just get the hell out.

One shouldn't, however, apply this principle willy-nilly – there's no sense in going to, say St. Andrews in Scotland just because you happen to live in Cornwall, or vice versa. Besides, this distance may be a little too far – the two most important rules of thumb in deciding on exactly how far away from home your choice of university should be, are:

1)   Go far enough from your parents that they won't know what you're up to.
2)   Go not so far that you're unable to reach them in an emergency.

Anything from 100 – 300 miles is probably ideal. This means that mum and dad almost certainly won't be popping down unexpectedly on a Sunday morning to catch you drugged up to your eyeballs and in bed with your tutor, but equally, should Granny take a turn for the worse, and you need to return home quickly, your journey won't take on the epic qualities of a Tolkien adventure.

In conclusion, the fact that something like 20% of students end up settling down in the town where they graduate suggests that there's a lot to be said for heading for pastures new, but think carefully about where you flee to. It just might end up being your home for life.

CHOICES, COURSES & STATISTICS

CHANGING YOUR COURSE IN THE FIRST TERM

It is interesting to note that all but the most exclusive universities have a few courses that never fill up properly. This is usually because the subject matter is heart-stoppingly dull or the course leader is a notorious alcoholic and the university rife with tales of how he turns up to lectures drunk, naked and covered in jam.

Now, if through choice, ignorance or sheer stupidity you have picked such a degree, *don't worry*, there's still time in the first term to bale out and switch to something else.

In fact, should you pull out of your degree in the first few weeks you could be in a rather unique and enviable position, as your university will try to do everything in its power to keep you (losing too many students gives a bad reputation and costs them serious money) and with there being guaranteed dropouts on virtually every course in the first term, you have a multitude of options.

In fact, you *can* be pretty cunning about this. If you really wanted to study say, English Lit at Liverpool Uni (but it required five straight A's) put yourself down instead for the university's least popular course: Theology and Town Planning. Then, when you and a lonely Hippy start the course in Autumn, go complaining to your personal tutor that the course isn't right for you, you're very depressed and thinking of leaving. Finally, after a few minutes of tears, suggest that you could only really stay on if they could find you a place on the English Lit course. This usually works like a dream, especially if you are an attractive young woman, but be aware of time restrictions. Most universities have a 3-4 week period at the beginning of the first term when course swapping is relatively easy. Beyond this it's down to you as to how well you can play the role of a depressed but stunning leggy blonde.

NB. Should this tactic fail, and you find yourself stuck doing 'Fish Management' at Bangor University instead of Media Studies, don't come trying to find us, we have moved.

INTERMITTING

Intermitting is a good last line of defence against being kicked out. In a nutshell, it means having a year out of your degree to "take stock". It usually applies to students who have gone through some personal crisis and need a break, but can be utilised by the terminally lazy, should the ever-hopeful powers-that-be feel that giving you time to pull yourself together will mean they'll still get their money. They avoid the doomsday scenario of losing a student, you avoid doing anything for a year. It's a comfort to know it's there.

COURSES WITH THE BEST MALE TO FEMALE RATIOS

Medicine	
Nutrition	♂ ♀ ♀ ♀ ♀ ♀ ♀ ♀ ♀ ♀
Sports science	♀ ♀ ♂
Nursing	♂ ♀ ♀ ♀ ♀ ♀ ♀ ♀ ♀ ♀ ♀
Biological sciences	
Psychology	♂ ♀ ♀ ♀ ♀
Agriculture and related subjects	
Veterinary science	♂ ♀ ♀ ♀
Forestry	♂ ♂ ♂ ♂ ♂ ♂ ♂ ♂ ♂ ♂ ♂ ♀
Physical sciences	
Physics	♂ ♂ ♂ ♂ ♀
Mathematical sciences and informatics	
Mathematics	♂ ♂ ♀
Computer science	♂ ♂ ♂ ♂ ♂ ♀
Computer systems engineering	♂ ♂ ♂ ♂ ♂ ♂ ♂ ♂ ♂ ♀
Software engineering	♂ ♂ ♂ ♂ ♂ ♂ ♀
Artificial intelligence	♂ ♂ ♂ ♂ ♂ ♂ ♂ ♂ ♂ ♂ ♂ ♂ ♂ ♂ ♀
Engineering and technology	
General engineering	♂ ♂ ♂ ♂ ♂ ♂ ♂ ♂ ♂ ♀
Civil engineering	♂ ♂ ♂ ♂ ♂ ♂ ♂ ♂ ♀
Mechanical engineering	♂ ♂ ♂ ♂ ♂ ♂ ♂ ♂ ♂ ♂ ♂ ♀
Aeronautical engineering	♂ ♂ ♂ ♂ ♂ ♂ ♂ ♂ ♂ ♀
Electrical engineering	♂ ♂ ♂ ♂ ♂ ♂ ♂ ♂ ♂ ♂ ♀
Electronic engineering	♂ ♂ ♂ ♂ ♂ ♂ ♂ ♂ ♂ ♂ ♀
Architecture, building and planning	
Architecture	♂ ♂ ♂ ♀
Social studies	
Economics	♂ ♂ ♂ ♀
Sociology	♂ ♀ ♀ ♀
Social work	♂ ♀ ♀ ♀ ♀ ♀
Psychology	♂ ♀ ♀ ♀ ♀ ♀
Mass communications and documentation	
Communication studies	♂ ♀ ♀ ♀
Languages and related disciplines	
English	♂ ♀ ♀ ♀
French	♂ ♀ ♀ ♀
Humanities	
History of art	♂ ♀ ♀ ♀ ♀
Philosophy	♂ ♂ ♀
Creative arts	
Fine arts	♂ ♂ ♂ ♂ ♂ ♂ ♂ ♂ ♀ ♀ ♀ ♀ ♀ ♀ ♀ ♀
Drama	♂ ♂ ♀ ♀ ♀ ♀
Craft	♂ ♀ ♀ ♀ ♀
Education	
Primary all ages (upper and lower primary)	♂ ♀ ♀ ♀ ♀ ♀ ♀ ♀ ♀

Based on current figures from the UCAS website

STRANGE COURSES

Ever felt the urge to learn Aromatherapy in German? What about three years of wine-tasting? Or how about getting into the minds of hardened criminals, whilst at the same time learning to upholster a settee? The courses below are legitimate, if a little bizarre. So if Geography, Computer Science, Law (or whatever you've chosen) starts to seem a little trite in comparison, remember that Blacksmithing at Lancashire is waiting for you with open arms…

**ARCHEOLOGY &
PHYSICAL EDUCATION**
(Chester College, University of Liverpool, 3yrs)

VIKING STUDIES
(University College London, 4yrs)

COMPUTER SCIENCE & WELSH
(Swansea University, 4yrs)

WINE STUDIES
(Brighton University, 2yrs)

EMBROIDERY
(Manchester Metropolitan University, 3yrs)

**FOOD STUDIES /
REMOTE SENSING & GIS**
(Bath Spa University, 3yrs)

SCIENCE & FOOTBALL
(Liverpool John Moores University, 3yrs)

ACUPUNCTURE
(Brighton University, 3yrs)

**WELSH &
AUSTRALIAN STUDIES**
(Cardiff University, 3yrs)

BLACKSMITHING
(Central Lancashire, 3yrs)

**EQUINE BREEDING
& STUD MANAGEMENT**
(Writtle College)

DISASTER RISK MANAGEMENT
(Portsmouth University)

GERMAN & HEALING ARTS
(University of Derby, 3yrs)

JAZZ STUDIES
(Wakefield College, 2yrs)

MEAT TECHNOLOGY & MANAGEMENT
(Leeds Thomas Danby College, 2yrs)

FOOTWEAR DESIGN
(De Montford, 3yrs)

**CRIMINOLOGY &
TEXTILE FURNISHING DESIGN**
(London Guildhall, 3yrs)

GAMEKEEPING
(Millennium Institute, 1yr)

GENDER STUDIES & TOURISM
(South Bank University, 3yrs)

The lecturer of Cricket Science at Sussex University

A FEW INTERESTING STATISTICS...

- 41% males / 50% females starting university said that drinking, clubbing and sex were what they were most looking forward to do.
- Only 8% students look forward to their university course.
- 66% female students are capable of cooking, cleaning and taking care of themselves, compared to only 50% male students.
- 20% boys still call their mothers as soon as they need money, recipes or advice.
- 23% students are not looking forward to the amount of work expected.

(Statistics taken from a student survey conducted by Orange)

THE UK'S TOP TEN BEST AND WORST UNIVERSITIES*

Based on ratings for teaching quality, research quality, employment, student/ staff ratios and dropout rate, the Sunday Times came up with the following (we'll leave you to figure out which is which).

Cambridge University	**Glasgow's Caledonian University**
Oxford University	**Napier University**
London School of Economics	**Southampton Institute**
Imperial College London	**University of East London**
York University	**University of Abertay, Dundee**
University College London	**South Bank University, London**
Warwick University	**University of North London**
Nottingham University	**University of Paisley**
Durham University	**North East Wales Institute, Wrexham**
Sheffield University	**Thames Valley University**

The University of Sheffield
SCHOOL OF NURSING
& MIDWIFERY

*Statistics taken from Sunday Times League Table 2001, compiled using data from the Higher Education Statistics Agency, the Quality Assurance Agency for Higher Education, the national funding councils and the universities themselves.

STRANGE PLACES TO STUDY

#1 THE ROYAL HOLLOWAY UNIVERSITY OF LONDON
(as remembered by former student Kirsty Gascoin)

Visible from Junction 13 of the M25, the chimneys, turrets, gables, balustrades and classical urns of RHUL are a set of dreaming spires populated with Oxbridge rejects, wannabe luvvies and rugger buggers, diluted a little by the usual great unwashed student underbelly of followers of alternative lifestyles and substance abuse. Founder's Hall itself is a fabulous piece of neo-Baroque architecture, based on a château in the Loire. Lucky students get to live there in their first year – while the less fortunate are relegated to the entirely uninspiring breeze-blocked edifices of Athlone or Cameron Halls (definitely not pictured in the prospectus) and more commonly known as Cell Block H.

Royal Holloway was a place that attracted a variety of students. During my time there, my friends ranged from the son of the owner of the Coca-Cola South East Asia franchise, with his house overlooking Kowloon Bay in Hong Kong, to someone from the council estate in Mitcham where they filmed 'The Bill'.

Being the smallest and most far-flung part of London University, there was a paucity of fun not known in the other London Colleges. Trips into town were limited by the last train back to Egham being at 10.30pm; some students turned instead to other forms of entertainment. Royal Holloway College was built in the late 1800s for Thomas Holloway, a Victorian philanthropist who raised the money to build his college for women by marketing patent medicines, among them, 'Holloway's

Ointment' and 'Holloway's Pills', a renowned laxative. Obviously, taking pills at Holloway had a sound historical basis, and many students felt that they were simply upholding the strong sense of tradition at the college. Indeed, since the pills taken were no longer laxatives, students could simply be seen as following the college's epithet of "a unique blend of tradition and innovation". Added to this, the fact that magic mushrooms grew abundantly within the 120 acres of parkland owned by the university, made the lack of facilities less important. Forget clubbing in London, tripping in nearby Windsor Great Park, and stumbling back in the dark along the A30 towards Staines afterwards was where it was at if you didn't fancy going to balls or participating in the incest that the college, then with only 3000 students, had to offer. For real on-the-edge excitement we'd walk out to the edge of Staines (a town famous then for only having one picture postcard – of the local fleapit cinema, and famous now only because Ali G stands outside this same cinema in his latest video) and wait at the end of Heathrow's Runway 3, betting each other a Student Union pint not to duck as a 747 hurtled into land inches (if you were on magic mushrooms) above our heads.

Being named Royal Holloway inevitably meant that the royals wanted to get in on the act, as they always seem to do when something has 'royal' as part of its name. I received my degree in the Royal Albert Hall see, from Princess Anne. Having been part of the great curtsy debate, I had on my oldest pair of Dr. Martens and was honourably proletarian until the last minute of actually receiving my degree, when a small curtsy did slip out.

I remember the Princess Royal also came to the college one summer afternoon to visit the Picture Gallery, the contents of which include paintings by the best known Victorian artists, such as Millais, Frith and Landseer, as well as a couple by Tony Hart. (Some students spent their entire college careers failing exams in the Picture Gallery simply because they were planning how to steal the entire collection and thereby negate any need to pass exams in order to make money.) I stayed away, being too busy plane-spotting, gathering fungi or being chased out of local pubs by the embryonic Staines Massive, and returned to college to hear that one of our number had been arrested and was being held overnight on charges relating to kidnap and possession of a replica machine gun, according to The Staines and Egham News. However, it later transpired that a jumpy bodyguard had overreacted when the Princess had unwittingly wandered into the middle of a water pistol fight. Apparently. It was all pretty cool at the time, though.

Is your university in the middle of nowhere?

Are you living next door to a psychotic hippy or is your tutor a vampire? If so, drop us an e-mail explaining exactly how weird and perverse your campus/ university actually is and we'll include it in the next update of the book. A few hopefuls for the next update include Bretton Hall, Lancaster University, St Andrews, Keele and just about anywhere in Wales.

♂ MALE TO FEMALE RATIOS ☿

TOP TEN UNIVERSITIES FOR MALE TO FEMALE RATIO	% MALE	% FEMALE
CRANFIELD UNIVERSITY	76	24
IMPERIAL COLLEGE OF SCIENCE, TECH AND MEDICINE	67	33
MANCHESTER UNIVERSITY INSTITUTE OF SCIENCE & TECH	67	33
LOUGHBOROUGH UNIVERSITY	63	37
BATH UNIVERSITY	58	42
HERIOT-WATT UNIVERSITY, EDINBURGH	58	42
LONDON SCHOOL OF ECONOMICS & POLITICAL SCIENCE	57	43
COVENTRY UNIVERSITY	55	45
QUEEN MARY & WESTFIELD COLLEGE	54	46
PORTSMOUTH UNIVERSITY	54	46

TOP TEN UNIVERSITIES FOR FEMALE TO MALE RATIO	% MALE	% FEMALE
BISHOP GROSSETESTE COLLEGE	21	79
EDINBURGH QUEEN MARGARET COLLEGE	21	79
BRADFORD & ILKLEY COMMUNITY COLLEGE	23	77
STRANMILLIS	24	76
ROYAL VETERINARY COLLEGE	25	75
LANCASTER UNIVERSITY COLLEGE OF ST MARTIN	25	75
BIRMINGHAM COLLEGE OF FOOD, TOURISM & CRT STUDIES	27	73
CANTERBURY CHRIST CHURCH COLLEGE	27	73
ROEHAMPTON INSTITUTE, LONDON	27	73
BRETTON HALL	28	72

DON'T SUFFER IN SILENCE

Feel like you're doing the wrong course? At the wrong university? In the wrong country? Of course it's easy to fall into the 'grass is greener' syndrome when you discover that your friend's degree only requires one essay a year and has much more attractive people in it, while yours is piled high with work and full of students who have been touched by the ugly stick. This is not the best reason in the world for swapping courses (though understandable) whereas if you passionately feel that you should have picked A.I. but was bullied into Sport Science by your Rugby-obsessed mother; then the sooner you act the better chance you have of transferring. Let your personal tutor know immediately of your doubts and they should let you know what possibilities/ opportunities are available. If you wait too long, you might have to see through the year before starting your new course afresh, which will, of course mean one extra year of studying and one extra year of accumulating debt!

ARCHETYPES

With the cultural and racial diversity that now exists throughout British universities, the old chestnut of what constitutes a 'typical student' is, these days, a redundant one. However, against all odds, there are those who still cling to a set of characteristics as ludicrously stereotypical as a Frenchman with a beret, stripy shirt and a bunch of onions.

Below we present a celebration of archetypes, which, despite immense social change, have prevailed doggedly throughout the ages.

Art Students

Natural enemy: Everyone else

Distinguishing features: Vacant and sullen expressions, tatty old dungarees with carefully splattered paint, Fifties poplin dresses worn over Seventies flares, silly hat, piercings and bizarre facial hair (favoured more by the male fraternity, though not exclusively)

Official name: Xavier / Orlando / Poppie / Chloe

Mating call: 'Do you want to see my etchings?'

Drug: Absinthe

Pin-up: A 3D collage of themselves, made of silver foil, sweets and their own excrement

Most Likely to say: 'My work is a post-modern parody of itself'

Destiny: Teaching art in a crappy secondary school / the dole

Engineering Students

Natural enemy: Anyone who's read a book that isn't by Terry Pratchett

Distinguishing features: Supermarket jeans, Korn T-shirt, home-cut hair, room decorated with pin-ups of large-chested females sat astride motorcycles. Weekends are invariably wasted away playing computer games with geeky mates

Official name: Martin (there are no female Engineering students, or rather none worth mentioning)

Mating call: 'Please have sex with me, I'll pay you'

Drug: Happy Shopper lager (drunk alone in room)

Pin up: Lara Croft

Most likely to say: 'Oh, there you are, anyone would think you've been trying to avoid me'

Destiny: Engineer

Rugger-Buggers

Natural enemy: Gays, lesbians, foreigners, art students, the disabled, left-handers, the blind and anyone who doesn't match up to the requirements of Hitler's Aryan Race

Distinguishing features: Ex-public school types with thick neck, low brow, tiny eyes, over-developed jaw, soft skin, ruddy complexion, braying voice, the old Hugh Grant haircut, Tory scum. Never seen out of their precious rugby shirts except on special occasions when they'll wear an evening suit with dickie bow and pour a bottle of champagne down their trousers while singing 'Eskimo Nell'

Official name: Toby/ Ben/ Jeremy/ Adam/ Giles/ Miles/ Rupert/ Barnaby/ James

Mating call: 'Show us your tits'

Drug: Lager by the gallon

Pin-up: Jordan/ Maggie Thatcher

Most likely to say: 'Show us your tits'

Destiny: Merchant banking/ parliament/ law courts/ prison

Ravers

Natural enemy: The Drug Squad

Distinguishing features:

Men: Obligatory silly hat of some kind, Bermuda shirt, expensive trainers, bad posture and vampire like pallor (caused by a lack of good night's sleep and the onset of scurvy)

Women: Pigtails, glitter on cleavage, tiny silver skirt, boob tube, silver platform trainers

Official name:

Men: Jez / Josh / Davey / Dosh / Quantum / Mr Natural / DJ Insertyournamehere

Women: Kat / Kati / Kath / Katerina / Kelli / Kirsti / Kim

Mating call: 'Christ I'm really coming up'

Drug: Yes please

Pin-up: Howard Marks

Most likely to say: 'Sorted…bangin'… largin' it… mint… cooking… cool… …whack… …twenty aspirin please'

Destiny: Web designer/ born again Christian

The Strange Silent Ones

Natural enemy: Themselves
Distinguishing features: Unknown
Official name: That bloke next door… the weird one
Mating call: Disturbing low moaning noises heard through wall at night
Drug: Loneliness
Pin-up: Hitler/ Thom Yorke
Most likely to say: Nothing
Destiny: Suicide/ homicide/ patricide/ matricide/ fratricide/ genocide

House Nazis and Note-Leavers

Natural enemy: Bacteria
Distinguishing features: Writing their own names on their food and leaving acidic note of steadily increasing hysteria regarding milk theft or blu-tac residue on walls Hobbies include collecting soft toys, listening to Maria Carey and Celine Dion and being smeared in their own excrement during sex
Official name: Joanne/ Brian
Mating call: No need, they have been dating a person with similar Nazi-tendencies since they were 16.
Drug: Mr Muscle
Pin-up: Not likely, it'll ruin the wallpaper
Most likely to say: 'Look everyone, I don't want to appear like a Fascist or anything but we've all got to live together, so would someone PLEASE CLEAN UP THIS FUCKING MESS!!'
Destiny: Suburbia

Activists

Natural enemy: People in suits, car-drivers, multinationals, carnivores, fox-hunters, anyone with a bit more money than them

Distinguishing features: Roll-up smoking, humourless skinny men with a day's growth of stubble, dreadlocks, Dr Martens and carrying a copy of 'No Logo'. Hobbies include Hunt Sabbing, leafleting and eating tofu

Official name: Spike, Bez, Badger

Mating call: 'Socialist Worker…Living Marxist' to be droned in an irritating voice outside Marks & Spencers

Drug: Cider

Pin-up: Mark Thomas

Most likely to say: 'If you eat a chicken McNugget, you might as well strangle a Ugandan child with your bare hands'

Destiny: New Labour/ selling out the day they leave university to work for Nestlé

Aesthetes

Natural enemy: Rugger-buggers

Distinguishing features:

Men: Homburg hat, cloak, bottle-green waistcoat, beard, pince-nez, cigarette holder, silver-topped cane, spats, copy of Finnegan's Wake and sheath of scribbled poems under arm

Women: Long copper hair, flowing muslin dresses, copy of Orlando under arm, room full of candles. Prone to occasional fainting fits and Ophelia complex

Official name:

Wayne Smith (prefers to be known as Theodore de Tocqueville)

Sharon Boggs (prefers to be known as Sylvia du Lac)

Mating call: 'Truth is beauty. Beauty is truth. Kiss me my darlin.'

Drug: Opium

Pin-up: Aubrey Beardsley

Most likely to say: 'I've written a new poem'

Destiny: Vanity publishing and alcoholism

The Unashamedly Posh

Natural enemy: The ashamedly poor

Distinguishing features: Tall, clear complexion, sensible hair (Alice bands for women), Armani jeans, Gucci anything, frightening cardigans, Burberry scarves, Barbour jackets, and brogues. Occasionally prone to strange ailments due to in-breeding. Utterly ignorant of popular culture, they will think that Fatboyslim is a diet program

Official name:
The honourable James Merryweather-Fortesque-Smythe
Lady Jemima Heuwshall-Wittingham

Mating call: 'Oh, go on, we're only second cousins'

Drug: Lashings of champers & cocaine

Pin-up: A picture of themselves snowboarding in Aspen, Colorado

Most likely to say: Nothing to the likes of you. In spite of what anyone tells you, nothing has changed in the last 1000 years. To them you are still a peasant crawling around in the shit and filth

Destiny: Working for Daddy

Nu-Goth

Natural enemy: Those who walk by day
Distinguishing features: Androgynous appearance, sallow complexion, lank dyed black hair, heavy eye make-up, piercings, grotty fishnets, freaky contact lenses, dog-collar, 12 inch platform boots, rubber bags with spikes. Like swans, they usually travel in pairs and are often indistinguishable apart (even if of the opposite sex)
Official name: Vlad, Morticia, Nosferatu, Dr Mabuse
Mating call: 'I want to shag your corpse'
Drug: AB negative
Pin-Up: Marylyn Manson
Most likely to say: 'Have you seen my pet snake?'
Destiny: Vicar/ Vampire

Generation 'Gap'

Natural enemy: Jez, the bearded Vegan who lives next door and makes annoying comments about how companies like Gap exploit the third world
Distinguishing features:
Men: Gap straight leg jeans, Gap roll-neck, Gap shirt, Gap coat, Tin-Tin haircut, mobile phone permanently to ear
Women: Gap boot-cut jeans, Gap roll-neck, Gap low cut vests, Gap coat, straight long hair, mobile phone permanently to ear
Official name: Insert any bland name here
Mating call: I ♥ you
Most likely to say: 'Text me'
Drug: Charlie and designer lager
Pin-Up: Jamie Oliver
Destiny: Daily Mail reading middle class respectability

Trekkies

Natural enemy: Darth Vader, Daleks, Cybermen, reality

Distinguishing features: Red Dwarf T-shirt, naff jeans, lank hair and bum-fluff moustache. Despite their BO and utter lack of charisma they seem to carry a horribly cheery demeanour. They can also speak Klingon

Official name: Gavin, Malcolm, Neil, Paul. (Like Engineering students, this one is strictly for the male of the species)

Mating call: 'Be my Scully, I'll be your Mulder'

Drug: Dope and real ale

Pin-up: Yoda, Lieutenant Uhura

Most likely to say: 'Dak Dok likk fakk cokk!' (Klingon for 'Oh, my God, I've wasted my life')

Destiny: Any mundane office job that will keep them in regular supplies of skunk and DVDs of 'Doctor Who'

Retro Boys & Hippy Chicks

Natural enemy: The last three decades

Distinguishing features:

Him: Corduroy flares, flowery shirt, suede jacket, floppy hat, huge sideburns

Her: Red PVC boots, flowery dress, white PVC mac, beads, huge sideburns

Official name:

Him: Spooner/ Terry/ Charlie/ Alfie

Her: India/ Luna/ Daffodil/ the Sea of Tranquillity

Mating call: 'Let's get high together and roll around naked in a fairy infested wood somewhere'

Most likely to say: 'I'm going to India this summer, to find myself'

Drug: Magic mushrooms/ LSD

Pin-Up: The Beach Boys

Destiny: Running a retro clothes shop in Brighton

Return Learners

Natural enemy: The under Thirties

Distinguishing features: They look and dress like your gran and granddad and can be found wandering round the university being overly cheerful in a desperate bid to fit in. Will also volunteer information in tutorials without prompting

Official name: Eric/ Geoff/ Keith/ Trevor/ Maureen/ Doreen /Eileen/ Pat

Mating call: 'I've still got my own teeth'

Most likely to say: (Sitting in front of a PC) 'can you get Radio 3 on this?'

Drug: Viagra

Pin-Up: The Hollies

Destiny: The oldies slot on Blind Date

The Self-Appointed Eccentric

Appearance: Top hat, flying-goggles, string vest, stripy leggings, flip-flops, and cape. Carries parrot in cage, stylophone or cabbage everywhere. Plays kazoo loudly in union bar. Usually sports a Salvador Dali moustache/sidewhiskers

Official name: Colonel Whoop-de-woo Toast-Buttocks

Real name: Steven Jenkins

Drug of choice: Jelly babies

Most likely to say: 'Brmmmmm! Beep beep! bluppflyybbb! Neep neepy smeepy!'

Mating call: 'Why not crawl inside my teeth, my little dodecahedron'

Pin -Up: A photograph of a bucket

Destiny: Holiday Camp entertainer

N.B. Despite his outlandish appearance, and reputation for madcap high-jinks, the self-appointed eccentric may, to your surprise; turn up one day on Blind Date as the token wally in chair 3, whereupon he will be chosen (purely on novelty value), and spend a week in Finland with a girl from Doncaster who the following week will expose him for the vacuous and utterly dull individual he really is

HOWARD MARKS

Once the world's most wanted man, Marks was, for twenty-five years, the biggest dope smuggler on the planet. This fresh-faced young undergraduate at Balliol College in the Sixties took one puff of a joint at a party and found his vocation in life, first selling the stuff to his fellow students, then moving on to much bigger things. Marks became a household name in the late Nineties, shortly after being let out from prison, with the release of his book 'Mr Nice', which spawned endless performances at festivals and literary events, a Channel 4 documentary and high-profile lobbying for the decriminalisation of cannabis, including him setting up the Cannabis Party during the last election (you can guess their policies).

We saw Marks performing a few years back and someone in the audience asked the (loaded) question-
'Did you ever know Bill Clinton when you were in Oxford?' (Clinton once famously claimed to have taken a puff on a joint but 'didn't inhale').
Marks replied with a twinkle in his eye-
'Yeah, I met him on several occasions. And I happen to know that he did inhale, and plenty more besides. I should know, I sold him the stuff.'
Career highlights: his cameo in 'Human Traffic' and being immortalised in the Super Furry Animals song 'Hanging out with Howard Marks'.

BYRON

The raffish, boozing, womanising, darkly sardonic poet of legend – 'mad, bad and dangerous to know' – studied at Trinity College, Cambridge, where he lasted exactly one term. During his brief stay he managed to achieve notoriety by forming a homosexual attachment to a choirboy and walking about with a pet bear on a chain. Miraculously, he wasn't actually sent down. He simply left to gallivant around Napoleonic Europe, boozing, womanising and scribbling verse. Three years later he published the fruit of his labour, 'Childe Harold's Pilgrimage', and, in his own words, awoke one morning to find himself famous.

STUDENT GRANT

Viz Comic creation, Grant Wankshaft, was a vicious, but amusing, stereotype of the comedy-catchphrase-quoting, PC student of the mid '90s. And with his goatee beard, clumpy boots and endless references to Vic and Bob, it certainly wasn't that far from the mark. Typical storylines included Grant pretending his dad's Christmas present of a car was won in a poker game. Has much changed since then?

PETER COOK

This Cambridge student played a significant role in revolutionising UK comedy in the early Sixties, by turning the University's annual comedy show from cheesy blokes-in-drag sketches to biting satire. It proved  such a success that the show 'Beyond The Fringe' toured the UK and the States, eventually making household names of its stars (Cook, Alan Bennett, Dr Jonathan Miller and Dudley Moore). The style transferred well to TV, in the form of a show called 'That Was The Week That Was', paving the way for future satirical comedy such as 'Not the Nine O' Clock News', 'Spitting Image', 'The 11 0' Clock Show', and Chris Morris. Cook's most beloved character was a chap called E.L. Wisty, a thin bloke in a grey mac who spoke with a nasally voice and would sit on a park bench reeling off surreal nonsense to anyone that cared to listen. Cook went on to help run Private Eye magazine, and eventually doubled up with Dudley Moore for a string of films, TV shows and albums. He is probably the only person to have a West-End hit while still at university. Other career highlights include his role of the devil in the original Sixties movie 'Bedazzled'.

THE GUY WHO GETS
BLACKED UP IN THE FILM 'SOUL MAN'

The plot: white actor C. Thomas Howell is forced by his rich but mean father to pay his own way through university, so in desperation he takes an overdose of suntan pills in order to win an African-American scholarship at an Ivy League College. You can guess the rest of the plot I'm sure, and while this film has some very funny moments and the best intentions (like tackling inherent racism within such a middle-class institution), it cannot avoid being jaw-droppingly tasteless. Kind of a Michael Jackson in reverse.

LEOPOLD & LOEB

In 1920s Chicago, Nathan Leopold and Richard Loeb, two local students, kidnapped and murdered schoolboy Bobby Franks as 'an intellectual challenge'. The two, who were also lovers, claimed to have committed the offence because they were bored, and wanted to prove their superiority by committing 'the perfect crime'. They failed. Loeb was killed in prison, and Leopold was paroled in 1958, dying of natural causes in 1971. The case inspired the Patrick Hamilton play, and Alfred Hitchcock film, 'Rope.' The only time you're ever likely to hear them mentioned nowadays is on old Woody Allen records.

"The reason I neglected my studies, Sir,
was because I was busy working
with my Dad on his plans to build a new
gymnasium for the College."

TARIQ ALI

Elder statesman, playwright and respected journalist, Ali was once the feared tyro of British student politics. As President of the Oxford Union in June 1965 he organised the first British 'teach-in' (a debate over Vietnam) which was televised. This essentially genteel event, however, gave no indication of the violence and notoriety which were to characterise Ali's later career — notably, the 'Grosvenor Square' riots. Ali organised these protests, together with Pat Jordan, under the banner of 'The Vietnam Solidarity Campaign'. The first, in October '67, resulted in 44 arrests. The second, in March '68, drew almost 28,000 protesters and was especially violent, with fighting between police and students lasting nearly two hours. The final march, in spite of the huge turnout of 100,000 and mounting hysteria leading up to it in the press, passed off without incident.

Little Tariq's face was pictured on every newsstand and bulletin in the land. He was invited to speak pretty much all over the world and hasn't looked back since. Now you're most likely to see him presenting 'Despatch Box' on BBC 2.

ESSAYS

'An essay is a collection of other people's thoughts, disguised to look like your own, in the judging of which, originality is heavily penalised.'

From 'A Liar's Autobiography' by Graham Chapman

Like whistling, masturbating and blowing smoke rings, essay writing is one of those skills that for many courses, your lecturers will simply expect you to have figured out for yourself*. Rarely will you encounter a tutor who will warmly take you to one side and explain the art of selecting quotations, or how to summarise your points concisely in a conclusion. And even more rarely will they give advice on your masturbation technique.

For these reasons, this chapter is dedicated to the art of essay writing, together with essential tips on research, meeting deadlines, cutting corners, plagiarism and downright cheating.

*if you are studying humanities/ languages etc, it is more likely that you will be given help in understanding how to write an essay, though if you fancy a challenge – ask your tutor to explain how to achieve 100% in your essays. You can get 100% for coursework in mathematics at university, so why not in essay writing?

RESEARCH

'Research' is, for many students, a four-letter word. (Actually it's an eight-letter word, but that is neither here nor there.) However, there are in any given subject, five guaranteed authorities you can quote to bolster whatever argument you may be making. Below are a few carefully chosen names to drop or leave hanging in conversation, the quoting of which will win you the respect of your tutor and fellow students…

"Five books are research, one book is plagiarism"

Cultural Studies/ Social Sciences

Karl Marx – Invented Communism, inspired revolutions around the world and suffered from boils

Gramsci – Cultural theorist and founder of the Italian Communist party. As a consequence he got up Mussolini's nose rather a lot, and ended his days in prison

Roland Barthes – Frenchman indirectly responsible for decades of NME journalism. Famously wrote an essay on the cultural mythologies of Daz and Omo washing powder

Noam Chomsky – Contrary, slogan-spouting radical-for-hire. The ultimate conspiracy theorist

Raymond Williams – Believed that culture is a form of industry. Ghastly. Tedious. Welsh

Economics

Adam Smith – Money-grabbing Scot and darling of the Right Wing. Influenced everyone from Gladstone to Ronald Reagan

Marx (again) – He crops up a lot in anything you're likely to be studying. Even metallurgy

John Maynard Keynes – The Elton John of Economics. Responsible for much of the Fifties and Sixties economic climate. Advocated mass spending to create full employment

J.K. Galbraith – Six foot eleven Yank and Keynes impersonator

Milton Friedman – Rabid, Thatcher-inspiring monetarist

English Literature

F.R.Leavis – Foaming-at-the-mouth literary autocrat

Terry Eagleton – Hip, leather-jacket-wearing Marxist. Interprets everything from Shakespeare to Carry On films with regards to the socioeconomic conditions of their time

Jacques Lacan – Structural linguist, whatever that is

Jacques Derrida – Unintelligible deconstructionistic, fey poseur. The ultimate Frenchman

Georg Lukàcs – Did not direct 'Star Wars'

Art

Gertrude Stein – Critic, scenester, and patron of Ernest Hemingway and Picasso.
Clement Greenberg – Famous critic and drunkard. His finest hour was the televised and slurred 'defection' from his position on Jackson Pollack as 'genius' to 'asshole and redneck.' But then he did like the odd G&T.
Guy de Bord – Rollneck-wearing French Situationist notable for being the real father of Punk. Shining moment – hurling a brick through a Parisian jewellers plate glass window with the attached message- 'Magic's Back!'. What a nutter.
Joseph Beuys – German artist. A fighter pilot during the Second World War, Beuys was shot down over Lapland. Seriously burnt, he was rescued by the Tartar people who wrapped his damaged body in Yak's fat and felt. On recovery, Beuys became (not unreasonably) a mystic and educator. His work often explores the magical properties of base substances such as honey, fat, metals etc. Also wore a cool hat.
Charles Saatchi – Art collector. Vilified throughout the Eighties and Nineties for creating an art market which he then manipulated, Saatchi nevertheless was true to a tradition of rich collectors who give youngsters (Damien Hirst, Tracy Emin etc) a break.

For other subjects, I'm afraid you'll have to find out for yourself, though Marx, Freud, and Chomsky are usually good for starters…

Although these five may vary slightly according to the whims of your particular faculty, if you stick with these you can't go far wrong. Firstly, reading them will mean you'll never have to read anything else (including the works they're actually commenting on), and secondly – since most of these people disagree with, and indeed, directly contradict one another – you can concentrate on their vast disagreements rather than the facts. Eventually you will be able to compose lengthy discourses entirely of their conflicting arguments while venturing no original opinions of your own. This is of course, what is expected of an academic essay.

RECYCLING

Bearing in mind that essay-topics rarely change, and that all academic prose is uniform and anonymous, it should be possible to recycle essays ad infinitum without anybody noticing. This practice can take one of several forms: -

A) YOUR OLD 'A' LEVEL WORK

Never underestimate the worth of even the shoddiest, most hastily prepared bit of tat you scribbled on the school bus. Sufficiently tarted up with quotations from any of your five key texts, it can be re-presented as a new and meticulously researched masterpiece.

B) HAND-ME-DOWNS

Most tutors give out pretty much the same essay titles year after year, so befriend a Second or Third Year and persuade them to let you copy their backlog in exchange for a drink / sex / pasta. Some essays have been doing the rounds like this for twenty years.

C) BUYING AND SELLING ON THE NET

Incredible though it may seem, some websites offer a service whereby essays on any particular subject can be downloaded for a small fee. While we could not possibly condone any student unscrupulous enough to benefit from this service, we must confess a certain admiration for their enterprise. Be advised however – mention this to anyone on your course and you might just end up handing in identical essays.

BIBLIOGRAPHY

It's bad practice for your bibliography to include merely the books you've actually read. Your tutor will be singularly unimpressed to see the same five names popping up again and again – so thicken the stock with as many obscure tomes as you can find, relevant or otherwise. (You don't even need to see the books. Just look up the titles on the Internet.) If you must glance over them, a useful trick is simply to read the first and last pages, and one chosen at random from the middle. Another neat trick is to nick titles, willy-nilly, from the bibliographies at the back of the few books you *have* read. As a last resort; make them up. With your tutors too busy trying to get off with freshers, or passing off post-graduates' research as their own, they almost certainly won't bother to check whether any of these books exist.

Well, perhaps.

The Berardi Five-Step Method of Essay-Writing

'The golden rule of essay writing is to never shy away from plagiarism, just do it with cunning'
Dr. A. Berardi

Discovered 15 years ago by the notorious Italian prankster and socialite Dr Berardi, this particular style of plagiarism has grown to become a standard amongst Universities in the west. In more recent years, its popularity has spread so far East and South that a rather primitive form of it was recently deployed on Vanuatu (a small Polynesian island), where a student at the local pig-farming college was found to have copied his entire essay 'the pig-myth' from some ancient scrolls found in a cave near his hut.

The Five Golden Steps

1) Go to the library. Root out a weighty book on your essay subject that hasn't been taken out of the library for a good few years and isn't on the reading list.

2) Do a little research on the author to ensure that he/she isn't too famous and hasn't written any other widely recognised works.

3) Copy huge chunks of the text directly into your essay in the knowledge that no one is going to be any the wiser.

4) Do not make any reference to the author in your essay and under no circumstances mention the book title in your bibliography.

5) To beef up your rather scant bibliography, go through a good many of the books on the reading list, opening each one at random and picking out general quotes that can be easily fitted into your essay, or any other essay for that matter*. (As mentioned earlier, reading the first and last lines of each book should give a vague idea of the contents, which can come in useful in tutorials if quizzed on the author.)

Congratulations! You should now have a first class essay, an impressive bibliography and one up on the University system. Welcome to the real world.

*Learn these quotes for exams and that'll help get you a first too.

URBAN MYTHS

Did you hear the one about the Philosophy student who, in his final year exam, when confronted with the question- *'What is the definition of bravery?'* answered with – *'This is.'*

And promptly left the exam.

And on a continuing theme, did you hear about another final year Philosophy student who, in his final year exam, when confronted with the age-old conundrum *'Why?'*, simply replied –

'Why not?'

These short tales have been doing the rounds at universities for umpteen years, and read, rather interestingly, like the Koans of Zen Buddhism.

(For anyone uninitiated in the mysteries of the East, Koans are documented tales of interaction between master and student.

E.g.: 'A monk went to his teacher and asked *'where can I find Buddha?'*

The master picked up his stick and shoved it firmly up the monk's nose and suddenly the monk was enlightened.')

MEETING DEADLINES

The business of writing an essay is further complicated by the fact that there is always a time limit. Though this can be anything from a week to, in the case of a dissertation, six months or more, you will, in all probability leave the work until the last possible moment (see 'the Gestatory Period Of An Essay' at the end of this chapter). There are therefore, several courses of action open to you.

1. GETTING AN EXTENSION

Disregarding the obvious excuses outlined elsewhere, you can claim one of the following to gain at least a few days' respite…

Trouble at home – Anything from your parents' impending divorce to the death of the family dog.

Heartache – Your girl/boyfriend has left you and you are incapacitated with grief.

Women's problems Always a good one, especially if you've got an old-fashioned tweed-wearing male lecturer who blushes at the mention of the word 'contraception'. He will not demand details of the problem at hand and would rather throw himself under a car than hear about your irregular menstrual cycle. N.B this will not work if you are a man.

2. FAKING A NERVOUS BREAKDOWN

For really hefty pieces of work, such as the 10,000-word dissertation, your bog standard excuses just won't cut the mustard. Extreme measures are called for, and faking a nervous breakdown is that extreme measure. This will take some planning. You will need:

A) A gullible doctor
B) A gullible counsellor
C) A gullible tutor
D) A tea cloth
E) A picture of 'Countdown' star Richard Whiteley
F) An ability to cry at will
G) A total lack of shame

Ideally, two weeks before your deadline, you should begin to display signs of mental instability. Start crying for no reason in the middle of conversations. Never wash or change your clothing, stare emptily into space for long periods, or wander around campus naked quoting the Book of Revelations with a tea cloth on your head. Then make an appointment to weep copiously before your doctor, who will promptly proscribe a course of Seroxat or Prozac, which you can sell to your friends. Next, visit your counsellor and weep copiously again, whining about the pressure on you, all the work you've got to do, your relationship with your mother, and how the pills the doctor gave you don't work. When the counsellor suggests perhaps trying to get you a reprieve, respond by screaming 'No! No! I must finish it! It's my life's work I tell you!' before collapsing in a heap. Before you know it, he'll be signing a special form requesting an extension on your deadline on the grounds of mental health. Finally, put your trousers on your head, glue a picture of Richard Whiteley to your arse and, dribbling, walk backwards into your tutor's room, hand him the form without comment, 'et voilà!'. With any luck he'll give you another month, which should more than compensate you for the loss of dignity and for the reputation you'll have earned as a 'psychopathic weirdo' that will dog you to your grave.

3. THE ALL-NIGHTER

When no more excuses can be made and you've reached the end of your fifth extension, you will inevitably find yourself with seven essays to write in the space of a single night. Beyond the difficulty of the sheer labour is the daunting task of simply staying awake. There are certain stimulants that will help you do this which are evaluated below.

COFFEE ★★★★

Reliable but limited. It probably won't keep you awake beyond 4.30 am, and can also give you a whacking case of heartburn after 45 cups which might upset your creative juices*. A further distraction is having to get up every five minutes, either to make a fresh cup or to pee.

PRO-PLUS ★★★★

Available over the counter at chemists, this is essentially a huge caffeine hit in the form of a tablet. If overindulged (as it often is by students) it can easily cause headaches and double vision, and give you an edginess akin to how you may have felt at the end of the Blair Witch Project. It also plays havoc with your bowels. Despite this, it's often a favourite for retaining a clear head.

RED BULL ★★★

Same as coffee but much, much more expensive.

SPEED ★

Do not – repeat – do not attempt to write your essays after a gram of this stuff. You'll probably have dashed off 150 pages by the crack of dawn, but not one of them will make the slightest sense. Even to you. See Spud's job interview in the film Trainspotting if you need convincing any more.

*If you've never experienced heartburn – it feels like rancid boiled beetroot is rising up from your stomach in an effort to dissolve your teeth.

LOUD MUSIC **

Playing Marilyn Manson or old Pixies albums at 138 decibels will keep you awake and set the pace for your typing skills, but it will also draw complaints from your neighbours as well as being a possible distraction to you too. Avoid 'The Dance of the Sugar Plum Fairy', or anything by Turin Brakes as they will definitely send you straight off, however loudly you play them.

A Cheeky Tale

"When I was at university, most of my social circle revolved around a couple called Pete and Eve, who were pretty big stoners and always had the best gear. A mutual friend called Shabby, who was work-shy to the nth degree, found himself in the very same position of having to write an entire term's worth of essays in a night. He took two grams of speed and managed to complete all of them, being particularly proud of one on Milton, which he read over approvingly the next morning before handing it in. He got it back a week later and was disappointed to see that he'd only received 48%. A note written by the marker read – *I would have given you a higher grade, but it's important to remember that the protagonists of Paradise Lost are Adam and Eve, not Pete and Eve.*"

Joe, Graduate of Nottingham Trent University

THE
GESTATORY PERIOD OF AN ESSAY

In order to achieve complete mastery of the form, one must never underestimate the importance of organising one's time properly. Make a chart if necessary. But most importantly, never ever leave it until the last minute.

There follows a template for how you will undoubtedly meet your deadline…

DAY ONE:

You are given the essay "Discuss Samuel Beckett's play 'Endgame' and its influence on post-war theatre, with particular reference to the works of Pinter, Osborne and Albee." – due in two weeks.

Spend the rest of the day in the bar.

DAY TWO:

Wake up hung over and lie in bed all day watching daytime TV, eating nice 'n' spicy Nick Nacks and smoking ashtray dog-ends.

Spend all evening in the bar.

DAY THREE:

Arise with a sense of purpose and resolve that you will definitely start work on your essay. Eat a hearty breakfast of toast and Marmite, pack pens, paper etc. and make for campus. Reject friends' suggestion of 'a couple of drinks' and proceed to the library. Grab a handful of books and sit. Stare out of window at happy students frolicking in sunlight. Sigh. Doodle funny face on paper. Listlessly flick through first book. Doodle your genitals on paper. Begin to feel hard-done-by. Mutter 'fucking Beckett' under breath. Give up, resolving to work later on in your room where there won't be any distractions. Join friends in bar in time

for second pint, feeling vaguely virtuous because you have at least checked out the books. Feel slight stabbing of guilt at 9.30 while downing another pint, but determine to start afresh tomorrow. Spend all evening in the bar.

DAY FOUR:

Awake feeling slightly the worse for wear. Drink enormous quantities of black coffee. Arrange books on desk and turn computer on. Become distracted by Mark Radcliffe on the radio. Type title of essay. Begin to feel slightly sick and drink pint glass of water. Open first book. Begin to feel really sick. Reason that you're never going to get any work done feeling like this and go back to bed. Sleep for thirteen hours, awaking at four in the morning. Turn on the video and watch the whole of Series One of 'Buffy'.

Go back to sleep again.

DAY FIVE:

Still feeling shaky. Convalesce by drinking tea, eating an entire bar of Dairy Milk, and watching daytime TV in your dressing gown.

DAY SIX:

Feeling better. First slight tremor of panic over essay. Make copious notes from books which, when viewed later, are entirely incomprehensible. Jack it in at 10pm and repair to bar, allowing yourself a frugal pint.

DAY SEVEN:

Just about to start essay when interrupted by Dodgy Martin from next door, who has just scored some 'amaaazing stuff.' Decide to take just one puff to help your creativity. Spend next 24 hours laughing, eating Snickers bars, Wine Gums and singing the theme from Bananaman.

DAY EIGHT:

Dodgy Martin round again. Bongs and pipes. Nod wisely when Dodgy Martin opines that 'essays are shit, man'. More theme tunes – this time Scooby Doo, Art Attack and TFI Friday. Have amazing insight into Beckett at 1.45 am, but fail to write it down and forget it four minutes later. Fall asleep in front of 'Buffy- Series Two.'.

DAY NINE:

Realising that Dodgy Martin is detrimental (nay, fatal) to essay writing, sneak out of room before he wakes up and repair to library. Struggle for four hours before coming up with opening sentence of essay – 'The influence of Samuel Beckett on post-war drama cannot be underestimated.' Feeling rather pleased with this, decide to decamp to bar to continue work. Feel rather raffish as you sit at the bar with notes and pint of lager. Interrupted by friend with news of 'fantastic party tonight.' Secretly resolve not to go, and feel warm glow of self-congratulation. More drinks in bar.

Realise you're still on first sentence. Drink more. Words swimming in front of eyes. Go to party. Meet rather attractive art-history student. Repair to his/her bed.

DAY TEN:

Still in his/her bed.

DAY ELEVEN:

Still in his/her bed. Knackered.

DAY TWELVE:

Finally leave, your conscience telling you it's to write the essay but really it's because you've run out of condoms and pot noodles. Resolve to work like hell, but instead meet friends at bar whom you can't help spilling the beans to about your last 3 days of sexual bliss. Retire alone to own bed at 1.30am, having entirely forgotten about essay.

DAY THIRTEEN:

Awake at four in the morning in icy cold sweat. Leap out of bed and switch on computer. Stare aghast at drug-induced notes which read 'Yoda perspired like Beckett into post-modern Boy George figure of theatre Britain.'

Have vision of self being thrown out. Have vision of self as tramp living on street dying lonely death. Have panic attack, in which you can't breathe. Calm down slightly and start typing at random – '…indeed, to underestimate the contribution of Beckett would be to close one's eyes to all innovations in theatre, from Shakespeare to Andrew Lloyd-Webber.' Do four pages then lie down. Awake at 2pm and re-read essay. Realise it doesn't make any sense at all. Rip it up. Go down to the bar and drown your sorrows.

DAY FOURTEEN:

Awake at 10am. Four and a half hours until essay must be handed in. Cry. Panic. Chainsmoke. Try to read five books in four hours. Re-type abandoned essay opening and continue typing randomly. Garnish with meaningless quotations culled from irrelevant books. Essay still only five pages long. Reformat, with triple-spacing and ENORMOUS typeface. Twelve pages – fantastic. Run to tutorial and arrive five minutes late. Hand in essay.

Receive another essay title, 'N.F. Simpson's oeuvre – the end of a cultural phenomenon or the beginning of one? Discuss.' Due in two weeks.

Spend the rest of the day at the bar....

DON'T SUFFER IN SILENCE

If you're having a problem with your coursework, then bring it up as soon as possible with the relevant tutor. You are much more likely to get a sympathetic hearing if you broach the subject 2 weeks before a deadline, rather than with five minutes to go.

Alternatively, consult your personal tutor.

LECTURES & TUTORIALS

Some lectures are tedious, unenlightened affairs, presided over by inaudible social misfits with speech impediments and monotonous voices, but we're prepared to admit that there are some bad ones as well.

OK, it's an old joke but, as with most comedy, there's a grain of truth in it. After all, it's a rare individual that can turn twelve pages of notes about the demise of the Sheffield Steel Industry into a spellbinding performance. As a consequence, you might occasionally want to find some other way to occupy your time while your lecturer is droning on. Doodling and text messaging are currently the most popular forms of time-wasting, while other useful props include:

• A good book • A walkman • A Game-Boy • Board games (Travel Scrabble, Ludo, or Junior Trivial Pursuit are particularly good) • a pillow (there is no shame in falling asleep during a lecture, even if you are the lecturer)

And in any case, should you miss/ fall asleep/ arse around in a lecture, you can always crib the notes from somebody else. For those of a mischievous and cruel disposition, humming and making farting noises with your hands under the desk, whilst maintaining an impassive expression on your face, is a great way of winding up a tutor. And if organised en masse, can induce a breakdown in the more fragile members of the scholarly community. However, if none of the above meets to your approval, you can always wile away the hours playing 'LECTURE I SPY'…

LECTURE I-SPY

CAN YOU SPOT?

a) The entire back row, surreptitiously text-messaging swear words to their friends in other lecture halls.

5 POINTS ☐

b) An attractive female student in a tight t-shirt whom the lecturer's eyes keep wandering towards, making him stumble over his words and dribble on his tie.

5 POINTS ☐

c) A psychothapic loner dressed in black (and sporting the only mullet on campus), who is writing the words 'kill kill kill' over and over again on his WHSmith pad.

10 POINTS ☐

d) The two students, who met on the first day of term and have acted like a married couple ever since, writing shopping lists for organic food and body-care products.

25 POINTS ☐

The student who's come to the wrong lecture, and is making his/herself conspicuous by continually looking around in a nervous manner but feeling too embarassed and English to actually get up and leave.

30 POINTS ☐

LECTURES YOU ACTUALLY WANT TO GO TO

In each university there is always a lecturer who fancies himself as a bit of a maverick, and gains a reputation on the circuit as something of a showman. This is usually due to cheap tricks such as wearing leather trousers, coming on with hands aloft to a burst of rock music, saying 'fuck' a lot, or ripping up and pissing on 'The Bible', or other such sacred text. However, despite the somewhat desperate shoddiness of their gimmicks, these guys generally give 'good value'.

Conversely, each university also has a lecturer who seems (from her flat-heeled shoes to the top of her Laura Ashley dress) the very embodiment of stuffiness, but who is, quite simply, an electrifying speaker, able to make even the most turgid subject as gripping as an Alfred Hitchcock movie.

GOOD LECTURES TO ATTEND

Film Studies – Free movies every day, followed by a hearty discussion.
Psychology – Glean an insight into your own fetid psyche – for free!
Any lecture involving an academic celebrity – i.e. Germaine Greer, David Lodge, Andrew Motion, etc. Get an autograph and, if you spot them up to no good, try and sell the story to the papers.
Anything that sounds really, really unusual – and/ or unfathomable (i.e. Chaos Theory, Shamanic Consciousness, Neo-Phantasmagoria, Psychic Monkey Linguistics). Once graduated, you may regret the pearls of wisdom that passed you by, so aim to attend at least one lecture per term, even if it's on Worm-Stretching in Stuart England. If nothing else, it may provide some original dinner party conversation in later life. In fact, a friend of ours swears that he actually studied the 'Importance of Hats in Shakespeare' for one whole term, during his three-year holiday at Bretton Hall.

It goes without saying that neither of these will be lecturing on any topic pertaining to your course. This doesn't matter – go anyway. Just as other people's newspapers on the train are more interesting than your own, other students' lectures are always infinitely more fascinating than the ones you have to drag your sorry bones along to.

HOW TO AVOID LECTURES

There is one sure-fire, time-honoured, fail-proof method of avoiding a lecture – don't go.

HOW TO SURVIVE AND EVEN EXCEL IN TUTORIALS WITHOUT REALLY TRYING

A short study in the art by David Mounfield

Tutorials are, of course, the lifeblood of university learning, where tutor and student sit, sometimes for up to two hours, once a week, in an atmosphere of mutual mistrust and silent paranoia. The tutor's job being to half-heartedly try to illicit any response to the subject matter that made up the reading list you lost two days ago, while your job is to respond with some degree of understanding.

Ghastly it can be, but these aren't like lecturers: they can fail you for not turning up. Attendance may be the minimum requirement to keep you off the vice-chancellor's list, (plus one essay a term), but this article is not about scraping by. It is about excelling at scraping by. Here's how it's done.

THE RULES

1. Arrive on time. Latecomers are always treated as an annoyance and will undoubtedly be an instant target for questioning from the tutor. If you do arrive late, make a brief apology and then wade straight into the debate with forthright opinions for about five minutes. It will let you off the hook for your bad time-keeping and give you brownie points for breaking the sea of silence that is the first five minutes of any tutorial. And it uses up time. Regard this *always* as your real job in any tutorial.

2. Always talk. It really doesn't matter what about. Everybody loves a good conversationalist, and no-one will be more relieved than your tutor to get away from the tedious matter at hand. Has an interesting event happened in the news?

Your tutor will have an opinion. Has he/she recently had some work published that they'd like to share with you? Your tutor will, no doubt, be delighted to discuss it. Imagine yourself to be a courtier and the tutor your ruler. Say what will please them, and give them the opportunity of hearing what is, to them, the sweetest sound of all; their own voice. If you play the part of a mirror; reflect back a flattering view of your tutor's insight and learning, and all will be well. Do not, however, be a sycophant. Occasionally put up a spirited defence against your tutor's opinions, as long as it uses up time. If the actual subject of the tutorial starts to loom on the horizon, it is your duty to wade in with some alarming new opinion on a trivial subject to get things back on track. Dare to be controversial; *'eyebrows should be taxed', 'all Mexicans are gay', 'compulsory shaving for the Welsh'. It doesn't matter.* Keep the conversation alive. It's only the minutes that count!

3. Steer the debate. When all tactics have been exhausted, there will be a portion of most tutorials that end up on the subject of the tutorial. It's a sad but unavoidable fact. But you are armed. It is a common and pitifully obvious tactic for the under-prepared student to "slipstream" in debate. For example; the tutor posits a question or point of debate. There is a pause. The mature student makes a nervous, fumbling but well-informed answer that illustrates a whole area of further discussion. The inexperienced know-nothings will then all eagerly jump on this bandwagon and ride it until their own lack of knowledge leaves it wheel-less five minutes later. Wait. Wait until you see the whites of their eyes, my friend. Then drop your bomb. Having looked serious and sage all through this early flurry of debate, as silence falls once again like a shroud on the room and the tutor wearily draws breath to start the whole process over afresh, come in with your bombshell. Say something like *"I hope I'm not speaking out of turn here, but one thing that struck me immediately about this text was what F.R. Leavis called "The tragic, inevitable effect of personal desire on the wider society". Does anyone agree?"* The tutor will immediately respond with the gratitude of a drowning man. At last! Someone who has bothered to do the reading! He will be doubly impressed as this was the quote around which he originally built much of his doctoral thesis, and you will know this because the mature student blurted this out to you twenty minutes earlier in the coffee bar. The others will, of course, now desperately jump into the debate and fill it for up to twenty minutes, which is exactly what you want. But it is too late for them; their trump has been played by you, and the brownie points are safe in your grasp. You need not speak again.

NB. These rules only really work, as far as we know, for the Arts and Humanities. Science students and the like may have to find different tactics, but then that really is your fault for trying to study something that will make you employable.

ONE-TO-ONE TUTORIALS

Some universities, Oxbridge in particular, conduct tutorials on a one-to-one basis. Just you, your tutor, and an hour of empty space to fill. Terrifying. No chance of letting the mature student fill up time with irrelevant questions, oh no.

And if you haven't done the reading (who does?) this is a golden opportunity for your tutor to uncover your inherent laziness, leaving you a marked man/ woman for the rest of the year. If, during one such tutorial, you find yourself floundering in a corner, about to give the whole game away, it's time to play your trump card by bringing up a subject dear to your tutor's heart. The vanity of lecturers being what it is, chances are he/she won't be able to resist the trap...

WAITING FOR LEONARDO

ACT ONE   SCENE ONE

THE ROOM OF AN OLD BUT DISTINGUISHED-LOOKING OXBRIDGE DON. HE WEARS A TWEED SUIT AND TIE AND SMOKES A PIPE. HE ONCE APPEARED ON 'NEWSNIGHT' IN A DISCUSSION ABOUT THE DISCOVERY OF A NEW DA VINCI, AND THIS HAS GONE TO HIS HEAD. HE SITS, CROSS-LEGGED AT HIS DESK. ENTER THE STUDENT, LOOKING PALE AND DRAWN.

DON: Ah....(LOOKS COVERTLY AT LIST OF NAMES ON DESK) Anthony. Sit down, sit down.

THE STUDENT DOES SO

DON: Ah, yes. I read your essay on Breugel the Younger (PRODUCES IT) and I found it very interesting in parts. I'm not sure I agree with your assertion that he was a major influence on Breugel the Elder. I think you may have become slightly confused, chronologically speaking. But anyway, on to other things. What did you think of Clark's 'The Nude: A Study of the Ideal in Art'?

STUDENT: (WHO OBVIOUSLY HASN'T READ IT)....Er...it was very nice. Oh..... and....interesting. I mean there's a lot of pictures of nudes in it aren't there? And a lot of sculptures of nudes as well...all over the place. I suppose people like nudes don't they? I mean... Ruebens did them, and...Picasso did them.....blue with their...bits on the wrong way round. And even today people are doing them left, right, and centre, and I suppose they always will do, and I think that is pretty much what Kenneth Clark is trying to say.

DON: (IN AN IRRITATED TONE)...Yes, yes but what of the Platonic   **75** form? What was Clarke saying about that?

STUDENT: He was saying……errrrrrrr….well….eeeeerrrrrrrrr

FLOUNDERING DESPERATELY HE PLAYS HIS WILD CARD

STUDENT: Oh!…..Da Vinci was keen on the platonic form wasn't he?… .in fact, didn't you once appear on Newsnight discussing Da Vinci?

DON: Ah, yes, I did as a matter of fact…

45 MINUTES LATER

DON:… And that Jeremy Paxman is an awfully nice chap. Not at all like you'd think he'd be from seeing him on the telly. I had a drink with him in the green room afterwards and he really was a very perceptive fellow…

DON LOOKS AT HIS WATCH:

DON: Good lord. Is that the time? Yes, we'd better finish now. Erm…I believe you have an essay for me, on Dali?

STUDENT: (CUNNINGLY) Er……….can I have your autograph, sir?……..

THE DON PRENTENDS NOT TO UNDERSTAND BUT SECRETLY BLUSHES WITH PRIDE

STUDENT:.it's just that I've never met anyone that's been on television before.

DON: But of course! (SIGNS AUTOGRAPH WITH A FLOURISH AND LOOKS DOWN FOR A FEW SECONDS TO TRY AND LOCATE HIS TOBACCO POUCH IN DESK DRAWER, AT WHICH POINT THE STUDENT QUIETLY SLIPS OUT).

DON: (TO EMPTY ROOM). Now what was I just saying?…….

THE
LECTURING FRATERNITY

'99% of lecturers give the others a bad name' – Ancient proverb

Unlike students, university lecturers have changed very little in the past 500 years. Like politicians they have nobly upheld the traditions of lechery, vanity and incompetence, while sauntering on in the futile hope that one day they will be immortalised for their body of work on 'the use of semi-colons in Shakespeare'.

Yet despite this, some still have the power to breath such enthusiasm and passion into the dullest of subjects, that they'd have you believe Mechanical Engineering to be the sport of the gods. Which kind you get is just a matter of luck really. So should you find yourself nodding off every afternoon to the drones of some bearded old fool, while your friends, inspired by their tutor, are experimenting with alchemy, ESP and time-travel, just remember – life can be cruel.

Dr Love
Description:
Middle-aged, married philanderer who preys on young students offering higher grades for sexual favours.
Appearance:
Leather jacket, checked shirt, Levi's, leonine mane of grey hair. Bears a vague resemblance to Melvyn Bragg.
Idiosyncrasy:
Sits on edge of desk in a flirtatious way during tutorials.
Most likely to say:
'Let's discuss this over a drink.'
Lecture style:
Soft silky voice and a propensity for running his hands through his mane whilst fixing his penetrating gaze on the large-breasted girl in the third row.

Dr In Da House

Description:

Dynamic young tutor, who still wants to be one of the gang. The only lecturer to be occasionally invited to wild student parties, he will generally embarrass himself by downing a whole bottle of whisky and throwing the television set out of the window.

Appearance:

Radiohead t-shirt, combats, short spiky hair, Liam Gallagher type shades.

Idiosyncrasy:

Openly smokes pot during tutorials.

Most-likely to say:

"In my opinion, Derrida was a fucking charlatan. That's right, I said 'fucking'."

Lecture style:

Quotes lyrics from Thom Yorke, David Bowie and Eminem. Once entitled a lecture 'Will the real Tristram Shandy please stand up.'

Disclaimer- Any similarity between the characters in this chapter and anyone living or dead is, of course, far from coincidental.

Dr Feelgood

Description:
Middle-aged and earnest single female, originally from North America. Overly demonstrative in her demeanour, she has yet to comprehend the taciturn nature of the English temperament and is prone to placing her hand on the arms of her students who will invariably recoil in distaste.

Appearance:
Laura Ashley dresses, silk scarves and Native American jewellery.

Idiosyncrasy:
Begins each tutorial with a ten-minute group therapy session, even though she teaches Geography.

Most likely to say:
"I don't want to know what you think in your essay, I want to know what you feel."

Lecture style:
Wild gesticulations of the arms and the occasional balletic leap.

Professor Dumbledore

Description:
Infinitely kind and worldly-wise lecturer, loved by both students and staff. Knowledgeable in not only his subject matter, but in everything to do with human nature. Can be found sitting on his favourite campus bench, smiling benignly for hours about nothing in particular. Loveably perplexed by computers/ mobile phones/ video recorders and electric razors. Personally knew Yeats, James Joyce and Freud. Rumoured to be able to turn water into wine.

Appearance:
A cross between God, Father Xmas and Gandalf. Still actually wears leather patches on the elbows of his jacket, corduroys that appear to have grown out of his skin and the same pair of brogues that he bought in 1927. Sports an eccentric hat of some kind, and invariably smokes a pipe.

Idiosyncrasy:
Habitually routes around in his ears with paper-clips/ pens/ your essay.

Most-likely to say:
'I am a universe inside my head.'

Lecture style:
A master storyteller, he has his audience hanging on his every word as he brilliantly illustrates the possibility of time-travel through amusing references to what his wife said to him that morning.

Professor Brainstorm

Description:

A jargonist of the highest order, this lecturer is incapable of describing anything in simple words (or 'nodes of meaning' as she would say). Young, dynamic and fanciable, she will cause male students' hearts to beat faster whenever she approaches, but sink whenever she opens her mouth. Despite her first book,'The decay of semiotic behavioural realisation systems', being completely unreadable, it has been a campus best-seller, thanks to the back cover featuring a sexy full-colour photo of its author in a little black number.

Appearance:

Young, sexy and well-dressed, with a neat line in patent leather trousers.

Idiosyncrasy:

Rumoured to be bi-sexual.

Most likely to say:

'The marginalisation of the hegemony of post-modern logistical difference is attributable to the delineation of Freudian Positivism, but only in as much as the Chomskyist theorem of didactic determinism co-interrelates to…'

Lecture style:

Completely incomprehensible. After five minutes the only pleasure one might get is when she bends over to pick up some dropped notes.

Dr Strangelove

Description:
Impeccably preserved elderly homosexual, commonly found at the more established universities (ie not an old Poly). Unswervingly decent, upstanding and professional, he has never acted on his desires, but will occasionally suffer moments of delicious melancholy after a tutorial with a Leonardo Di Caprioesque student. Almost certain to be a Classics scholar.

Appearance:
Elegant Saville Row tailored suits, bow tie and unusually flamboyant shirt. Meticulously coiffeured hair. Looks like Gore Vidal.

Idiosyncrasy:
Seemingly infinite supply of dry sherry in his top drawer.

Most-likely to say:
"My dear boy, you really should read Death in Venice."

Lecture style:
Florid and erudite, with an exquisite turn of phrase, and perfectly balanced sentences, but occasionally prone to throwing in the odd bitchy remark about the other lecturers.

Dr Dolittle

Description:

Lacklustre at the best of times, this most indolent of creatures will have been delivering the same lecture ('will man ever land on the moon?') for nearly 40 years. His absences from lectures strangely coincide with test matches, Wimbledon, The Grand National, Five Nations Cup and happy hour.

Appearance:

Slovenly. Always wears the same rumpled beer-stained charcoal grey suit.

Idiosyncrasy:

Since gaining his doctorate from the University of Doncaster in 1965, he has yet to publish a single academic treatise or article of any kind.

Most likely to say:

'Ah, your essay. Now. I've got it here somewhere, I'm sure I marked it but... ...ah, yes... ...now I remember... ... errrr... ...the dog rather got hold of it last night...'

Lecture style:

None. Simply puts on a video that is vaguely related to the subject and sits back to do the crossword.

Doogie Houser MD

Description:

This guy obviously did his 'O' levels at the age of seven, his 'A' levels at the age of 10, and passed his PhD before he could buy a drink in a pub, as he is head of the whole physics department despite being much younger than you. After winning the Nobel prize at the age of twenty nine, he will burn out and become a tramp.

Appearance:

Looks about 15, with bum-fluff, greasy hair and lolloping gait.

Idiosyncrasy:

Complete inability to communicate his knowledge, combined with a profound lack of social skills.

Most-likely to say:

'Pint of cider please… …what do you mean you want to see my ID, of course I'm over 18, I'm a member of staff. Oh for fuck's sake, put me down… …ouch… …you big bully, give me back my glasses…'

Lecture style:

Malformed sentences stuttered out at minimal volume, while his voice alternates between high-pitched piping tremolo and a basso profundo. Blushes upon being questioned by female students.

GAMES

1. Can you help Dr Dolittle get to his tutorial on time?

PROFESSOR BRAINSTORM'S WORDSEARCH

2. Can you find all the words in Professor Brainstorm's wordsearch?

C	Z	A	R	D	A	S	C	O	C	C	Y	G	E	S
F	O	P	Z	K	Y	V	A	P	R	T	Y	Q	V	L
A	R	O	C	V	G	I	R	A	Y	Q	T	S	T	M
I	O	P	Q	V	I	N	C	U	N	X	V	P	U	U
Z	A	H	N	Q	Q	K	H	X	Y	B	L	I	M	I
T	S	T	I	S	R	A	A	L	B	W	B	R	N	R
C	T	H	N	I	V	T	E	X	X	R	A	A	K	T
O	R	E	Q	D	C	M	O	X	E	Q	X	E	H	T
H	I	G	U	B	Q	O	P	T	Y	Z	O	A	G	Y
C	A	M	E	Y	I	O	T	M	N	L	L	C	Q	O
S	N	V	R	R	N	Y	E	L	K	V	O	Q	W	P
H	I	V	E	A	N	A	R	Q	B	L	T	I	B	P
C	S	C	M	H	I	B	Y	M	X	X	L	K	D	U
S	M	Q	E	C	J	W	X	C	O	R	Y	Z	A	G
E	I	S	T	E	D	D	F	O	D	W	L	C	Q	N

ESCHSCHOLTZIA
CZARDAS
COCCYGES
PYX
SPIRAEA
YTTRIUM
OPPUGN
OOMIAK
CORYZA
EISTEDDFOD
DJINNI
CHARYBDIS
QUINCUNX
AXOLOTL
APOPHTHEGM
XYLEM
QUINQUEREME
ARCHAEOPTERYX
YTTERBIUM
XYLOID
ZOROASTRIANISM

3. Can you unscramble this photo to discover which lecturer this is?

Answer: Doogie Houser M.D.

85

SIGMUND FREUD

'The father of psychoanalysis'

Born in Moravia in 1856, Freud studied medicine in Vienna, before switching to psychopathology, and from this, formulated his famous theories on the unconscious. These theories (including the notion that even infants have an inherent sexual awareness, dreams are manifestations of repressed sexual desire, and all men with beards are great lovers) earned him a great deal of notoriety and were vigorously opposed. In 1902 he became a lecturer at the University of Vienna, where, with Adler and Jung, he set up a society for tolerant and open-minded psychologists to discuss these controversial ideas.

Within only a few days, however, the three men were all quarrelling bitterly. Freud, determined to keep his role of 'father figure', infuriated Jung in his refusal to be psychoanalysed, and the two fell out. The final straw came when Jung called Freud's mum a 'fat cow', Freud gave Jung a Chinese burn and Adler wet himself.

The three never spoke again and went their separate ways. With the annexing of Austria by the Nazis in 1938, Freud (who was Jewish) fled to Hampstead, where he died a year later of cancer of the jaw, caused (and in a very Freudian way) by sucking on big fat cigars.

KEY IDEA(S):

The Oedipus Complex. This states that each male child harbours an unconscious desire to sleep with his mother and kill his father. This superceded the current theory of the day, the Julian Clary complex, which stated that every male child harbours the desire to sleep with his father and would kill for his mother's wardrobe.

RECOMMENDED READING:

The Interpretation Of Dreams, The Psychopathology of Everyday Life.

QUOTE:

"The great question, and one that has never been answered, and which I have not yet been able to answer, despite my thirty years of research into the feminine soul, is 'what does a woman want?'"

CLAIM TO NOTORIETY:

Took cocaine throughout most of his life, wrote on the benefits of it, and shared it with many of his friends, making him extremely popular at parties. Perhaps, however, Freud's single most important contribution to mankind came from the fact that, with his cuddly white beard, glasses and strong German accent, he set the standard for comic caricatures of pschoanalysts forever.

GERMAINE GREER

Unlike any other academic in the history of the world ever, Sydney lass Greer seemed to lead a double life during her tenure as lecturer in English Literature at Warwick. By day, a stuffy academic, poring over the finer points of Chaucer and Shakespeare, by night a sex-obsessive, orgy-attending, 'Rolling-Stone' cover-girl with a filthy mouth and a sharp tongue.

With the publication of her seminal work 'The Female Eunuch' in 1970, she became a spearhead for 'Second-Wave' feminists the world over, and appeared on the cover of 'Life' magazine billed as 'The Saucy Feminist Even Men Adore'. Now a fellow of Newnham College, Cambridge, she seems to have calmed down somewhat. Thank God.

KEY IDEA(S):
Marriage is nothing more than a legalised form of female slavery, with the repression of female sexuality in a male-dominated society thrown in for good measure.

RECOMMENDED READING:
The Female Eunuch.

QUOTE:
"I guess I'm just a starfucker really."

CLAIM TO NOTORIETY:
Appeared stark naked in a beaver shot in 'Suck' magazine in 1972. The caption read 'Germaine Shows Her Cunt.'

In the Nineties, still keen on a bit of controversy, she also made the news after bitchily describing fellow newspaper columnist Suzanne Moore as having *'birds nest hair, five inches of fat cleavage and fuck-me shoes.'*

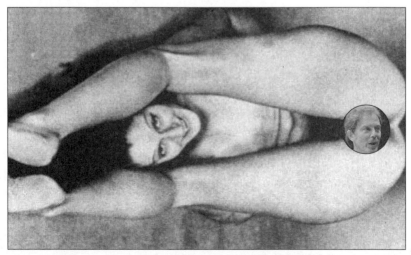

DR TIMOTHY LEARY

Throughout the Sixties and Seventies, Leary was partly responsible for spearheading the counter-culture revolution in the US, through his (much misunderstood) role as 'LSD- guru'. Far from encouraging mindless hedonism through psychedelic drugs, Leary was, instead, interested in their use for a new therapeutic form of Psychiatry. Whilst working at Harvard University, Leary achieved promising results by using LSD to help rehabilitate criminals and cure alcoholics. He went on (like Allen Ginsberg and William Burroughs before him) to suggest that psychedelic plants, when used in the right settings, can bring about profound and positive changes to the human psyche, not to mention a compulsion for sporting paisley shirts and clogs.

Before enough meaningful results could be made, however, LSD was made illegal in the US, and Leary was arrested in 1968 for possession of a small quantity of cannabis. The government, recognising a powerful and 'dangerous' figurehead of counterculture when they saw one, incarcerated him for 8 years for good measure. Leary escaped prison in 1970, fled to Switzerland, was extradited and finally released in 1976 when new evidence came to light that the eighth he was sent down for was in fact an old OXO cube.

Since his liberation he dedicated much of the rest of his life to championing new computer technologies, Chaos Theory and Cyberculture, yet he never successfully threw off the old tag of 'LSD guru'.

Though now deeply unfashionable, and widely scorned by Science and the Media, the lack of acceptance of many of Leary's ideas exposes much more the failings of society as a whole to take an interest in raising the level of human consciousness and develop the human spirit; something that Leary dedicated his whole life to. Hats off to the man.

KEY IDEA:
Psychedelics have the potential for generating spiritual growth in mankind.

RECOMMENDED READING:
Exo-Psychology, 'The Politics of Ecstasy', 'Chaos and Cyberculture', 'Start your own Religion'.

QUOTE:
"Tune in, turn on, drop out"

CLAIM TO NOTORIETY:
Faced with cancer in the late Nineties, he celebrated his impending death via the Internet.

NIETZSCHE

Born in 1844 in Saxony, the son of a Lutheran pastor, Nietzsche was a brilliant student, who was, at the age of 24, appointed Professor of Philology (the study of classical texts) at Basle University without even having completed his degree (a good trick if you can pull it off). There he lectured for ten years, although he came to acquire a deep contempt for the plodding methods of academia. He lived an extremely lonely life (partly as a result of growing one of the stupidest moustaches on record), throughout which his books were almost completely ignored, though his influence on twentieth century thought is incalculable.

KEY IDEA:
The Superman. Fatally misunderstood by the Nazis, this complex idea, which has nothing whatever to do with race or evolution, is best summed up by Nieztsche himself – "Man is something to be overcome. The 'overcoming' of man is in fact the overcoming of oneself – the mastery of one's desires and the creative use of one's powers." In a godless world where systems of morality are purely subjective, this is a challenge we all face. In a nutshell – try going without fags, booze, chocolate and masturbating for one month and you'll soon discover what a weak-willed pathetic individual you really are.

Anyone who can overcome themselves, according to Nietztsche, is a 'Super – man' or Super-woman (hotpants, red boots and whip optional).

Ironically enough, with such a deep-rooted belief in a godless world, Neitztsche's ideas sometimes echo uncannily the practices of many religion doctrines in their purest forms, particularly Buddhism.

RECOMMENDED READING: Thus Spake Zarathustra, Beyond Good And Evil

QUOTE: *"God is dead."*

CLAIM TO NOTORIETY: Went stark raving bonkers through syphilis, which he probably caught while a student (though God knows who would have gone to bed with such a misery arse as him). His final breakdown came in a remarkable fashion. Seeing an old man in the market place at Turin whipping his horse, Nietzsche ran to the animal, embraced it, wept copiously, then fainted.

SOCRATES

Born in Athens in 469 B.C., Socrates was the great, great granddaddy of western thought. His most famous pupil was Plato, who recorded most of his philosophy in 'Apology', and 'Phaedo.' Socrates shifted the emphasis of philosophy from speculation about the natural world to ethics and concepts. He was also reputed to be so ugly that fellow citizens would openly laugh at him in the street.

KEY IDEA:

The 'Socratic Method', which involved asking his pupils to define certain concepts, such as 'truth', 'justice', or 'love', through a dialect of questions and answers, thus revealing the inherent contradictions in the concepts (i.e. like every good lecturer, he didn't do a stroke of work himself.)

RECOMMENDED READING:

Never wrote anything. We only know of his works through the writings of Plato, Aristophanes and Woody Allen.

QUOTE:

'The only thing I am certain of is my own ignorance.' (This confession alone, of course, puts him head and shoulders above all other lecturers.)

CLAIM TO NOTORIETY:

Was prosecuted for 'perverting the young' with his ideas and sentenced to death by drinking hemlock (an evil concoction of Red Bull, Horlicks and arsenic) in 399 BC.

DON'T SUFFER IN SILENCE

If you're having a problem with a tutor and feel you're being victimised or even sexually harassed (though very rare, this does occasionally happen) the best thing to do is to go to the Education Officer at the S.U. right away. He or she will advise you of the proper channels of complaint, which differ from university to university. It's probably not a good idea to approach anyone else on the faculty, or your personal tutor at first, as you cannot be sure they will respond favourably to any accusations you might make.

THE LIBRARY

In theory, the library is where you spend the majority of your time at university, studying, revising, poring over dusty old tomes and up-to-the-minute periodicals, and scribbling down notes for those masterly dissertations that will set the academic world aflame. In practice, you're just as likely to use it for snoozing, flirting, chatting to your mates, scoffing sandwiches, or just idly browsing through books that are in no way related to your subject but seem infinitely more interesting.

But, as finals draw ever nearer, it's likely that more and more of your time will converge here, in a vain, last-ditch attempt to get your head down and finally try to understand what Post-Modernism actually is. During this period, the library can be as bustling as Times Square during rush hour, and the photocopiers, computers, short loan texts and the last slice of lasagne in the canteen as elusive as pubic hair at a Westlife concert.

THE CANTEEN

Usually located in the belly of this vast building, the library canteen is, perhaps, the very nerve-centre of the university campus. This is a place where friendships are forged, endless debates are fought and lost, and countless cups of coffee consumed, with everybody united under the banner of that well-worn phrase –

'God I've got so much to do, I must get back to it', followed by –

'Oh, alright, just one more cuppa and then I've really got to knuckle down'.

So, bearing in mind that this place can bring out the procrastinator in everyone, what is an acceptable length of stay and number of visits to the library canteen? Here's a simple rule of thumb:

- If the lady behind the counter knows your name, your studying is not going well.
- If she can predict with a stifling yawn what you're going to eat and drink and even has the correct change ready before you open your wallet, you're in big trouble.
- If she knows about your dad's problems with his verucas and is offering you advice on how to spice up your sex life with your partner then you're well on your way to failing.
- And, if you're starting to glow Homer Simpson yellow from eating nothing but their microwaved lasagne every lunch and evening for a whole year, then perhaps it's time to throw in the towel and just get a job there instead.

Despite these various invidious properties that the library canteen possesses, it can be a welcome friend during the heady months of late spring, when you're in need of occasional relief from those long heavy hours revising and studying in the carrel. Just remember though; even the heroes of Greek legends would have thought twice about doing battle with those rubbery burgers, festering salads and bulletproof spuds…

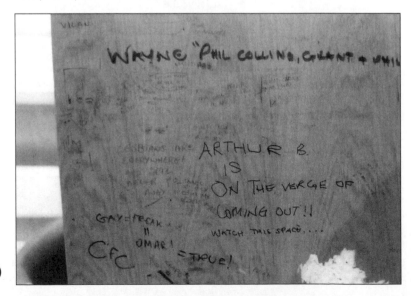

THE PHOTOCOPYING AREA

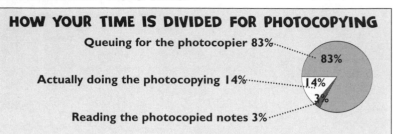

HOW YOUR TIME IS DIVIDED FOR PHOTOCOPYING

Queuing for the photocopier 83%

83%

Actually doing the photocopying 14%

14%

3%

Reading the photocopied notes 3%

It's a fact of university life that any book you really desperately need for completing your work will be both out of print and 'for reference only'. This will therefore, necessitate an enormous amount of photocopying, sometimes of the entire book (which isn't strictly allowed, so you'll have to do it in shifts, donning a disguise each time). For this reason, the photocopier queues in university libraries are always depressingly long and slow. Most universities have tried to cut down on this congestion by having photocopiers run on cards rather than small change. In reality it hasn't helped a bit, since most students' experiences of photocopying run along the following lines…

1) Join an unfeasibly long queue, moving forward with the speed of an old man eating soup.
2) Realise twenty minutes later that you've left your photocopy card at home.
3) Leave queue, and go to the machine to get a new card.
4) Realise you don't have change.
5) Waste ten minutes walking to the nearest cash machine.
6) Return to library with a twenty-pound note.
7) Spend 15 minutes in the library canteen eating a dehydrated pasty and a shrivelled sausage, just in order to get change.
8) Return to the card machine. Notice that there is now an enormous line of people in front of it. Join queue.
9) Finally get to the front of queue, insert your money, and get card.
10) Follow the queue for the photocopier and discover that it snakes all the way to the Waste-Management section on the fifth floor of the library.
11) Throw yourself out of fifth floor window.

HOW TO AVOID THROWING YOURSELF OUT OF THE FIFTH FLOOR WINDOW

A) Make sure you've got plenty of change on you.
B) Buy two photocopying cards, keep them in your wallet at all times and keep one fully charged as a back up.
C) Try to do your copying early in the morning when it's likely to be less crowded. Just before closing time is no good, as the queue by then will just bring back unpleasant memories of the toilets at Glastonbury.
D) Ask yourself how important it is to actually photocopy the thing in the first place. Couldn't you just read it and make notes?

THE STUDY BOOTHS

There are two kinds of library booths – the A.V. and the study-booth. The A.V. is, properly speaking, a kiosk, and is self-contained, with its own door, light, TV, video, and even CD player, whereas a study-booth is merely part of a big long table with partitions stuck on the top of it. You can get away with very nearly anything in an A.V. booth: having sex, smoking dope, hosting a romantic dinner for two, manufacturing a bomb, anything. Unfortunately, for this very reason, it is difficult to find one unoccupied, especially given the number of media students there are these days. Study booths, on the other hand appear, to the outsider, to function as little more than glorified cloakrooms. In any university library you will see countless booths that have been bagsied with a fleece draped over the chair, and a rucksack and a few books plonked on the table, leaving the owner free to wander around unencumbered, chatting to his/ her mates and hanging out in the canteen until closing time, when he/she returns to reclaim their belongings, secure in the knowledge that they've put in a solid day's work.

HOW YOUR TIME IS DIVIDED IN THE STUDY BOOTH

Daydreaming 31%
Checking out whom you fancy 17%
Reading the graffiti 14%
Replying to the graffiti 10%
Nibbling on snacks 8%
Nodding off and dribbling on your notes 16%
Working 4%

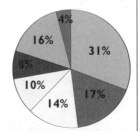

MOBILE PHONES

All university libraries take a very dim view of these, requesting students to switch them off upon entering the premises. There is a point to this. Isaac Newton would probably never have developed calculus if he'd been surrounded by the constant trilling of the theme tune to the Good Life and someone saying, *"Ah, Giles – I'm in the library. Whassup!"* However, most students would rather lose a limb than turn off their mobiles even for a second, and so will cunningly switch them to vibrate, and conduct clandestine, sotto voce conversations in the study booths (while the people they're talking to sit in the booths opposite). Some actually resort to going into the loo to continue their inane chatter. There are few things more disturbing than passing by a cubicle, and hearing a muffled voice proclaim, *"Hi there! Yeah, I wondered where you'd got to. I haven't see you for ages."* Which could leave you feeling incredibly paranoid, or worse, fearful that the owner of the voice is actually addressing his own turd.

TOILETS

Alongside the usual racist, homophobic and moronic scribbling found in every campus loo (who **are** these people??) library toilets can also be said to boast graffiti of a decidedly literary bent, foregoing such sentiments as "beware limbo dancers" for loftier statements like "'God is Dead' – Nietzsche. 'Nietzsche is dead' – God", "Proust woz 'ere" and "André Breton was a wanker." If you have neither the time nor the inclination to read any books, a quick glance at the lavvy walls should at least give you a few humorous quotations to colour your essays with.

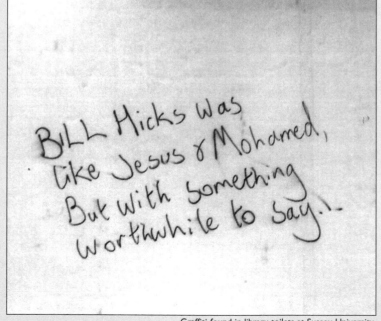

Graffiti found in library toilets at Sussex University

COMPUTERS

Your library is sure to have rank upon rank of perfectly serviceable PCs, but unfortunately there are always more students than computers available, and getting to use one is like trying to get a Nu-Goth to wear a pink flowery shirt. Having finally gained access, however, you will find that the library PC is actually no fun at all. All Internet usage is strictly monitored for obscenity, and anything even slightly dodgy will get you thrown out on your ear. Even if you *could* look up – 'hairyfatandnaked.com" – you probably wouldn't want to if you're seated between a mature student and a willowy first year studying R.E., with the library assistant periodically peering over your shoulder. And while the Internet can be indispensable for research, bear in mind that it is not always the most reliable source of information. Type "famous quotations" into a search engine to find what Tolstoy said about Shakespeare, and you're more than likely to wind up with "Steve's Hilarious Red Dwarf Quotes Page." Though with the odd bit of tweaking, you could try and pass a few of them off as authentic off the cuff witticisms from the great Russian novelist.

ILLICIT DINING IN THE LIBRARY

Since the dawn of university life and beyond, students have been stealing themselves off into quiet corners of the University Library to have a crafty nibble on a cheese sandwich.

Despite this being such a commonplace activity, it is possible to get into trouble for stuffing your face in the library, and bringing knives, forks, napkins and a carafe of red wine is not advisable.

Sneaking food in is easy, provided you have a bag. If you haven't, buy a cheap gun holster from a toyshop and wear it under your coat. They work perfectly in the art of discreetly storing a sandwich about one's person.

Once the food is successfully inside the library, choose your picnic spot carefully. The Short Loan section is a big mistake, as it has a constant stream of students and staff, while scoffing among the bookshelves can leave you prey to being caught unaware. Instead, either seek out a study booth which is so remote and hidden that it houses the skeleton of a forgotten Ph.D. students from the 1970s, or find one that gives a full commanding view of the corridor you are in, so that no librarian has the chance to creep up on you and catch you with a mouth full of Spaghetti Bolognese.

NARCOLEPTIC BOOK SYNDROME (NBS)

A worryingly persistent problem, Narcoleptic Book Syndrome has been present in all university libraries since their inception in the late 1300s.

The effects of NBS are sudden and overwhelming: the victim sits down in a study carrel with a short-term loan set text that must be at least skimmed through by next week/tomorrow/this afternoon, and despite his/her best intentions and steely resolve, within a minute of the book being open, debilitating waves of sleepiness overcome them. Some may briefly struggle against the inevitable, but in 90% of cases, the victim is spark out in a deep sleep, snoring gently and dribbling on the introduction page within ten minutes. Effects of the disease have been known to be even more spectacularly rapid when handling books with no pictures in.

Recent scientific evidence however, *has* discovered large residues of the soporific herb valerian (often used in the paper-making process) prevalent in the paper used for dull academic texts and there have been some suggestions that if enough of this substance inadvertently finds its way into the blood stream it can make the reader feel drowsy. But when tested on normal healthy patients, it was discovered that they had to lick over 400 pages of a particularly long and tedious biography of Marx before feeling any ill effect.

So NBS remains a mystery, but should you find yourself suffering from any of these worrying symptoms, our best advice is to go for a bracing walk, grab a coffee in the library canteen or swap to Fine Art.

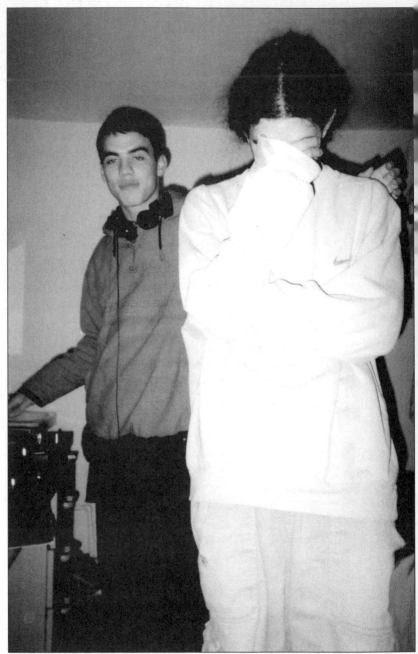

That traumatic moment of discovery when you realise that the laundry fairy doesn't exist

LIFESKILLS

Let's cut to the quick. Obviously you are very excited at the thought of leaving home and being able to do many things that have previously been denied you. But be aware that freedom has a cost. You have up 'til now most probably been living in an artificial environment where many important life-supporting tasks that you are barely aware of have been managed for you. In particular (and you may want to sit down before you continue reading) the following childhood friends will not be going to University with you:

- The Laundry Fairy
- The Washing-Up Elf
- The Tidy-Up Pixie
- The Sock-Sorting Sylph
- The Magic Money Machine

It was all an illusion perpetrated by your parents to keep you in an extended state of adolescence, for reasons which only 20 years of Freudian analysis will uncover. Help, however, is at hand...

#1 CLEANING THE KITCHEN
(or HOW TO AVOID HOUSE ARMAGEDDON)

1) **Try and make a house rule of 'washing up as you go':** Then watch as arguments of epic proportion erupt over whose eggy frying pan has been left in the sink for two weeks.

2) **Rule of thumb:** If you find it hard to cross the kitchen due to your trainers sticking to the lino, it's probably time to give it a wash. Equally, if you can't remember what colour your work surfaces are, it's also time for a spot of cleaning. Then watch as arguments of epic proportion erupt over whose turn it is to do this.

3) **Make a washing-up and cleaning rota:** Only girls can do this. No-one knows why, but in all-male student households, despite agreeing wholeheartedly to the rota system, men find it impossible to understand the concept of "turns" and also, due to some quirk of nature, they cannot read the charts.* They will grow restless and angry when challenged about it being their "turn" and start shouting irrational nonsense. To conclude, whether your household is male, female or mixed, rotas never work  for more than two weeks anyway, before someone goes away for the weekend, thus missing their turn and throwing the rota totally off-kilter. Then watch as arguments of epic proportion erupt over who should take responsibility for their washing up duty.

4) **Get a house kitty going for cleaning provisions:** This money can then be spent once a month to buy bleach, cloths and the like which will then sit forever untouched under the sink. More likely it will be secretly used to buy a bottle of cheap vodka by the house boozer, leading to arguments of epic proportion over where the money has mysteriously gone.

In reality, the only things that will keep your place habitable are an iron will, and some degree of honour amongst your housemates. Choose them wisely…

*For the male student, rotas are actually able to bend time in ways that could be of interest to quantum physics.

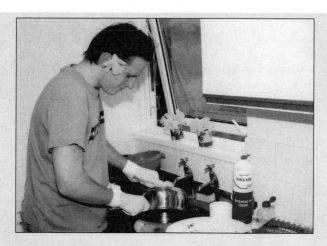

#2 CLEANING THE BATHROOM

HOW TO REMOVE HAIR FROM THE PLUGHOLE

With long hair deeply unfashionable for men it's the ladies who are usually to blame on this one. Congealed lumps of matted hair are often the most common cause of blocked sinks and baths. Under no circumstances try and remove this revolting stuff with your fingers, your hands will never feel clean again. Caustic soda will shift the stuff but probably kill off half the world's fish stocks in the process (it's a wee bit toxic); your best bet is to 'borrow' the tweezers from the most unpopular person in your household and wrench it out with them.

HOW TO REMOVE A FLOATER

1) Go out and eat a plate of black pudding, then bombard it with your own.
2) Weigh it down with toilet paper and flush twenty times. (Remembering to leave enough loo paper for your next visit).
3) Throw a lit firework at it and run for cover.
4) Fish it out and stick it in the bed of the perpetrator of the crime.

HOW TO REMOVE SKID MARKS IN THE LOO

Whatever you do, this requires swift action otherwise these buggers can set like concrete.
1) Erosion. If you're lucky, a few flushes might wear it away.
2) Pressure hose (i.e. peeing on it). Easier for the boys though, as it does require a fair degree of accuracy.
3) Use the toothbrush of the most unpopular member of the household.
4) As a last resort, use that strange brush that always sits at the side of the toilet.

HOW TO UNBLOCK A TOILET

Unbend a coathanger and waggle it around the U-bend in the hope of shifting whatever horror might be lurking there. If that fails, move house.

THE VEXED ISSUE OF TOILET PAPER

Running out of toilet paper is a perennial problem, especially if you live with, or are, one of those girls who endlessly uses it for everything from removing make-up to creating a 3D papier-mâché sculpture of Jamie Oliver. Some students, however, manage to last three years without buying a single roll of Andrex. This is done by cunning and petty theft. Fruitful hunting grounds for the enterprising cheapskate include: pubs, public loos, other people's houses, cafes and, of course, the library toilets.

POPULAR SUBSTITUTES
(In order of popularity)

1. Newspapers
There's usually some kicking around the house somewhere, but be prepared to end up with the mirror image of yesterday's headlines on your cheeks until your next bath.

2. Kitchen roll
A nice replacement, but will usually require you bunny hopping into the kitchen, with your trousers round your ankles (much to the surprise of your flatmate, who's in there making a cuppa) then bunny-hopping back.

3. Unraveling the empty cardboard tube
Yes, we've all had to use this unsatisfying substitute at some time in our lives. And, yes, the cardboard's stiff unyielding texture will, as always, leave you walking round like Frankenstein's monster for the rest of the day.

4. The flannel of your most unpopular housemate
Soft on the bum but you can only really do this once, before he/she starts to suspect the brown stains on it.

5. Rizlas Painstakingly gum 24 of these together and pray for the best (it's best not to use the blue ones).

Even superheroes need to go to the toilet sometimes

WASH DAY (an editor confesses all)

Now, if you are insulted at the thought of being told how to use a washing machine then please skip this section*. If, however, there are any nagging doubts lingering (such as – what is a washing machine?) then it won't do any harm to read on. Besides, this section comes more as a confession than a step-by-step guide, though in the process we hope to save you from committing similar acts of sheer stupidity, and therefore experiencing that sinking feeling when you take a new white T-shirt out of the washing machine only to discover it to be bright pink and resembling an accessory from the Ken and Barbie wardrobe.

TEMPERATURE

During my first year in halls, we shared a launderette in the basement, which housed a group of strange looking machines designed for washing clothes. I vaguely remembered seeing my mum pulling wet clothes out of one of these sinister metal beasts in our utility room back home.

Unaware of how to properly use the damn things, I decided to apply the principle of 'the hotter the better', under some misplaced notion that if I boiled my clothes at 100 degrees they would come out better than new. It took many months of crushing disappointment, as yet another new flowery shirt came out resembling an accessory for Action Man (Hawaiian-style) before I made the discovery that 40 degrees or below is a much more ideal setting if you fancy saving your wardrobe from the incredible shrinking man syndrome. In fact, according to the nice lady round the corner who runs the dry cleaners, unless there's a particularly nasty Tommy K stain on your latest pair of 501s, it's actually just as effective to wash clothes in cold water. Either way, the important thing here is to learn what the correct setting is for each item of clothing, which brings us rather neatly onto the next section.

---

* This is bound to apply more to our female readers, as, statistically, it's over 50% of all male students who are shocked to discover that there is a whole mystical process from which dirty clothes return clean and folded into their drawers.

READING THE LABEL

Obvious as it may at first appear, you'd be surprised how many people don't bother with this. If it says hand wash/ dry clean only, it means just that. Stick that new silk dress in the machine and you can kiss it goodbye. Idiotic as it sounds, in my second year (by which time I should have known better) I attempted cleaning a soiled suit by…..you've guessed it….. putting it in the washing machine. I even carefully set the machine on a low temperature, thinking how sensible I was being. Needless to say, the crumpled, sodden mass that I optimistically hung up to dry two hours later was never used again for anything other than cleaning the floor.

SEPARATING WHITES AND COLOURS

The only legitimate occasion for apartheid is, of course, wash day. There is a wonderful Eddie Izzard sketch I remember seeing once where he describes that familiar sinking feeling when you diligently separate your whites and coloureds, only to discover, that once all the whites are in (and the machine is in full swing) a rogue coloured sock has suddenly pressed its mischievous face at the window of the washing machine, hell-bent on wreaking havoc with your pure-white knickers/ pants/ T-shirts/ wedding dress.

This kind of pathos in life can't always be avoided, but can be reduced by not throwing all colours and whites willy-nilly into the machine and hoping for the best, as dyes from non-fast coloureds will happily turn your entire wardrobe a shade of grey (a bit like what happened to the plasticine in Infant school when you mushed it up for long enough).

Never try and clean your friends in a washing machine

LIFESKILLS

TOP 5 TIPS FOR THE LAUNDERETTE

1) Take plenty of change: Well at least enough for washing and spin-drying; you'd think change would be readily available in a coin-operated launderette, but this is sheer optimistic folly.

2) Take your own washing powder: And when you're up to advanced techniques, fabric conditioner. The stuff you buy there is a rip off, is probably made out of whales and will bring you up in a green rash.

3) Take something to read: Why not take that important textbook that you've been putting off for the past few weeks, because it looks a bit like heavy going. After the novelty of watching your clothes spin round for ten minutes, hopefully you'll get bored enough to give it a read. Of course, what also might happen is that you'll end up having a natter with a stranger, and in the process make a new friend. We'll leave you to decide which is more important.

4) Make use of the tumble drier: Don't neglect to tumble dry your clothes to save time, even if you have drying facilities at home. Clothes are approximately 75,000 times heavier when wet, and the bin-liner you used as an impromptu laundry bag will either split and dump your clothes all over the pavement or snap your spine.

5) Minimise on ironing: Once you've chucked everything in the tumble drier, the temptation might be to bugger off and buy some fags. Do not do this. We are about to reveal a magical trick that, if followed to the letter, will allow you never to look an iron in the eye again. The *moment* the tumble dryer stops, and you've checked everything is properly dry, quickly get all the things that need ironing and neatly fold them. This will bring creasing down to an absolute minimum, as the fabric is still hot and highly suggestive. Leave your washing sitting in the tumble dryer for even a couple of minutes after it's stopped however, and you're entering into a world of crease-shaped pain.

A quiet word about bed sheets

It is possible to go for months without changing your bed sheets. Nothing really unpleasant will happen, there will just be an almost imperceptible sensation as you climb into bed of something being not quite right; a sort of greasiness, a total lack of crispy freshness caused by 3 billion microscopic bed bugs all licking you at once with their weird alien tongue-nodules.

If you manage to lure anyone into your bed for the purposes of sexual congress either ensure they are very drunk, or be the first to get into bed and contrive to distract your unwitting partner while quickly attempting to displace the numerous small particles of debris which have collected on the bottom sheet – breadcrumbs, toenails, pubes, miscellaneous fragments of biological matter etc – with vigorous flicking gestures. All things considered, it's probably best to give them a clean once in a while…

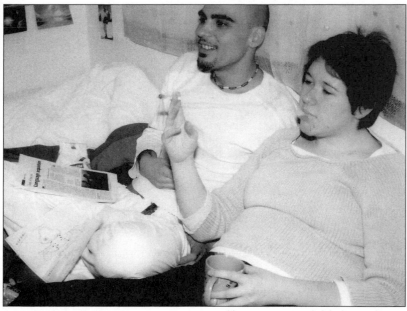

Never use someone else's bed as an ashtray…

…but if you do, when challenged deny everything

COPING WITH THE LOCALS

There are, of course, numerous regional rivalries in the U.K., most of which have been going on for hundreds of years. These include North vs. South, Manchester vs. Liverpool, Scotland vs. England and, of course, Upper Piddlington vs. Lower Piddlington. While these factions shouldn't affect you unduly, if you happen to be an upper-class southerner studying in Glasgow, I'd consider learning the art of self-defence. And while there are some cities (eg. Brighton, Oxford, Sheffield) that have integrated well with their student populations, there are countless others for whom friction between 'town and gown' is still a problem. Below are a few useful pointers that might indicate that your new home might not be 100% welcoming.

BEWARE:

1) A large army or navy base nearby ('student bashing' is still a big problem in places like Farnham and Plymouth, because of this)
2) A preponderance of Eighties-looking nightclubs, bestrewn with pools of vomit and blood. They are usually named 'The Roxy', 'Razzle's', 'The Ritzy', 'Glitzy', 'Mizery' or any word where a 'z' is substituted for an 's'.
3) A population who have a supernatural immunity to the cold, and view you with suspicion and contempt if you venture out in sub-zero temperatures in anything more than a short-sleeved shirt, low-cut-top, mini-skirt and flip-flops.
4) A town centre awash with scary-looking adolescents, drinking cider, necking, and hanging around outside Burger King.

If you do end up in any of the above locations, don't worry unduly, all cities in the UK have their good points as well their bad (with the possible exception of Middlesbrough) and all it usually requires is a knowledge of which notoriously rough areas to avoid, and whether the city centre is relatively safe at night. It is, however, all too easy to make the mistake of going into the wrong pub...

THE
SLAUGHTERED PUPPY

Located down a forgotten back-street in the city centre, you may be mistaken in believing this place to be a homely and unpretentious place for a flagon of ale. Absolutely not. This is strictly a no-go zone.

Inside, it will boast a snug corner (where two evil-looking, wizened old men play an endless game of cribbage) a main bar consisting of a juke-box playing Johnny Cash, a 90 year-old bleached-blonde barmaid called Lynne wearing a neon blue boob-tube, and a dozen or so blokes resembling Robert de Niro in 'Taxi Driver'. As you enter, these chaps, all of whom boast many interesting-looking facial scars and tattoos, will look up from their conversations about their recent court appearances and fix you with a gaze of soul-freezing contempt, indicating that your

presence is about as welcome as ham sandwiches at a bar mitzvah. At this juncture the only thing you can do is order the most masculine possible drink at the bar (hint – avoid shandy) down it in one, nod to those present as if suggesting close personal links to the Kray family, and walk casually to the door. Then run like hell. N.B. this advice applies equally to both sexes.

THE FIRKIN NIGHTMARE

The other boozer to avoid like the plague is the spanking new place located slap-bang in the centre of town. This corporate abortion (usually called something coyly-rude like 'The Cock And Fanny') has a sign outside that proudly boasts that it has been in existence since the year 2002, and inside is *enormous*, with beige carpeting, gleaming chrome everywhere, a hundred mock-Victorian wall-lights, and thirty-five video screens all showing Britney Spears. It might appear at first glance to be a pleasant, clean environment, the sort of place you could take your parents for a nice plate of breaded scampi and French Fries, but after 8pm it becomes the habitat of an enormous tribe of pissed-up, shaven-headed, sportswear-sporting knuckle-draggers, who have a grudge against society in general and students in particular. If you turn up alone on a Thursday evening and sit down to leaf through 'The Tao of Pooh' these Neanderthals will remove your teeth one by one then scalp you for good measure.

DEALING WITH FRIENDS
WHO HAVEN'T GONE TO UNIVERSITY

It goes without saying that there is bound to be at least one or more of your old school friends who won't have followed you into higher education, choosing instead to settle down in your old hometown with a steady job. After only a year at University, you might be surprised to discover that meeting these old mates *can* be tricky. Obviously your lives have taken different paths, and they may well have experienced things unfamiliar to you (having babies/ earning more than £5 per hour/ filing for divorce) while you too will have had experiences unknown to them (working in a lap-dancing club/ eating toenails on toast/ being forced to read Jean Paul Sartre).

These differences can manifest themselves over time and if you're not careful, lead to the unfortunate situation as described on the following page.

HAVING AN OLD MATE VISIT YOU AT UNIVERSITY
ACT ONE SCENE ONE – THE UNION BAR.

KERRY AND PAMELA (HER OLD FRIEND FROM HOME) ARE SEATED WITH
CLAIRE, ZOE, AND DONNA, KERRY'S NEW UNIVERSITY CHUMS

DONNA: …So what do you do, Pamela?

PAMELA: I work at Andy's Records. It's quite good actually, I…

KERRY: (INTERRUPTING) Have you heard who Angie got off with at the Eighties night?

CLAIRE: Not Rob from the union?

KERRY: No.

DONNA: Tony?…..Veggie Andy?…… Sophie??

KERRY: No! You'll never guess…………………it was Toby.

DONNA: I thought Toby was gay?

KERRY: No, he's bi. He used to go out with Katrina, remember?

ZOE: What, the one who had her clitoris tattooed?

KERRY: That's the one. Anyway – Jason's mate Fat Leo is furious because…..

AN HOUR PASSES IN WHICH EVERYONE CONTINUES IGNORING PAMELA.
PAMELA MEANWHILE HAS RESORTED TO DOWNLOADING THE RECIPE FOR
BAKED ALASKA ON HER WAP PHONE, FOR WANT OF SOMETHING BETTER TO
DO…..

CLAIRE: ….but I thought Nigel had had another sex change?

PAMELA: (STANDING UP) Er, Kerry. I'm a bit tired. Can I have the keys to your room?

KERRY: Aren't you coming clubbing?

PAMELA: No, no. I don't feel like it.

KERRY HANDS OVER THE KEYS AND PAMELA LEAVES

DONNA: Christ Kerry, your mate Pamela's a bit dull, isn't she? Anyway, where was I? Oh,
yeah, Melanie is furious 'cause Toby slept with her flatmate's mum………

Of course it may be the case that you and your old friend simply drift apart. This
happens. It will happen also with friends you make at university. But it's important
to remember that you're not the only one going through changes – your old friends
too will be experiencing a different kind of life from the one you both knew at
school. But if you think the relationship is worth keeping, make. sure to put the
effort in.

SPONGING FROM YOUR PARENTS

Further education is an expensive business and, unless you happen to be, say, Prince William or a kleptomaniac, you'll be reliant on your parents.

Most parents accept this with equanimity, and are fully aware of the fact that they'll have to stump up, not only for fees and accommodation, but also for what you might like to refer to euphemistically as 'a little something to keep me going.' Let's face it, no matter how many part-time jobs or overdrafts you manage to get, you're always going to need the odd £20, £50, or £10,000 to keep the wolves from the door.

Some parents will, however, need a little gentle persuasion before they finally cough up. There are several methods you can utilise, through either letter, phone call or email to get them to hand over the readies: -

1. GUILT

Dredge up some past event, such as:
• The time they didn't let you go to Alton Towers.
• The time they promised you a pony for Christmas and then didn't get you one.
• The time they wouldn't pay for you to have karate lessons.

Cunningly suggest that this has ruined your whole life. Guilt-stricken, your parents will re-mortgage the house and send you the money in a big bag.

2. THREATS

"Okay mum and dad. Cards on the table time – in 35 years you'll both be drooling, gibbering wrecks and you'll need someone to look after you, so hand over twenty quid, or I'll put you in that home we saw on 'Watchdog'."

3. EXAGGERATE THE COST OF THINGS

This works particularly well if:
a) Your parents are over sixty.
b) They live in the north and you go to university in the south. Tell them that a haircut costs £150, a teapot £75, and a bag of crisps £2.50. They will be scandalised by this, but will hand over the extra cash.

N.B. if they come to visit you, keep them away from the shops.

4. LIE

Only an idiot would say "Yeah, I need £25 for an eighth of skunk, and I could do with a couple of E's for the party on Friday night, so that's another £15" to his/her parents, unless they happened to be Howard Marks and Cerys from Catatonia (both, curiously, Welsh). Tell your folks you need the money for something educational, like an angle-poise lamp, or a textbook.

N.B. think this through, otherwise you'll find yourself saying "Yeah, I need £25 for an eighth of textbook, and I could do with dropping a couple of angle-poise lamps for the party on Friday night, so that's another £15."

5. DENY THAT YOU WANT ANY MONEY

A tricky double bluff, this. Say things like "No I'm fine, no really. Look, you can't keep sending me money like this, it isn't fair on you. I'll be okay. I didn't really want to eat today anyway, and if I get hungry later I can always have a rummage in the bins by the back of the refectory. What? No, I couldn't. Oh go on then, just £20, Oh alright, £50."

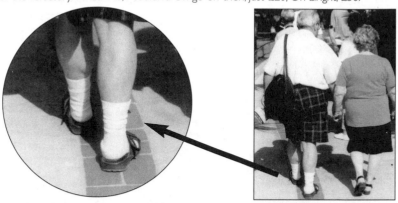

Safety tips for Women / Don't suffer in silence

It may come as a rather alarming statistic to know that sexual assault after drink-spiking is the UK's fastest growing crime against women. With this in mind it is a good rule of thumb, when out in pubs and clubs, to ensure that you never leave your drinks alone for anyone to tamper with.

For peace of mind, we'd also recommend investing in an attack alarm. They cost less than £10 and should be available from the Student Union (if not, kick up a fuss). While they're unlikely to summon immediate help, if you are approached by someone who you think is out to harm you, set your alarm off in their ear and you should stun them long enough to make a run for it or to find help.

Be aware of what is going on around you when using the cash machine, especially late at night, as you can be an easy target for muggings, especially if you've had a skinful.

Student houses are notoriously easy picking for burglars, as they know that they'll be a dream to break into, and they'll find plenty of electrical equipment, CDs and the like. Don't make it easy for them by being relaxed about your security. Make demands on your landlord to secure the windows and doors well. In big cities like London, Birmingham, Manchester, Coventry etc where student accommodation is generally found in the poorer areas, you can count yourself extremely lucky if you don't get burgled more than once during your student years.

When in potentially aggressive pubs (see 'coping with the locals' earlier on in this chapter) don't advertise the fact that you're a student; it's not uncommon that you'll attract a group of pissed-up arseholes who will take this information as an invitation to cause trouble. A friend of ours narrowly avoided being beaten up in a pub in Manchester last year for wearing a Hawaiian shirt. If he'd let on he was a student as well, I don't think he'd be alive today.

HOW TO LIVE IN A HALL OF RESIDENCE

BY RICHARD COWDRY © 2002

THOUGH WE ARE BUT POOR STUDENTS, STILL WE ARE ENTITLED TO A DECENT PLACE TO LIVE AND A REASONABLE QUALITY OF LIFE. IT IS THEREFORE OUR RESPONSIBILITY TO MAKE LIFE AS PLEASANT AS POSSIBLE FOR EACH OTHER

UNFORTUNATELY, FOR SOME PEOPLE THE CONSIDERATION OF OTHERS APPEARS TO BE AN ALIEN CONCEPT...

SCRATCH!

PERHAPS THE SINGLE LARGEST CAUSE OF UNHAPPINESS AND TENSION IN A HALL OF RESIDENCE IS

NOISE

LOUD, OBNOXIOUS MUSIC IS THE BLIGHT OF MODERN SOCIETY — FROM THE IRRITATING WALKMAN BEHIND YOU ON THE BUS, TO THE BASS LINE SENT THUDDING THROUGH YOUR WALL FROM YOUR NEIGHBOURS STEREO

B-DUM
B-DUM
B-DUM
B-DUM
B-DUM

It's like a giant heartbeat

NEVER BEFORE HAVE THE IGNORANT AND THE INSENSITIVE HAD SUCH AN OPPORTUNITY WITH WHICH TO EXPRESS THEIR PERSONALITY

THIS IS ME!

BITE ME

IF YOU PLAY YOUR MUSIC TOO LOUD: YOU ARE A

SELFISH JERK!

THE TRUTH IS:

No one wants to hear your music and you are destroying other peoples enjoyment of life - your neighbors and in extreme cases, everyone in your block

OUR POINT BEING:

TURN IT DOWN, PAL!

Ah, fuck you...

AND IT'S NOT JUST MUSIC; YOUR NEIGHBOURS PLAYSTATION OR TELEVISION SET CAN BE AS ANNOYING AS THEIR STEREO.

UNDER NORMAL CIRCUMSTANCES TELEVISION WOULDN'T BE A PROBLEM, BUT...

...HOW LOUD DOES IT NEED TO BE?

I LOVE ACTION MOVIES

BOOM CRASH AARHH

PEOPLE LEAD THEIR LIVES AT DIFFERENT VOLUMES. IF SOMEONE IS A MAXIMUM VOLUME PERSON, IT'S NONE OF YOUR BUSINESS — UNLESS THEY'RE LIVING IN THE ROOM NEXT DOOR!

TO BE CONSTANTLY ASSAULTED BY NOISE IS FOR MANY PEOPLE QUITE DISTRESSING. EVERYONE SHOULD BE ENTITLED TO PEACE IF THEY WANT IT. TO BE DEPRIVED OF PEACE AND QUIET CAN DRIVE SOME PEOPLE TO THE BRINK OF DESPAIR!

ACCOMMODATION

One of the most important decisions you can make for your first year at university is choosing where to live. End up sharing a cramped bedsit on the wrong side of town with a neurotic, bedwetting Slipknot fan and chances are that you won't make it to the end of the first term. And with rent accounting for the biggest chunk of your outgoings, getting a decent place to live with people you like can play a crucial role in maximising your enjoyment of university life.

The most important piece of advice to offer is, of course, to start looking as soon as possible. Whether you're a fresher wanting to move into halls, or a second year looking to share a house with friends for the first time, the sooner you start looking the more choice you will have. But what do you look for, should you choose catering or non-catering, how do you deal with unscrupulous landlords, why does everyone keep nicking your food and how do you get rid of fleas? All will be revealed...

Eurgh!

FINDING UNIVERSITY HOUSING IN YOUR FIRST YEAR

With few exceptions, we thoroughly recommend living in university accommodation in your First Year if you can, as it is, on the whole, cheap, convenient, clean and comfortable. It is also usually tied to offering student friendly contracts (so you have the option not to rent over the summer, for example) and you are less likely to get large hairy men coming round with big hammers and threatening to break your legs if you are behind on the rent. More importantly, living in halls/ uni accommodation is an excellent means of socialising; put ten people in a corridor with one tiny kitchen, a couple of showers and a loo, and they'll have no choice but to talk to one another, even if it's only to say "hurry up in there I'm nearly shitting myself," or "who's nicked my sausages?"

Also relevant is the fact that uni accommodation provide a crucial buffer between living at home and having to fend for yourself in 'the real world.' As for reformed drug-addicts and released long-term prisoners, halls are a sort of 'halfway house' which grant you a degree of independence, while still taking care of the more daunting tasks such as security, bills, cleaning and paying the rent. Though, unlike the reform homes of addicts and criminals, by the end of your 9 month stay there's every chance that you will be smoking 40 a day, drunk every night, addicted to Pro-Plus and plotting to kill the bloke in room 49 who keeps you awake every night practicing Embrace riffs on his electric guitar.

THE OPTIONS

University accommodation usually falls into one of the three categories below:

1) **Halls** (catering/ non-catering)
2) **Student house** (shared)
3) **Village complex**

And while the buildings don't vary much beyond being joyless concrete tower blocks, your style of accommodation can make a big difference to your quality of life, so choose carefully…

Catering:
PROS: Sociable, convenient, easier to budget and guaranteed hot meals every day.
CONS: Little opportunity to develop your cooking skills and a lack of freedom to eat when you want (if you fancy a lie-in you'll probably miss your breakfast). Plus, of course, the food might be terrible.

Self-Catering:
PROS: Freedom for that late-night greasy fry up, you can eat in the nude, nick other people's food, learn how to cook (in theory) and learn a lot about potential future flatmates by sharing a kitchen with them.
CONS: Washing up, cooking, buying food, sharing a skuzzy kitchen and constantly having your food nicked.

Single sex:
PROS: Get more work done
CONS: Get more work done

Own room:
PROS: You are completely free to indulge in perverted acts and eccentricities while keeping the place clean/ unkempt according to your own tastes. Plus you can study without hindrances.
CONS: It can be an uncomfortable social barometer and quite lonely living on your own if no-one ever visits you And in the long dark night of the soul, there's no-one to stop you playing Pink Floyd's 'The Final Cut' over and over again before sinking a bottle of whiskey.

Shared room:
PROS: You might make a life-long friend with whom to share late-night chats and have farting competitions with. You might also learn about the art of living if they're more sophisticated than you. And if they're witty and popular you can leech off their success.
CONS: There's every possibility that you could move in with a loony, someone you really, really don't like, or, worse still, someone who plays Phil Collins albums. Plus there's the lack of privacy with sharing and having to put up with someone else's snoring, different sleeping patterns and the awful noises they make when they bring someone back for sex.

FURNISHINGS

Regardless of where you study (unless it's somewhere really posh like Durham, Oxford, Cambridge etc) your room will no doubt be kitted out with the following items:

One perfunctory pine desk

On which the student from last year will have either left fag marks, doodled their genitals or stuck bubble gum underneath.

One single-sized bed

Comfortable enough for one, but for two will cause un-ending misery and sleep deprivation every time you have someone over for the night.

One anglepoise lamp

The spring of which will break in term 2, leaving the head lolling about on your desk like a sleepy dog. After a week or two of this you will have to construct some improbable structure out of rulers, pencils, loo roll and superglue to hold the damn thing up. It will rarely last more than a few hours before crashing down again.

A cheap carpet

In some kind of indistinguishable brown/ grey/ blue colour, and containing a strange yellow waxy lump that mysteriously bears the odour of raw sewage.

A wardrobe

Containing either no coat-hangers, or about 4,000 of them.

A sink

Ideal for taking a crafty pee in during the night, though try and be discreet if you share with someone, and always remember to run the hot tap afterwards (though this does have the unfortunate consequence of filling your room with the smell of hot wee).

A strange object

Somewhere in the room (either under the bed, or back of the cupboard) you will discover an object left by the previous year's student. This can range from the mundane (an odd sock/ joss-stick), the bizarre (a photo of someone's knob with pins sticking in it) to the downright frightening (a severed ear).

DECORATING YOUR FIRST ROOM

Unless you are an art student whose room contains nothing but four terrapins and a poster of yourself in the nude, you will undoubtedly invest in at least some of the following when decorating your first room:

- **A Klimt/ Dali/ Monet/ Klee poster**
- **Kitsch posters of TV cartoon heroes**
  (eg Button Moon, Zippy and George, Scooby Doo etc)
- **An ethnic throw**
- **A photo collage of mates from home**
- **Tea lights**
- **Wind chimes**
- **A poster of your favourite iconic**
- **cult-action hero**
  (eg Bruce Lee, Sean Connery as Bond, Michael Caine as Carter, Nick Berry from Heartbeat etc)
- **A statue of Buddha**
- **A cuddly toy**
- **A dying/dead spider plant**
- **A stolen pub ashtray**
- **A Police cone**
- **An acoustic guitar**
  (with one string missing)
- **Fluorescent stars on the ceiling**
- **A lava lamp**
- **A collection of arty postcards**
- **A horse**
- **A beer can/ fag packet pyramid sculpture**

MISSING THE BOAT

If you are late in the game for whatever reason (maybe you are changing university or going in through clearing) don't panic; last minute solutions are often available, either through the University Accommodation Service or the Union. They should be able to find any spare rooms that pop up at the last minute. This happens quite a lot, with people changing their mind or having personal reasons for not attending their courses at a late date. Failing that, they will have lists of private landlords, B&Bs, lodgings and student house-shares looking for new victims for their satanic sex cult, that you can contact. These should have been vetted for safety and appropriateness, so with any luck you won't be living with the new Rosie and Fred West. While these solutions may often not seem ideal in the short term, once you're there, you can always be scanning the notice-boards and chumming up with folk to find better deals.

GETTING YOUR OWN PLACE IN THE SECOND YEAR

Come the second year, it is highly likely that you will want to find private accommodation with a few friends. While we all know the kind of people who are those lucky, charmed-lifers who can swan in at the last minute, pick up a gem of a place for next-to-nothing in the cool part of town with an attractive landlord who keeps on forgetting to collect the rent, don't expect it to happen to you. Renting privately comes with all the potential nightmares of having to shell out cripplingly large deposits, not paying the bills on time and getting cut off, being ripped off by dodgy landlords, getting your stuff nicked etc etc. But it doesn't all have to be blood, sweat and tears. To avoid being lumped with the dingiest, foulest hellhole in town run by Mr Rigsby from 'Rising Damp' though, take note of the following…

WHERE AND WHEN TO START

The University Accommodation and Housing Office should be your first port of call as they will have lists and names of local reputable accommodation agencies. Other places to look include the local and free papers, university notice boards and accommodation websites. The most important rule is: **start the search as early as possible and get a holding deposit down on anything decent.** There is a school of thought that says coming back a week or two before Autumn term and looking at the last minute can work, but you have to ask yourself, *'do you feel lucky Punk?'*

LETTING THROUGH AN ACCOMMODATION AGENCY

The great majority of rental stock is held by these companies whose level of malignancy usually depends on how short of rental accommodation an area is; considering that it's a seller's market in most university towns, they will tend to be as evil as possible on behalf of their clients, i.e. the landlords. Read carefully before signing anything, and ask around to find out the reputations of various agencies. You may have viewed a beautiful little flat, but if your guarantors (i.e. mum and dad) are going to receive threatening letters the first time you are a few days late with the rent, it may not be worth it. Generally, those agencies that rent to students a lot will be more understanding and accommodating, if you'll excuse the pun. But it's doubtful whether they'll have the nicest houses.

Some agencies will charge you a fee for finding you a place; some will even charge if they don't, just to have you on the books; which is not legal. Many will charge for "drawing up" (i.e. opening a filing cabinet and fishing out a standard form) a contract; they may charge for collecting references and setting up direct debits to guarantors and even inventory checks. Most will require a guarantor such as a parent or relative who has to sign a legal undertaking to underwrite the contract financially should you default. This means they have you by the short and curlies. They will also ask for a month's rent in advance, and as much again as damage deposit. Most landlords regard this deposit as a free holiday or new kitchen fund unless you are very neat and keep a very close eye on the inventory. This is worth bearing in mind if you think the deposit will help fund your next move; normal wear and tear is allowed, but legally it's very hard to define.

RENTING THROUGH PRIVATE LANDLORDS

These can be contacted through the local free papers, on the grapevine (many good student houses are passed from generation to generation), by keeping an eye on student notice boards and, again, through the Accommodation Office. Renting directly off a landlord can have its advantages; they get to know you, you get to know them; mutual trust, tolerance and understanding can build up and sometimes they can even become your friend or lover (though not very often).

The biggest single advantage of renting off a private landlord is they don't tend to be as coldly legalistic and bullying as agencies when things go wrong; the downside is they don't always have much interest in repairing things like heating and roofs. OK, neither do agencies, but, unlike landlords they are legally obliged, and have teams in place to do such repairs. So when viewing a property, take as much time to study the landlord as the house; a bad one can be worse than rising damp and burst water-pipes on a January morning.

A typical landlord

WHERE TO LIVE?

Any estate agent will tell you that location is the most important factor to consider when choosing your accommodation. And a mere hundred yards either way can mean the difference between domestic bliss and household hell. So what should you look for? Here are a few pointers: -

1) Try and move into your local student ghetto. Every town and city has a cheap, slightly skuzzy area that is largely inhabited by students. It might not exactly be South Kensington, and may suffer from umpteen burglaries, but you are more likely to have sympathetic neighbours who don't complain about parties, the old fridge in your front garden and your tendency to play The Pixies at full volume at three in the morning.

2) Choose somewhere within walking distance of the university if you can. Places on the outskirts of town and/ or notoriously dodgy estates may be cheaper, but this can be a false economy as you end up blowing all your cash on buses / trains /petrol / hospital bills. If your university is out of town, like Keele, Warwick and Sussex, then pick an area near a cheap bus or train link.

3) Try and ensure you have all of the following close at hand:

> A) A cheap supermarket/ corner shop
> B) A 24-hour garage
> C) A good pub
> D) An off-licence

If only letting agents cottoned on to the importance of these things, they would advertise student accommodation with phrases like 'Only three minutes from Patel's Mini-Mart', and 'A stone's throw from Thresher's'.

NEIGHBOURS

'Everybody,' as the famous Aussie TV soap theme tune goes, 'needs good neighbours.' Unfortunately, 'good' (as in pleasant, non-complaining, sane and non-prying) neighbours are rarer than a knob gag at a church sermon. There are many different kinds you might end up with – from the ranting psychopath and his girlfriend who spend twenty four hours a day yelling at their six offspring to 'get in here *now* you little bastards!' to the softly-spoken, infinitely polite bank manager who is quietly planning a campaign to get you evicted. If you're lucky you might end up with someone who seems really together and laid-back but to improve your chances of avoiding the 'neighbours from hell' try avoid moving into any house that has:

A) A Union Jack / 'Sun' campaign poster/ picture of Jesus in the window.

B) An enormous motorcycle in the front garden that is constantly being overhauled by a gargantuan, sweaty, tattooed, scowling man clad in a vest.

C) A lawn so immaculate that it looks as though it has been trimmed by hand with nail-scissors, and a Rover so highly-polished that it blinds anyone who comes near.

D) A twee, wrought-iron sign on the front gate that boasts the name 'Cedar View', 'The Old Coach House', or 'Chez Nous'.

Even if you do lead a silent monk-like existence, the kind of neighbours whose abodes boast these accessories will, almost inevitably, manage to find fault with your behavior and engage in action that will result in either your imprisonment or hospitalisation. With anyone slightly more reasonable you can avoid all-out war simply by obeying the following steps:

1) Don't have a party on any day other than a Saturday. Weekday parties are taking the piss a bit and Sunday is, of course, the Lord's Day. Do, however, warn your neighbours about parties beforehand and send them an invite. They're very unlikely to come but at least, having had prior warning, they have the option to go spend their weekend with the in-laws on the Isle of Wight.

2) Put your rubbish out on the right day. There's nothing more likely to annoy the street than a huge pile of rotting rubbish-sacks being savaged by gangs of marauding seagulls, rats and street urchins.

3) Don't have band practices in your bedroom or play loud music all day long with the windows open. No explanation needed.

4) Don't keep large, exotic wild animals (horses, chimpanzees, Bengal tigers) in your back garden.

But take heart; should you earn the disdain of your whole neighbourhood, at least it won't be for very long. Before things get really ugly, you'll probably have moved on, and begun the process over again. This is the sole consolation of rented accommodation.

THE ASSURED SHORTHOLD
OR 'FIXED TERM' CONTRACT

• If you are renting an entire flat or house, this is almost certainly the contract you will be signing, and the term is normally six months. This means that the landlord is obliged to let you live there for six months, unless there is a breach of contract, and even then the landlord has to obtain a court order to get you to leave. Which, incidentally, can take up to three months. If you bugger off early, you will still be bound by law to pay the rent for the remainder of the contract, although it may be possible to find a replacement with the agreement of the landlord. You have the right to know your landlord's name and address, and frankly you'd be mad not to. Keep an eye open for clauses that give you responsibility for keeping the windows clean and the garden neat, these are legal obligations, breach them at your peril.

• Technically, this contract doesn't have to be in writing, but you can make your landlord send you a "Statement of Terms" which lays out things like the date the tenancy began, amount of rent, when it is due etc. It is a criminal offence for them not to send you one of these within 28 days of a written request.

• If your rent is paid weekly, the landlord is required to provide a rent book that you fill out and they sign each week – remember to always get a receipt for cash. Most letting agencies take rent out of a nominated bank account by direct debit, try and avoid it being yours, or try for a rent-book /monthly-cheque-from everybody system, and still ask for receipts.

Conversely, if you are lodging with your landlord (sharing kitchen, toilet etc) you have very few rights. They need only give you a week's notice to leave, and a mere bellowing of "get the fuck OUT!" is legally binding. The upside is you normally only have to pay a week's rent in advance and a week's rent as deposit, you don't need to sign anything, and you can give them a week's notice also. They won't ask for a guarantor in all likelihood either. But be aware; if you do sign anything, you may be bound by it.

HARRASSMENT & UNLAWFUL CONVICTION

This happens more than one would hope. It's hard to define harassment, but it includes threatening or excessive phone calls, unannounced visits, cutting off utilities, intimidation or unreasonable demands. Any landlord has to give you at least 24 hours written notice before entering your house, and is never under any circumstances allowed to let him/herself in without your permission.

Remember, you are legally entitled to stay in your home (even if you've defaulted on your rent and smashed the place to bits) until your landlord has obtained a court possession order against you, and even then, only official court bailiffs can carry out the eviction. Furthermore, and rather ironically, you have to be in to let them evict you.

If you've got a psycho on your hands don't mess about; call the police. If things are merely getting dire, talk to the Student Welfare Officer who may point you in the direction of mediating services such as the Council's Housing Advice unit or some other body, or they may try via the Accommodation Office to mediate for you direct with the landlord. No landlord who rents to students wants to be put on a University blacklist, so they do have some muscle. The best move initially, if you feel you can do it, is to try and reach agreements directly with your landlord or their letting agency.

DEPOSITS & INVENTORIES

As was mentioned earlier, deposits are often viewed by landlords and agencies as a way of paying for Christmas. The onus is very much on you to prove you haven't done the damage they claim has been done, excessive to normal wear and tear. Some agencies will be much more stringent than others; again a reason to ask around the older student population. The following tips will give you a greater (let's say 30% for the hell of it) chance of getting the money back.

• Write to your landlord at least a month before leaving, asking him to inspect the property. Then get cleaning!! Thirty quid for hiring a carpet cleaner and a tin or two of paint is often money well spent. Replace missing stuff and repair what you can.

• Be there for the inspection, and get your landlord/agency rep to agree on what is/isn't damaged, based on your inventory copy that YOU WILL HAVE KEPT SAFE FROM THE START and get it in writing. You could agree in writing to get stuff fixed before you leave; believe us it will be cheaper than their invoice. Then get it done and send evidence of the repairs.

• Arrange to make a final payment of utilities for the day of your move and return your keys. At that time, make a written request of your landlord to return your deposit within seven days, unless your contract specifies otherwise. Remember; KEEP COPIES OF ALL CORRESPONDANCE – YOURS AND THEIRS.

• If they are still withholding all or part of your deposit, ask for receipts of work done, purchases etc – if you still disagree with the amount held back, write explaining why and set a new date for return of monies. It won't work but it will make you feel better.

• Finally, if they've still got their nasty little mitts on your dough and you feel you have a case, you can take them to Small Claims Court. This can be a lengthy process, and even if you win, the court has no enforcing powers to make the reluctant landlord pay; they can merely request that they do. Or the skinflints can claim poverty and set an absurdly low monthly repayment scheme.

ACCOMMODATION TERMINOLOGY
(AND WHAT IT REALLY MEANS)

LUXURY	GROTTY
SPACIOUS	POKY
EXCLUSIVE AREA	MILES FROM ANYWHERE
NEWLY-FITTED BATHROOM	IN 1972
ALL MOD CONS	FLOORBOARDS, ROOF, WALLS
G.C.H	GROTTY COLD HEALTH-HAZARD
GARDEN WITH PATIO	TWO-FOOT-SQUARE STRETCH OF SCRUBLAND WITH A BREEZE-BLOCK AND A DOG TURD ON IT
IDEAL FOR STUDENT	A SHITHOLE
SINGLE-BEDROOM	A BROOM CUPBOARD WITH A CHILD'S BED IN IT
DOUBLE-BEDROOM	JUST BIG ENOUGH FOR ONE
FIVE BEDROOM	ACTUALLY TWO BEDROOMS BUT ONE HAS BEEN DIVIDED BY A CURTAIN TO FORM ANOTHER ROOM, ONE USED TO BE THE LIVING ROOM AND THE OTHER IS AN UNCONVERTED ATTIC, WHICH CAN ONLY BE REACHED VIA A STEPLADDER PERCHED ON A SUITCASE

YES, FRIENDS, THESE ARE NOISY TIMES WE LIVE IN. WHY DO PEOPLE HAVE TO **SHOUT** SO MUCH? WHY NOT JUST TALK — IT TAKES FAR LESS EFFORT AND DOESN'T STRAIN ONE'S VOCAL CHORDS. HALLS RESIDENTS SHOULD REALLY MAKE AN EFFORT TO TALK AT A REASONABLE VOLUME. RESIST THE TEMPTATION TO ANNOUNCE YOUR PRESENCE BY TURNING CONVERSATIONS INTO

SHOUTING MATCHES

REMEMBER: YOU ARE ALONE BUT YOU AREN'T; BEHIND THOSE THIN WALLS YOU ARE SURROUNDED BY DELICATE EARS

CERTAIN PEOPLE HAVE TO PROVE THEIR EXISTENCE BY MAKING THEIR PRESENCE KNOWN TO OTHERS. IF YOU REQUIRE EVIDENCE OF YOUR EXISTENCE, KEEP A DIARY — IT'S QUIETER

Dear Diary, Today I was NOISY!

FOR SOME PEOPLE, SEX PROVIDES YET ANOTHER EXCUSE FOR MAKING AN ANNOYING RACKET.

Unngh! YAAAAH! SCREAM! WHAM BAM!

Hey, I can't help it, man!

Hyuk!

YES YOU CAN: EXERT A LITTLE SELF-CONTROL!

...AND MOVE THAT BED SO IT DOESN'T KEEP BANGING AGAINST THE WALL!
THUD! THUD! THUD! THUD! THUD! THUD! THUD! THUD! THUD! THUD! "THUD!" THUD!
VIRGIN GAZETTE

SIMILARLY, PLEASE TRY TO SCHEDULE YOUR LOVER'S QUARRELS FOR A TIME OTHER THAN 3AM...

YOU DON'T LOVE ME! SOB!

SHUT UP! JUST SHUT UP! CRASH!

WHO TO LIVE WITH
A SHORT QUIZ

You must select the two housemates who will be the most bearable to live with from the list below. (Answers at bottom of page.)

#1 DODGY MARTIN
AGE: 20
DEGREE: Art History
CHARACTERISTICS: Veteran dope-smoker and paranoid conspiracy theorist. Never goes into tutorials. Rises at four in the afternoon and goes to bed at six in the morning, in between which he lies on the sofa watching old episodes of Columbo. Smells pretty bad.
SECRET CRIME: Washing his willy with your face flannel.

#2 SEB
AGE: 18
DEGREE: French with politics
CHARACTERISTICS: Incredibly posh moneyed ex-public schoolboy from Hampstead. Wears designer jeans and drives a Jag. Organises social events, such as trips to Rimini and paintballing expeditions that you will invariably get caught up in.
SECRET CRIME: Never has any food in the house but nicks plenty of yours.

#3 DIANE
AGE: 33
DEGREE: American Literature
CHARACTERISTICS: Attractive, affable, mature student, who has dropped out of her job as head of marketing at the British Museum to go back to university. Already has a degree in Canadian Literature from the same university. Stays in a lot working on her essays over bottles of red wine.
SECRET CRIME: Throws out meals you've left unfinished without asking.

#4 MELISSA

AGE: 18
DEGREE: Visual and performing arts
CHARACTERISTICS: Sleeps with a different bloke every week and drinks like a fish. Never, ever, ever, ever has any food in the house. Room looks like a skip (discarded bra fusing with plate of mouldy spaghetti etc). Slobs around the house all day in a dressing gown listening to Radio 1.
SECRET CRIME: Pisses in a pint glass she keeps by her bed.

#5 'ADAMANDSUE'

AGES: 20 and 19 respectively
DEGREES: Biology / Media Studies
CHARACTERISTICS: Couple who have been together since meeting in Freshers' week. Do all their shopping and cooking together. Watch the television in their room. Stock the fridge with their food. Leave little notes for each other all over the house, which say things like *"I love you scrummybum."*
SECRET CRIME: Shag on the living-room sofa whenever you're out and leave sperm stains on the cushions.

ANSWER: Dodgy Martin and Melissa
Why?
Well, for all their faults Martin and Melissa are extremely laid-back and are unlikely to be annoyed by any of your equally annoying excesses, which, after a couple of months will be a godsend, whereas Diane will make you constantly guilty for not being as industrious as her, as every Saturday you awake to find she has cleaned the house from top to bottom and is consequently in a filthy mood even though you never asked or even expected her to do this. As for Seb, after two weeks of his chinless, public school mates dropping by the house making racist and homophobic jokes you will want to break their legs, while AdamandSue, not long after the third week will split up, each bending your ear about the other long into the night. Shortly after this they will get back together and turn against you again. They will repeat this pattern every two months until you finally go insane.

THE ADVISABILITY
OF LIVING WITH THE OPPOSITE SEX

If at all possible, you should try to number amongst your flatmates at least one of the opposing gender. If you're a bloke, female flat mates will most likely represent the single civilising influence in your life. There are few things more horrible than a house occupied by four twenty-something males. Generally, after two months such an abode resembles one of those Samuel Beckett plays in which the characters sit up to their necks in rubbish. A female flatmate will at least make you think twice before drying your rugby socks in the toaster, or watching 'Robot Wars' in your pants.

This is not to suggest that all-female households cannot be disgusting either, far from it. We have seen places that would make Harry Enfield's 'The Slobs' blush and choosing the right men for co-habiting can have an equally moderating influence. Living with the opposite sex can also of course increase your chances of meeting a potential partner. When their friends come round for a movie night or pop in for a chat you can turn on the charm and be thankful that you've been encouraged to use the washing machine now and again.

As to male-female ratios, two girls and two guys is ideal. It takes two women to curb a man's excesses and vice versa, but a single woman with three men will be driven demented by their bad habits, while a man living with more than two women will find that when their periods synchronise, it can be like re-living James Caan's experiences in the film 'Misery'.

And finally, if you've attended a single-sex school or have no brother or no sister, living with the opposite sex is certainly an educative experience and a crash-course in male-female relations. It's hard to place the opposite sex on a pedestal when you've seen their skidmarked pants on the bathroom floor.

TOP TEN FLATMATE CRIMES

1) Stealing the last of the milk in the morning even though you bought it.

2) Stealing the last of the bread in the morning even though you bought it.

3) Never ever buying toilet roll.

4) Using your razor/ make-up/ sanitary towels.

5) Playing the same record over and over and over again until it drives you mad. (And always something utterly shit like Shania Twain.)

6) Leaving a ring of scum around the bath.

7) Farting excessively.

8) Denying that the unknown numbers on the itemised phone bill are anything to do with them.

9) Letting their smeggy friends sleep/shag in your bed while you're away.

10) Using all the cups and plates as ashtrays so that your morning mug of tea starts to taste disconcertingly of Golden Virginia.

HOUSE MEETINGS

If yours is a relatively amicable household, the only house-meetings you should have to endure will concern financial matters, i.e. rent and bills. This invariably means everyone tediously wading through 47 pages of an itemised phone bill and trying to figure out who made that 3-hour phone call to a Petrol Station on the Isle of Man. This may all seem well and good but even the logistics of trying to get all your housemates in the same room at the same time to do this can be a feat in itself.

So, having spent a month tracking down housemate number 4 (who is ALWAYS round at his boyfriend's and only comes back once a week to change his pants) you all finally assemble one evening in the living room, like the suspects in an Agatha Christie story, when suddenly housemate number 2's mobile goes off, drawing her out of the room. Meanwhile housemate number 3 has rolled a joint while waiting for number 2 to get off the phone, number 4 has started telling stories of his recent sexual conquests and within five minutes the meeting is forgotten, the bills go unpaid and disaster lurks rounds the corner.

Inevitably the following month, when the phone is cut off, the next house meeting will turn from being a chilled out affair to a full-on slanging match where months of pent-up frustrations over each other's annoying habits are revealed through a stream of vitriol and plate smashing. To avoid this, and everyone falling out over money matters, you require just two things; being honest with each other over what is owed (particularly with regards the phone bill) and stumping up your cash on time. Manage this and your household should remain as harmonious and peaceful as a Buddhist temple (until your next house meeting that is, when you have to tackle the thorny subject of the breakdown of the washing-up rota...)

Introducing the new range of
STUDENT furniture from

Tired with the plush furnishings of your university accommodation? Never fear, your landlord will be ordering all his furniture from Shabitat's exciting new-season catalogue. Some of our most popular ranges are detailed below and are sure to be featured in your future off-campus abode.

SETTEE
This beautiful Seventies monstrosity offers no comfort whatsoever but does incorporate the following features:

- Broken springs
- Fleas
- Capacious back lining for the collection of coins, Rizlas, pens and TV remote control
- Generous collection of brown stains
- Old man's smell
- Auto-slip cushions
- Fire-friendly!

£19.99

CHEST OF DRAWERS
Made of finest MDF and chipboard and badly painted in lurid violet with attractive graffiti. All drawers now feature the new easy-jam trademark with drawers able to stick closed, half-closed or fully open at your own inconvenience.

All drawers also come replete with flimsy, paper-thin bottoms that give way under the weight of a single sock. New features include disturbing German porn mags left in bottom drawer at no extra cost!

£4.99

BROKEN IRONING BOARD
You can't put it up, you can't take it down! Try ironing on it and watch your spirit crumble. Comes complete with disturbingly sticky top and kitsch Fifties lukewarm iron!

FREE with every order over £1!!!

Shabitat

THE PENSIONER'S FRIEND

For those who like to live on the edge, this extremely inefficient throwback to the days of the Coronation and The H-bomb will provide not only a modicum of warmth at close range, but also a very real chance of a slow, unpleasant death. Leave this unattended for just a few seconds and watch your house turn into Hiroshima!

£2.99

THE FRIDGE

A perennial favourite, our latest model now features:

- A revolutionary new loud shuddering noise alternating inexplicably with periods of eerie silence!
- A guaranteed non-shuttable freezer compartment door.
- A 'Big enough to sink the Titanic!' pre-formed glacial ice-block which includes five frozen peas and the remnants of a fish finger.
- Now with mould as standard!

£14.99

WEIRD THING

No bedroom is complete without this…thing! Is it a commode, a wine cooler, a butter churn? Your guess is as good as ours as you have hours of fun trying to find a use for the bloody thing!

8s 6d

STUDENT HOUSEHOLD
WILDLIFE SPOTTER'S GUIDE

What better place to witness the glorious bounty of God's creation than the student house. In the comfort of your own squalor, you can sit for hours and watch the procession of an endless variety of creatures, both small and much smaller.

Simply tick the box if you manage to spot one of these rare beasts, and when all boxes are complete it's probably time to reward yourself with a midnight flit.

THE WOODLOUSE (Porcellio scaber)

This cheeky little fellow is a shy one, and often prone to curling up into a little ball if disturbed (we mean disturbed in the sense of 'discovered', rather than 'distressed and worried upon being told that the lifespan of a woodlouse is very short.'). Grey-brown in colour, he deplores solitude and is always found in the company of his mates. Loads of them.

HABITAT: Dark, damp, rotting places. Look for them in the kitchen under the bread bin, in the breadbin or in the bread. Also found down the side of the bath, and in the bottom of the wardrobe.

☐ *2 POINTS*

THE SILVERFISH (Lepisma saccharina)

An elusive and beguiling creature (being neither silver nor a fish), the silverfish spends much of its time scurrying around behind the fridge and cooker wallowing in decomposing matter that at one time might have been a bit of bacon. The best time to spot him is late at night (when you return from the pub slightly drunk and with the nibbles) when, on turning on the kitchen light, you notice a strange scurrying on the floor like several tiny wind-up mice having panic attacks. On rare occasions this can actually be an hallucination brought on by the excesses of alcohol/ Ketamine but usually it is simply a plethora of these sweet little creatures trying desperately to figure out what the sun is doing shining at midnight.

HABITAT: Cool, damp, humid places, especially basements, bathrooms, laundry rooms and under the fridge.

☐ *5 POINTS*

THE FLEA (Ctenocephalides)

This bold chap is usually either a cat flea *(Ctenocephalides felis)* or a dog flea *(Ctenocephalides canis)* and boy, is he itching to meet you! As tiny as the speck of dust he is often mistaken for, Mr. Flea will, no doubt either have been left in your abode by the pets of the previous tenant, or introduced by 'Flabby' your new feline house mascot. Lying dormant through winter, he wakes up when the weather warms up a bit, rushing to bite you as if you were a pie and he was Johnny Vegas.

HABITAT: Your carpet and sofa are his Savoy hotel, from which it is impossible to evict the bugger.

☐ *10 POINTS*

THE SNAIL & SLUG (Mollusca)

These two pals, one the proud owner of his own home, the other a wandering vagrant, are generally not seen in the house itself, but their presence can be noted by the horrid, slimy trail they leave in their wake (a bit like politicians). Snails and slugs are gastropods (from the Latin *gastro* meaning 'stomach' and *pod* meaning 'foot'), which is really quite freaky if you think about it.

HABITAT: Any room nearest the garden (usually the kitchen.) Pop outside the back door late at night in your pyjamas and feel your stomach turn as you experience that unpleasant sensation of snail-shells breaking beneath your bare feet.

☐ *SLUGS – 10 POINTS*
☐ *SNAILS – 15 POINTS*

THE COCKROACH (Blattoidea blattida)

At 400 million years old and able to survive a nuclear blast, the Cockroach is certainly one of nature's success stories. One day, when man has died out he will mutate, take over the world and bear an uncanny resemblance to Geri Halliwell (but with a few more limbs). A shiny brown colour with horrible spiky hairy legs, roaches like to eat rotten food, then shit in it, so they're far from ideal party guests, but luckily they're not very common in this country, preferring a hotter, more humid climate.

HABITAT: Anywhere there's food i.e. under the cooker/fridge/washing machine and in school canteens.

☐ *25 POINTS*

ACCOMMODATION

THE MOUSE (Mus musculus)

Cute he may be, but the mouse is still a pest —
shredding your essays to make his bed and crapping
on your floor. The house mouse is more commonly
heard than seen, as he likes to lurk under the
floorboards and scamper out in the wee small hours
in search of cheese.* A mouse can scare the life out
of you if you wake up in the middle of the night and
hear a rustling in the corner, which sounds almost
exactly as if a serial killer was tapping gently at your
door. If you want to get rid of mice you could always
get a cat. Animal lovers, happy to squash ugly looking
cockroaches and woodlouse always have a problem
with killing mice, and prefer to catch them and
release them in the nearby park. The only problem
with this is that they return within five minutes.

HABITAT: Small holes in the skirting-board, often
with a door with a tiny handle and a plaque reading
'J. Mouse Esq.'

☐ *50 POINTS*

THE STRIPED HYENA (Hyaena hyaena)

Although rare in this country, the striped hyena will,
on occasion, wander into student households if it
smells a rotting carcass or two. Disappointed when it
discovers the smell to originate from your laundry
pile, this fierce scavenger is likely to lurk behind the
sofa, wait for you to go for a pee, then leap out and
devour your Chicken McNuggets before your
return, thus leading you to blame your flat mate. The
hyena can also be identified by his laugh and if you're
watching 'Baddiel and Skinner' doing another one of
their terrible improvised comedy shows and there's
a laugh in the room, you've got a hyena.

HABITAT: North East Africa, India, Asia (extending
north to the Caucasas), Southern Siberia and around
the bin area of your back garden.

☐ *2000 POINTS*

*Mice apparently don't actually like cheese that much.

BEING DRUNK IS ALSO NO EXCUSE FOR BEHAVING BADLY AND CAUSING A DISTURBANCE.

IF YOU ARE A SELFISH FOOL WHEN DRUNK, YOU ARE PROBABLY ALSO ONE WHEN SOBER. TIME TO CHANGE YOUR WAYS?

FURTHER SUGGESTIONS FOR HIGH-VOLUME PEOPLE:

RESIST COOKING FEASTS AFTER 12 PM ~ THE CLANKING OF PLATES AND DISHES WILL INTERRUPT THE MUCH-NEEDED REST OF YOUR NEIGHBOURS.

IF YOU MUST ENCOURAGE SOCIAL GATHERINGS, AT LEAST DISCOURAGE SHOUTS OF MERRIMENT (MAY I SUGGEST TRYING SIGHS OF MERRIMENT).

DO NOT ARRIVE HOME DRUNK, START COOKING, THEN FALL ASLEEP UNTIL THE SMOKE FROM YOUR BURNING FOOD (USUALLY TOAST) SETS OFF THE FIRE ALARM.

BY MAKING THIS NEXT POINT, I RISK SOUNDING LIKE THE ULTIMATE KILLJOY. NONETHELESS:

LAUGHTER IS OFTEN A DELIGHTFUL SOUND! SOME PEOPLE THOUGH HAVE BEEN UNFORTUNATE IN THIS RESPECT AND HAVE BEEN CURSED WITH AN EXCLAMATION OF MIRTH WHICH SOUNDS LIKE A PIERCING SIREN OR THE WHOOPING BARK OF AN ANIMAL IN DANGER!

IF YOU HAVE A LAUGH THAT CAUSES DISTRESS TO OTHERS ~ TRY TO CONTROL IT!

"But I can't help it!" YOU EXCLAIM. I DON'T BELIEVE YOU. A PERSONS LAUGH SAYS A GREAT DEAL ABOUT THEIR PERSONALITY; PEOPLE WITH DISGUSTING, OBNOXIOUS-SOUNDING LAUGHS TEND TO BE HIGH-VOLUME TYPES WHO USE THIS UNPLEASANT NOISE AS YET ANOTHER WEAPON IN THEIR PERSECUTION OF PEACE-LOVERS EVERYWHERE.

ANOTHER SERIOUS THREAT TO HALLS HARMONY IS THE INCONSIDERATE USE OF THE DOORBELL...

IT SHOULDN'T COME AS A SURPRISE TO KNOW THAT NOONE WANTS TO BE WOKEN UP AT 3AM.
A LOUD FRONT DOORBELL OR BUZZER CAN BE A BIG PROBLEM IN A FLAT OF 12 STUDENTS, ALL WITH DIFFERENT LIFESTYLES, SCHEDULES AND GROUPS OF FRIENDS.
PEOPLE WHO HAVEN'T ENDURED THE HALLS EXPERIENCE (OR SOMETHING SIMILAR) MAY ASSUME THAT NO ONE WOULD DARE TO RING THE DOOR-BELL AFTER EVEN MIDNIGHT AND RISK WAKING THEIR NEIGHBOURS...
I REGRET TO INFORM YOU THIS IS OFTEN NOT THE CASE...

OCCASIONS WHEN THE BELL IS RUNG IN THE DEAD OF NIGHT OCCUR FAR TOO FREQUENTLY...

NOTHING IS WORSE THAN THIS FOR CREATING A BAD ATMOSPHERE

EVEN WHEN THE BELL REMAINS SILENT, ONE CAN'T SLEEP IN ANTICIPATION OF BEING WOKEN UP AGAIN.

LACK OF SLEEP MAKES PEOPLE EDGY, DESPERATE AND MEAN...

CONTINUALLY BEING WOKEN UP AT NIGHT CAN TEST ONE'S PATIENCE TO IT'S LIMITS.

WHY THEN ARE MORE MURDERS NOT COMMITTED IN HALLS OF RESIDENCE?

A PLEA THEN TO HALLS DWELLERS EVERYWHERE

DO NOT RING THE DOORBELL AT A TIME WHEN YOU THINK PEOPLE WILL BE ASLEEP!

RMC '02

HOUSE PARTIES

House parties are usually quite different from the ones held on campus, which tend to be relatively subdued affairs owing to the restrictions that the university imposes. In a place of your own however, you can really let yourself go. Drinks are spilt, drugs are consumed, windows are broken, drunken arguments are had, and furniture is smashed to smithereens – and that's before any of the guests turn up. So if you do decide to throw a party, expect to discover several of the following:

1) Dozens of bottles of booze cunningly concealed all over the house in strange places (like inside the oven or at the bottom of the cat's litter tray) by different people so that no one will nick them.

2) A flat-mate sulking in the corner because the compilation CD he spent three days assembling has been taken off after the second track and replaced with 'Abba Gold.'

3) A party of friends (none of whom you recognise) who have colonised your bedroom and are sitting around smoking joints, playing the acoustic guitar and will not budge an inch when you try and evict them on the grounds that 'it's your bedroom and you want to go to sleep.'

4) Someone throwing up in your garden.

5) Three self-conscious male virgins sipping cans of Heineken in the kitchen and seriously discussing the relevance of Marx in today's post-modern society.

6) A couple in the corner having a blazing row, the subject of which no one can distinguish until a gap between songs, when you suddenly hear '…*I would if you washed it more often.*'

7) Someone E-ing their head off and dancing madly in the centre of the room when no one else is (and no music is playing).

8) Someone desperately trying to phone a taxi despite the noise, and screaming the address down the receiver.

9) A couple shagging in the toilets.

10) An enormous queue for the toilet (due to the couple shagging in there).

11) Someone who has lost his girlfriend and keeps going round asking everyone 'Have you seen Lisa?' suspecting (quite rightly) that she is in the toilet shagging his best mate.

12) A hippy standing barefoot in the back garden looking up at the stars.

13) Someone trying to organise a search party for his mate who, after consuming two E's, a line of speed and half a bottle of tequila, has wandered off into the night wearing only a dressing gown and one shoe.

A common mistake when organising house parties is to assume that you actually have to do anything other than get some booze in, move the furniture to another room to create a dance area, and tell people to show up. In actual fact, provided plenty of people do turn up, this should be enough for a successful party* as long as you don't:

- Begin the party too early (except for a few lonely souls, no one ever appears until the pubs close, so you'll just sit around on your own for hours feeling like a failure).
- Leave any valuables around the place. (The oddest things go missing at parties – electricity meter keys, books of poetry, pepper pots, toothbrushes. The golden rule is: if it can be nicked, it will be.)

*Saying that, "Themed Parties" can be a good laugh, as long as the theme is not too complicated or obscure. The chances are that only a fraction of your guests will bother turning up in fancy dress, but this can be just enough to create an especially debauched ambience. Old tried and tested favourites include Togas, Seventies, Night Wear and 'Come as You Were.'

THE MORNING AFTER THE NIGHT BEFORE

The scene of a party is never very pleasant the day after. You will awake with a throbbing head to a house that smells like a cross between a compost heap and a dead dog. Hundreds of empty cans, bottles and fag butts will litter every possible surface. With a pounding head and nausea in your stomach you will grab a black plastic sack and begin to tidy up in a desultory manner. At some point a bloke you've never seen before in your life will emerge shakily from one of the rooms, say, "Great party, man," and stagger out. You will never see him again.

From this point on you will realize the great boon of tidying up after a party – the booty. You will find fags, lighters, drugs, even bottles of spirits that people have squirrelled away and forgotten about. According to the official laws of parties, all this stuff is now YOURS.

HOUSE HORROR STORIES

THE QUIET AMERICAN

"Dave Nelson, this American student we knew, couldn't find anywhere to live so his friends agreed to let him kip behind the sofa in their living room. This was his abode for the next six months — a two-foot by six-foot space that contained a sleeping bag and his innumerable Pink Floyd albums. Occasionally the other housemates would forget he was there, and start necking on the sofa with their girlfriends, only to be reminded of his presence when a high-pitched American voice screamed out "*Can ya keep the bloody noise down?!*"

THE BOA WAR

"Three squeaky-clean female Media Studies students at Coventry University were looking for a fourth flatmate, so I put them in touch with a friend Ashley who was looking for a room. Having more than a passing interest in reptiles, Ashley wondered how the girls felt about sharing a house with a six-foot Boa Constrictor called 'Ag'. The girls were reluctant at first, but Ashley re-assured them it was all quite safe and Ag would be kept secure in his room at all times. What he failed to reveal however, was Ag's specialist dietary needs. For every month Ashley would receive a large delivery of frozen rats, which he rather thoughtlessly dumped into the freezer, not thinking the girls would mind seeing a sea of petrified rodents every time they reached for the fish fingers.

Unfortunately the arrival of the rats coincided that afternoon with the escape of Ag, who, being fond of small spaces, wedged herself tight into one of the girl's knickers' drawers. The discovery of this (followed by a scream) and the frozen rats in the freezer (followed by another scream) was too much for the girls, and Ashley was swiftly ejected and replaced with the clean-living sporty yuppie-type they had always dreamed of."

Editor — from his days at Coventry University

THE SMALLEST ROOM

"We left house-hunting for our second year a bit late, and in a fit of panic took the first flat we saw. It had all the joys of being cramped and grotty while still costing the same as the bigger, better place that our friends had secured — in fact one of the bedrooms was so small it was possible for our tallest friend to touch all four walls when he stretched out on the bed. The real horror however was the loo. It was so tiny you literally couldn't close the door when sitting down. It opened straight out onto the hallway, so morning ablutions were an interesting affair, involving shouting to the others that you were off for a number two and the hallway was out-of-bounds for ten minutes. This arrangement was not popular with lady visitors either (as you can imagine).

One afternoon when I thought I was alone and venturing into battle with a particularly reluctant log, one of my colleagues came into the flat with a newly acquired female friend with whom he had romantic ambitions. Their passionate embrace in the hallway was cut short upon her seeing my undignified form caught mortified on the loo. It was at this precise point that my anal prisoner was set lose from its bonds, dropping into the bowl with a mighty rectal fanfare, shortly followed by a resounding splash, reminiscent of an Olympic High-Diver mis-timing a particularly tricky jump. This, accompanied as it was by an astoundingly nasty wave of odour, rather broke the mood for them both, and made introductions awkward all round. I am sad to say the relationship was not a long one."

Kristian, a Brighton University Graduate

SAFETY AND REPAIRS

After many years of fire and gas related student deaths, this is one area where the law is firmly on your side. Do not be slack about these issues; they may save your life.

Gas

The landlord has to show you a certificate on demand from a Corgi-approved installer that the gas appliances have all been checked recently and regularly, and comply to current safety regulations. If they cannot do so, contact Welfare immediately – and don't move in. Danger signs on gas fires and water heaters include stains, soot or discolouring, and an orangey/yellow rather than bluish flame. Symptoms of carbon monoxide poisoning include headaches, dizziness, chestpains and nausea. Not to be confused with hangovers. If you smell gas, contact Transco's emergency line on 0800 111 999. If you have a possibly unsafe appliance and the landlord isn't moving, contact the Environmental Health Gas Safety Adviceline on 0800 399363.

Electrics

Your landlord has a duty to make sure all sockets, wiring and appliances are safe and up to scratch. Keep an eye out for sparks from switches, plugs that get hot and sockets that look like they were installed during the First World War. To avoid potential electrical fires, try to avoid plugging your computer, printer, hi-fi, Playstation, amp, electric heater, mobile recharger, lamp and hairdryer all into one socket with a multi-adaptor.

Furniture and Fire Safety

All upholstered furniture must comply with fire-safety standards in rented accommodation. This means they should pass ignition resistance tests, but these should not be undertaken by you, late at night with the end of a joint. Be suspicious of any item that is over ten years old or is furnished with ghastly paisley patterns.

All houses in Multiple Occupation (not joint tenancies) should be fitted with a smoke alarm system, fire doors and emergency lighting. If they don't, contact the Council's Environmental Health Officers. There are no set rules for non-HMO's, but try to get smoke alarms and firedoors fitted by your landlord. At very least get him/her to buy you some battery operated alarms, which you should check regularly, as inevitably the first time it goes off when someone burns the toast, the battery will be ripped out, forgotten about, and the next pork being roasted might be you.

Repairs

In broad terms, the outside, windows, heating, water and utilities are their responsibility – the inside is yours. You are responsible for not trashing the place, keeping it secure and protecting it while you're away; e.g. don't leave the bath running before leaving for the summer. You are also obliged to undertake minor maintenance duties such as unblocking sinks, cleaning fixtures and fittings, and putting in new bulbs.

Insurance

You may be covered for your expenses if you take out good personal possessions and house insurance, such as that offered to students by Endsleigh. It is a good idea to take out some insurance on your personal posessions anyway; burglary of student houses is an increasingly popular sport amongst the criminal fraternity- one house, many computers and hi-fi, lots of security lapses and comings and goings. Perfect. You may also want to consider fitting a lock to your room and windows for this very reason (and to keep housemates out of your diaries when you go away). You don't want them to know what you really think of them.

Don't Suffer in Silence

For problems ranging from electrical safety to disputes with your landlord, your first port of call should always be your S.U. Housing Officer.

Advice on a whole plethora of housing problems can also be found on the Students Union Website www.nusonline.co.uk, while for free advice on your legal rights, try contacting your local Citizens Advice Bureau. You will be able to locate your local branch through their website, *www.nacab.org.uk.*

Never let people like this into your house

MONEY & JOBS

Back in the golden days when everyone was nice and policemen would share their cigarettes with passers-by, governments showed their respect and support for Higher Education by offering students reasonable grants, housing benefit, dole in the summer and even a small allowance for class B drugs. Sadly, with Socialist principles in this country gone to the dogs, all these benefits have disappeared and these days you can expect to leave university with debts of around £12-£15,000 hanging over your head.

All this can be frightening and worrying, especially if you're studying Fine Art, so this chapter is devised to offer as much practical advice as possible on your finances, ways of saving your cash and a few hare-brained money-making schemes, some of which are barely legal, and others which definitely aren't.

COPING WITH THE BANK

At the beginning of term the banks will throw themselves at your feet in the hope of having you as a customer, and will offer you everything from a CD player to an evening of free sex with Danni Minogue and 'H', formerly of Steps. Do not be fooled into thinking they have your best interests at heart. You will, in all probability, be paying back whacking great interest on your overdraft until the day you die. This is why they want your custom.

Our advice is; forget the freebies and concentrate on what's on offer over the long term. Compare the APR with other banks and find out how long you can keep your overdraft going once you've graduated. Often the rule of thumb is: the bigger the incentive, the less they're offering. Saying that, we've heard 'H' can do amazing things with his tongue.

In fact, for all their friendly 'we love students' image, banks are, for the majority of you, going to become your first tyrannical master. But if you're a smart cookie you should be able to minimise the good spanking they're longing to give you by following the steps below:

- **Don't go over your free overdraft limit.** If you do without telling them, they will impose a one off penalty fee and start charging you an exorbitant rate of interest on the excess. They may even charge a whopping penalty for any extra activity in the account once it has reached this stage, and you will recoil in horror as the cash machine eats your card one morning, squirts skunk scent at you and bites off your fingers for good measure. If, under dire circumstances, you do need to go over your limit, go see your student account manager beforehand. And with enough grovelling, wailing and promises to wash their car, they might, if you're very lucky, organise a temporary extension to your overdraft at a lower rate of interest.

- **Get to know your bank.** More specifically, get to know your student account manager. You'll get a lot further by ringing up and saying "Hi, is Alex there?" (but don't do this if he/she is not called Alex). Even bankers find it harder to send round someone to break your legs if they are on first name terms with you. One student we knew got so friendly with his student account manager that he left university with a £12,000 overdraft; not a good idea, but you've got to admire the levels of charm that must have involved.

- **Open an account with a local student-friendly branch.** Unless you have a long and amicable relationship with your branch at home, it's usually preferable to transfer your account to a campus/ local branch. This allows the all-important human contact element, plus campus branches are generally more tolerant and understanding of the needs and foibles of the student.

- **Try and minimise your debt with the bank/ credit card.** In the long run the rates of interest with the Student Loan Company are much better, and with skill you can avoid giving it back to them for years.

Credit Cards: The work of the devil

Knowing that you're going to leave university with horrendous debts anyway, getting the odd credit card or three may seem the ideal way to generate the extra bit of cash you need in order to splash out on that Fender Telecaster/ motorbike/ yacht you always wanted. This is understandable, but can easily lead to the nightmare of spiralling debt, blacklisting and being kneecapped when you leave university (unless your parents are rich/ mad enough to pay off all your debts the day you finish).

Sure, credit cards are interest free from point of purchase for about fifty days, but do any of us really have the strength of will (or the funds) to pay it all back each time in full and on time? Pay a credit card late and you'll have the most horrendous late payment charges. (You can usually avoid these charges by ringing up and apologising and saying it won't happen again but this will only work the once).

And don't be fooled by credit cards' low introductory offers; it's the standard APR that is important in the long term and can make a big difference. Don't forget, most banks have low or no-interest overdraft facilities for students, so try your utmost to keep your day-to-day debts with them.

If you already have credit card debt or are keen to get one some just to spite us, remember that you can minimise your interest by transferring to a new credit card every six months or so, taking up their low APR introductory offers.

Useless and futile ways of trying to cheat money out of the cash dispenser

1) Insert your card and immediately type in PI to thirty decimal places, from memory. This will bring down the entire banking system and your cash machine will spew cash out confetti-like into your waiting hands.

2) Ask for an insane amount of money such as £4,000,000,000,000. Cash machines are known to suffer electronic indigestion when dealing with such large amounts, and with any luck yours will burp up a couple of twenty-pound notes to relieve the pain.

3) Superglue a piece of string to the end of your card, request some cash, wait until the screen says 'Your Request Is Being Processed', count to four and then whip the card out in one swift movement. This will generate the computer equivalent of a seizure, and for about 30 seconds the system will approve the withdrawal of any amount.

4) Approach the cash machine disguised as a member of the royal family. Cash machines are notoriously patriotic, and, even if your account is as dry as a Jack Dee one-liner, they wouldn't dream of offending royalty, and will cheerfully hand over ludicrous amounts of money to you and even finish with a little curtsey.

5) Oh, what's the point going on?

Earn over 5 pounds an hour as a Harry Enfield lookalike

GETTING BLACKLISTED

What this means it that your name and details will be included on a vast database, which can be accessed by any business organisation in seconds (usually accompanied by a blaring klaxon and the appearance of several burly security guards to hurl you out onto the street.) Blacklisting will preclude you from having a bank account, getting a mortgage, receiving a loan, or buying anything in instalments for the next seven years. This might not seem like a big deal when you're at uni, but will be a right royal pain in the arse when you leave.

HOW DO YOU GET BLACKLISTED?

If you annoy your bank by continually running up enormous overdrafts that are way over your limit, and ignoring their angry letters, then eventually they'll lose their patience with you, stop your account and – likely as not – sell your debt on to a collection agency. The collection agency will then contact you and ask for the debt to be repaid in monthly instalments. They will usually demand a payment that is ten percent of the original debt (i.e. 200 pounds on a debt of two thousand.) **Ignore this.** They're trying to pull a fast one. Legally speaking, they can't insist on any specific sum without taking you to the small claims court (which they won't want to do – A. Because it costs money, and B. Because the court might agree on a repayment even smaller than the one you're offering). If necessary contact a solicitor who deals in legal aid to help you work out a repayment more in accordance with your meagre 'earnings.' You'll probably be able to get away with paying something as tiny as five or ten pounds a month. Of course, this means that it'll take you the next two decades to square the debt, but what the hell – you'll be blacklisted for the next seven years anyway.

BAILIFFS

Of course, it's likely that the debt agency will try to scare you into forking over the cash by threatening to send over the firm of 'Hefty and Kneebreak' (i.e. two shaven-headed, neckless sacked policemen or failed security guards) to impound everything you own. If the bailiffs do turn up, then it's vitally important that you remember the following points:-

1) You <u>DON'T</u> have to let them in, whatever they may say. (You don't have to let anyone in your house, not even the coppers if they don't have a warrant.)

2) If they force their way in, **call the police immediately.** (It's a good idea to call your solicitor as well, since the police may otherwise regard the whole thing as simply a domestic disturbance.)

3) They can't take anything that isn't yours. Simply claim that all the objects in your house belong to other people. (A solicitor friend recommends that, prior to the bailiffs arrival, you affix 'post-it' notes bearing other people's names to anything of value – i.e. 'Steve's Video', 'Kathy's Computer', etc. This should put the bailiffs off because they know that if they take anything belonging to anyone else, their firm will have to provide a brand-new model free of charge.)

EXTRA FUNDING

If you are totally broke, a single parent, over 25, disabled, doing a teaching degree, or come from somewhere really depressing, like Coventry, there is a chance that you could be due a bit more money. Below is a list of grants/funds currently available to the needy*.

HARDSHIP FUNDS AND EMERGENCY/ CRISIS LOANS

Each university is allocated extra funds by the government to help out anyone that gets into dire straits with their finances. If this happens to you, go talk to your welfare officer to see what's on offer, as the universities are not always keen to promote the fact, fearing that everyone will plead poverty in the first week and bleed them dry. In normal circumstances, you'll have to apply for an emergency loan first (which will have to be paid back) but once you've drunk this, there's still the chance to apply for a hardship fund which you won't have to repay. To earn this free cash, you'll need to provide your last two month's bank statements, a blood sample, and sell one of your kidneys to prove how hard up you really are.

OPPORTUNITY BURSARY / EXCELLENCY ACTION ZONES

In 2001 the government made available some extra money for any towns/cities, which fell under the banner of 'a bit of a shit-hole'. Places turning out a low percentage of students, areas where the household has a low income or no history of higher education in the family have been singled out as 'excellency action zones' and if your home fits this criteria you may be eligible for an extra £2,000. Of course, there is no guarantee the government will continue to run this scheme. Typically, they set these things up, then the money runs out the following year. But if you come from Middlesbrough or mid-Wales for example, it wouldn't do any harm to check it out.

DISABILITY GRANTS

Forms for these can be picked up on campus from your finance officer. These grants cover a wide range of dibasitilies including dyslexia.

*though, knowing this government, by next week they'll have removed all the funding

STUDENTS WITH DEPENDENTS

If you are a single parent/ have a partner earning less than £7,000 p.a. you could be due some extra money. Again, ask your finance officer.

SCHOOL BURSARIES

Some schools offer cash incentives for certain degrees (usually ones that could lead to fill the ever-growing list of job vacancies in certain sectors of the job market. We're talking here mainly about teaching and dubious research jobs at the MOD). Although it's obviously important to pursue any chance of extra funding whilst at university, perhaps more importantly, it's time to do a little soul searching and ask yourself – if the government needs to offer cash incentives to encourage students to study certain degrees, what's the catch?

The answer is that spending four years on a PGCE, specialising in science, to prepare yourself to be a physics teacher in a secondary school is perhaps the most masochistic and painfully stupid act known to man. If you think secondary teaching has even the remotest bit of glamour ('the reward….the holidays… the corduroy') think back to what a handful you were when you were fifteen, and ask yourself if you'd enjoy having to face a class of stroppy 15-year olds every day for the rest of your life. And as for the people who help the government build bombs to sell to third world countries – how do they sleep at night?

Poor but happy....because they've got each other

MONEY SAVING STRATEGIES AND SCAMS

PAYING BILLS

In shared accommodation the problem with bills isn't paying them (although, lets face it, that is quite a big problem); the real problem is getting every one else to pay their bit. For this reason, try not to be the only one who puts everything in their name. This will make you the muggins responsible for collecting all the money from your slack housemates, which, believe us, is a thankless task. Instead, try and make sure everyone in the house has their name on each bill, so you are all jointly and severally liable. Or better, share the bills out so you all have a bill "weapon" with which to threaten the others into paying. It's sort of like the cold war and the theory of Mutually Assured Destruction, only with bills instead of nuclear weapons. If you do pick the short straw and have to be responsible for the phone bill it's a good idea to get pin numbers generated for each house member which show on the phone bill who made which call. BT and Cable will do this for a small fee.

DIRECT DEBITS

Do this for as many of your outgoings as you can and it will help enormously in your monthly budgeting. Often utility companies will let you set how much you want to pay each month, relieving the sting of a whopping great payout as the electricity phone and gas bills all roll in at the end of term, swallowing up all the money you'd been saving for a debauched weekend in Ibiza. You can also get discounts for paying by direct debit and, provided your landlord doesn't mind, you can change suppliers to get cheap combination deals for gas and electricity.

COUNCIL TAX

Check carefully that you are getting your full discount on this for being a student. Councils, being like a very old cat (i.e. slow, dopey and given to sudden bouts of random bad-tempered viciousness) are often prone to making cock-ups and trying to reclaim overpayments to them can be real grief, especially if, like with the entire staff of Doncaster Council, they've already blown your cash on a world cruise.

PAYING THE TV LICENCE

Where would we be without the good old TV licence? OK, rid of Chris Moyles and The Weakest Link for a start, but that isn't a reason not to pay up. For the more unscrupulous among you however, it is worth noting that TV detector vans are a scam. Far from containing high-tech equipment that can detect from 10 miles away that you're tuned into Channel 4 watching Countdown in your pants, all they really have on you is a list that tells them which households haven't coughed up the readies. Remember this and consider what can be done. You don't have to let them in and they do have to prove you've got a telly. And even if they spot it or you're daft enough to let them in to watch Neighbours, they will usually give you a period of grace to buy a licence if you play dumb and apologetic. That said, don't blame us if you get lumbered with a fine.

STUDENT UNION CARD

Don't forget to carry your Student Union Card everywhere. It's amazing where and when you can get money off with it. Your union will have a list of places locally and nationally where the card will get you money off anything from clothes, films and drinks to garden furniture, moustache wax and plastic surgery.

BUYING A HOUSE

This is only an option if your parents are sickeningly rich, but if that's the case, see if you can persuade them to buy you a house with two or more bedrooms. You then get to rent out the rooms, cover your mortgage and bills, and you even get the power to evict your mates if they don't do all the washing up and cleaning for you.

FAGS

If you must indulge in the dreaded weed, try switching to rolling tobacco; it will save you heaps of money in the long run and if you use filters it's better for you (relatively speaking).

SAVING ON ELECTRICITY

Try switching the fridge off at night to cut down on the 'leccy bill.

When renting or buying a student house, don't set your expectations too high

Charity Shopping

Gone are the days when almost every student's wardrobe was almost entirely made up of stained collarless shirts, grotty old cardies and grandma's cast-offs. With Charity Shop chic currently at an all-time low amongst the majority of students (particularly in the South), they no longer represent a goldmine of retro chic, but do still possess that faint but ever-lingering smell of piss.

With a good eye, however, a creative flair and the courage to reject the latest over-priced high street uniform, charity shopping can still be a fun and cheap way to find some unique additions to your wardrobe. And, if nothing else, it is invaluable for finding that perfect number for an Eighties-themed party. Here are a few tips for how to get the best out of these much-maligned lucky dips...

1) Don't expect to get a bargain in Oxfam. It's almost as expensive as Gap these days. Look for smaller causes (Help The Aged, Scope, P.D.S.A.) or obscure local ones. Any place called, for example, 'Mrs. Fotheringay's Aid Organisation To Help The Stray Cat That She Feeds' is bound to be cheap.

2) If you're studying anywhere near a small town or village, it's definitely worth your while going there on a clothes-buying expedition. Charity shops in little, out-of-the-way places are nearly always less expensive than their savvier big-city counterparts.

3) Charity shops, being more business-minded these days, have sales just the same as any other high-street outlet. Keep your eyes peeled for signs reading 'Winter Coats ½ Price', '2 Trouser-legs For The Price Of 1', and 'Everything 99p.'

4) Try volunteering for an afternoon each week. It'll only be a couple of hours of your time, and not only will you be helping the less fortunate, you'll also have first dibs on any bargains that come in (and you'll get a discount.)

Of course, the other advantage of kitting yourself out in charity shop clobber is that you will at least look a bit more individual than the Gap and Top Shop-clones who surround you. Don't take this too far however – wearing a sombrero, jodhpurs, a 'Bryan Adams' T-Shirt and diving-boots might well mean that nobody talks to you for the next three years.

BUDGETING

At the beginning of your first term at university you will be given access to a large chunk of cash, quite possibly more money than you have ever got your hands on before. At first glance it probably seems an enormous amount. But before you get over-excited at the possibility of being able to afford a new car, designer wardrobe and a brand new laptop, you need to get your head round the dreaded weekly budget. The bald truth about budgeting is that some people are better at it than others. To generalise grossly, older students are better at it than the young, women (if they keep away from clothes shops) are better at it than men, and science students are better at it than arts students. So if you're an eighteen year-old male drama student, the chances are that right now you're probably staring morosely at the tin of beans that is all you've got to eat for the next three months, and wondering why on earth you spent six hundred quid on an original Seventies Space Hopper.

But don't despair – working out your income and expenditure on a weekly basis can help you conserve cash, and stop you from being unpleasantly surprised by a bill you've completely forgotten about. To do this you need to:

1) Divide the original amount by how many weeks there are in the term.
2) For each week subtract your weekly rent.
3) For each week subtract the amount you are likely to spend on food.
4) For each week subtract an amount for bills such as electricity, gas, phone calls, as well as travel, clothing etc.

And having performed these mathematical feats you will finally discover the stark reality of your financial situation, as your amount of money transforms from LOADS to BUGGER-ALL.

Put all thoughts of this as far from your mind as you can

CASE STUDY OF HOW TO PLAN YOUR BUDGET ON A WEEKLY ALLOWANCE OF £120

WEEKLY EXPENDITURE OF
STUDENT (A)
SENSIBLE STUDENT

RENT – £60
FOOD/HOUSEHOLD ITEMS – £20
BOOKS/EQUIPMENT – £3
CLOTHING – £5
TRAVEL – £5
TELEPHONE – £3
ELECTRICITY – £2
GAS – £1
TV LICENCE – 50P
ENTERTAINMENTS – £20
TOTAL – £119.50

This leaves you with a whole 50p to go crazy with. Don't spend it all in the same shop.

WEEKLY EXPENDITURE OF
STUDENT (B)
NAUGHTY STUDENT

RENT – £60
FOOD/HOUSEHOLD ITEMS – £20
ELECTRICITY – 1.50
GAS – 1.00
TAXIS – £10
PIZZA DELIVERY – £15
5 NIGHTS OUT DOWN THE BOOZER – £40
AN EIGHTH – £20
LINE OF CHARLIE – £20
3 HOURS ON MOBILE TALKING CRAP WITH FRIENDS – £10
SHOPPING BONANZA IN GAP/FCUK/ HENNES/ JIGSAW/ M&S – £50
HAIRCUT AT TONI AND GUY – £25
6 HOURS ON THE INTERNET SEARCHING FOR NAKED PICTURES OF JIMMY SAVILLE – £12.50
TICKETS FOR ABBA REUNION GIG IN PARIS – £50
NIGHT AT CREAM – £60
FINE FOR NOT PAYING TV LICENCE – £500
TRACTOR – £12,500
TOTAL – £13, 395

As you can see, student A may be a sensible, goodie-two shoes who only drinks ginger beer, shops at Primark and listens to Cliff Richard records without irony, but he/she will not leave uni with the bailiffs knocking on the door.

Student B on the other hand, is a total slacker who would rather pay someone to make them a sandwich than get off their fat lazy arse and make it themselves. Although they make everyone jealous by their careless spending and new shiny tractor, they will, over their years at uni, rack up a debt so vast that Bono from U2 will make a plea to the World Bank to write it off.

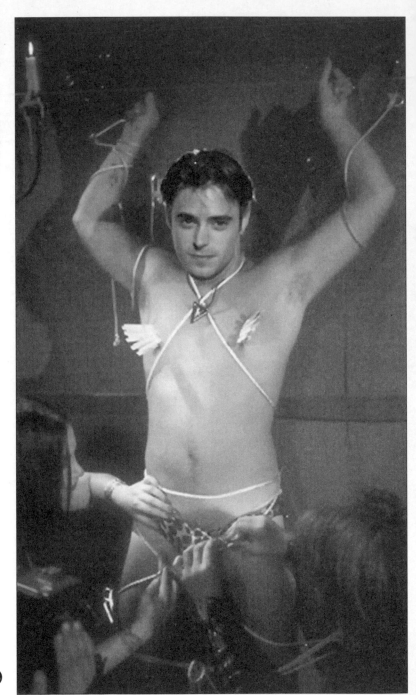

THE BUDGET QUIZ

So, how good are you at budgeting? Simply answer the question below and see bottom of the page for how well you did.

You have twenty quid to last you the next twelve days. Do you spend it on...

A) Five tins of beans, four tins of soup, three tins of tomatoes, two packets of pasta, a bag of potatoes, a big pack of Golden Virginia, some rizlas, a four-pint carton of milk, a tub of marge, three loaves of bread, a box of tea bags, a box of cornflakes, a tin of corned-beef, a bag of onions, mild cheddar, a jar of Branston Pickle, a bag of carrots, a tin of rice-pudding, and a packet of jammy dodgers?

B) One tin of beans, a loaf of bread, and twenty-four cans of Heineken?

C) A haircut?

D) Twenty quids worth of calls on your mobile?

E) Electronic farting machine?

F) A signed photograph of Jamie Theakston?

G) A hamster?

H) Magic beans?

The answer is, of course, D). Five minutes of sobbing on the phone to your parents should be enough to get them fretting and prompt them to send a little something your way, to 'see you through the month.'

JOBS

*If your finances are in dire straits, the solution (aside from theft or doing a 'Mr. Ripley')
will invariably point towards the dreaded part-time job. Welcome to the dull,
unrewarding and glamour-free world of pulling pints, washing up, burger flipping,
telemarketing, care working, shelf stacking, and toilet cleaning.*

*It is generally recommended that your job should take up no more than 15 hours
per week during term time; any more than this and your studies are bound to suffer.
Most students find part-time jobs off their own backs (by simply going round local
bars/ supermarkets etc and asking for work), but you may be lucky enough to have
an employment center at your university which should be your first port of call when
job-hunting, saving you going round town and knocking on doors with a hang-dog look
on your face.*

*Of course, not all jobs can be dismal, many people enjoy the sociable element to
bar-work and tipping in restaurants can be rewarding if you know how to put on the
charm, but, more often than not, the part-time job can be a real stinker.*

40% of students now work part-time to
supplement their income

BAR WORK

PROS: If you're good with people, able to add up, and get a friendly pub, bar work
can be quite fun and sociable. Plus the hours should suit your timetable pretty well.
CONS: The pay is never great and long hours on your feet can be draining, as can
having to deal with obnoxious drunks who, when you are sober and tired, will make
Nick Cotton seem like a nice person.

FAST FOOD DELIVERY/COURIER WORK

PROS: Earn a reasonable wage as you whizz around on a clapped out old moped,
pretending you're in some Sixties Italian movie.
CONS: Earn slightly less money as you spend two weeks in hospital after being
mown down by a bus.

WAITING/ WAITRESSING

PROS: If you're good at it, are charming to boot, and it's quite a swanky restaurant,
you can clean up on this one with lots of tips and a reasonable rate of pay. And if
customers are rude and surly you can still get immense satisfaction by discreetly
'coughing up' a few extra ingredients into their food.
CONS: Long hours on your feet, no time for socialising and if you drop scalding hot
soup on someone you'll instantly get the sack. Not always the most PC of
environments, girls can still expect the occasional boss whose idea of saying he likes
you is to give you a big slap on your arse.

DATA-INPUTTING

PROS: Quite good rates of pay, your own chair and free coffee.
CONS: Sedentary, mind numbingly dull and repetitive.

CALL CENTRES/TELESALES
PROS: Relatively stress-free, flexible hours, a comfy chair and usually better wages than bar/ shop work.
CONS: Sedentary, mind numbingly dull and repetitive. And if it's commission-based, avoid like the plague.

SHOP WORK
PROS: Pilfering the stock and sloping off into the stock room for a sly fag.
CONS: A monkey can do shelf stacking, and some of the people you'll be working with will resemble them. (Till work is slightly better paid, but is sedentary, mind numbingly dull...etc)

PROMOTIONAL/SKINWORK
PROS: Dressing up and running around pubs and clubs giving out flyers and free samples can be a laugh, and is sometimes well paid
CONS: You will lose all sense of dignity as you wobble around in a giant panda costume day after day while little kids prod and kick you.

STEWARDING – A CUSHY NUMBER
Depending on the size of your campus/ university, your NUS should have quite a few jobs on offer in the way of stewarding/ supervising gigs, club nights and other events. If you can secure yourself one of these jobs, you have landed on a potential goldmine. Forget cleaning dishes in the local pizza hut – this work is sociable, pays quite well and provides a fairly regular income. But, more importantly, it offers on-campus employment, the chance to meet loads of people, and the opportunity to get into gigs and club nights for free.

These jobs are, naturally, much sought after – so to avoid disappointment, approach your union the day you arrive at university, find out who is responsible for these jobs, and keep pestering them until they finally give in and offer you some work, or at least put you at the top of the waiting list.

STRANGE AND SEEDY JOBS

If none of the above appeal, and you are willing to go down the line where the distinctions between respectability, decency and immorality and downright illegality become somewhat hazy, then read on. We are not necessarily condoning the following jobs, but have to admit that they show cunning and enterprise.

LAP/POLE-DANCING

If you don't have an issue with the sleazy and exploitative nature of this work (which, understandably, many women do) this can be a remarkably lucrative profession (as much as £500 a week, with tips) and an increasing number of female students are taking it up as a way of funding themselves through university. According to several female students we met who have undertaken this kind of work, some complained of feeling 'cheapened, dancing about in front of about twenty-six Japanese businessmen wearing nothing but a g-string', while others confessed to having enjoyed it and one even claimed to find the experience 'empowering'.

The one thing that all the girls did agree on was that their initial worries of being 'touched up' proved to be unfounded, for if one of the clientele lay so much as a finger on them, a posse of burly, unreasoning bouncers would forcibly eject undesirables from the premises. In fact, their main concern seemed to be that one day they'd look down to see who'd just slipped them a tenner in their pants and find themselves staring into the face of their personal tutor/ their old piano teacher/ their dad.

DRUG-DEALING

While not wishing to encourage anyone to take up such an activity, it cannot be denied that a small percentage of entrepreneurial students in every university manage to pay their way through uni by dealing to their fellow alumni.

The obvious advantages to this are that, not only will you make heaps of money for doing very little, but you'll also get invited to every party on campus.

The big disadvantage with dealing drugs in whatever quantity is, of course, that it is, unfortunately, illegal. Whereas a copper may turn a blind eye to the cannabis plant in your airing cupboard, he/she is unlikely to ignore the suitcase full of the stuff you keep stashed at the bottom of your wardrobe.

Get caught with a sufficient amount of any drug and you're looking at a hefty prison sentence. In fact, even if you don't get caught, unless you've got a very cool head on you at all times, you will be plagued by intense paranoia that everyone you know, from your friends to your tutors, are in fact plain-clothed policemen. It could even be us.

LIFE-MODELLING

There is always a demand for life-models (i.e. people who stand around for ages in the nude while others sketch them.) Visit the art department, local art college, community centre, night-school, or anywhere you know there are life-drawing classes held, and put your name forward. You might think you'd have to be a Venus or Adonis for this work, but nothing could be further from the truth. Classes actually prefer the saggy, ugly, or even obese, as they often make more interesting subjects.

It pays quite well, normally about eight pounds an hour, but you'll frequently have to work at short-notice (when someone else drops out, say). Also, you may have to travel around – obviously classes don't want to have to draw the same old carcass week in, week out, so you'll tend to get passed from college to college. This can be a good thing – if you earn a reputation as a reliable model, then art teachers will recommend you to other institutions.

As to the work itself, it's not that strenuous – all you have to do is get naked before a load of artists and hold a pose for a certain length of time. You'll get a break every half hour, but even so try to avoid poses that tax you physically (avoid balancing on one leg, the lotus position and smiling) as cramp is the life-model's bête-noire. The best thing is to portray a reclining Samson or Psyche – if you're a dab hand, then you'll even be able to get some kip in.

Finally, it is important to remember that the embarrassment doesn't stop at the modelling sessions. Be prepared to see larger-than-life depictions of your rude bits at exhibitions, galleries, craft fairs and café bars all over town. For you the phrase 'Private View' will take on a whole new meaning.

Confessions of a life model

"I was booked for a modelling class at an old folks home in Rottingdean. I turned up, to find a roomful of octogenarians eagerly clutching their pencils. I asked if there was anywhere to change and was directed to the Ladies. I stripped, put on my dressing gown and returned to the class, where I disrobed and struck a pose. Two dozen wrinkled, toothless jaws hit the floor as one. It turned out they didn't know what "Life Model" meant, and were only interested in clothed subjects. Still, I'm sure it gave a few old-timers a thrill, or at least thinned out their number." – Anonymous

BOOZE AND FAG RUNS

If your uni location is favourable to a quick jaunt over the water, this potentially lucrative (if ever-so slightly-illegal) venture simply requires a small van, a passport, a ferry to your nearest overseas destination, and a visit to the nearest hypermarket to clear them out of booze. If the authorities question you on your return, simply explain it's for personal use (although they definitely won't believe you.) If you're doing this regularly, then vary the ports you're using, otherwise the customs men will smell a rat (even a student can't drink 30 cases of vodka and smoke 50 dozen packs of Drum in a month).

All that's left to do is simply flog your cut-price booze and ciggies to all and sundry. The downside of all this is that if Customs and Excise get suspicious they may put you under surveillance, which might entail your having to drink the 30 cases of Vodka and smoke the 50 dozen packs of Drum in one month after all.

JOBS TO AVOID

- Anything that is commission-based pay – i.e. your pay directly relates to how many time-shares you sell/ how many people you swindle
- Anything advertised on a sticker on a lamppost saying NEED MONEY NOW? EARN UP TO £5000 A WEEK!
- Anything stuck up on a handwritten card in a newsagent's window that involves stuffing envelopes for a seemingly very generous rate.
- Any job where you are asked to "invest" money to start up "your own exciting new business opportunity".
- Prostitution
- Teaching

The Great Charity Shop Swindle

Volunteer for a couple of afternoon shifts at Oxfam or Help The Aged. Once there, you will be offered the pick of the crop of the kitsch memorabilia which floods in every day before it's put on the shelves. Certain charity shops forbid the sale of any item to their staff before it has been officially priced, but if you have an understanding manager, he or she will generally ignore this, and let you have it for next to nothing when it's fresh out of the bin bag. After a couple of weeks you should have accumulated enough 1970s Action Men, World's Greatest Dad mugs, cheese-cloth shirts, velveteen pictures of crying clowns and Village People Albums to set up a stall at a none-too-local car boot sale and flog it for a handsome profit. One acquaintance of ours actually made five hundred pounds in a week using this scam.

Not recommended if you have a conscience.

THE DOOMSDAY OPTION: CHANGING YOUR IDENTITY

If all else fails, and you are being chased by debtors, banks, recovery agencies, bailiffs, and large men that bear more than a passing resemblance to Phil from Eastenders, then you might have to consider the option of changing your identity. There are several ways in which you can accomplish this:

1) DEED POLL – It's remarkably cheap and easy to do this. Shell out a few quid, fill in a form, and you can walk straight out into your new life as a different person. Under no circumstances choose a comedy name. 'I.P.Freely', 'Norma Snockers' or 'Arthur Lager', may seem funny at the time but will quickly grow wearisome. There was, of course, the famous case of the man who – pissed off with his bank – changed his moniker to 'Barclays Bank Are Bastards' and then got Barclays to issue him a chequebook in that name. This sounds like a great wheeze but, then again, he was stuck with the name Barclays Bastards.

2) CONVERT TO ISLAM – Another good plan – there's no way anyone is going to cotton on that Mohammad Rashtar Jamil was once Kevin Pryce. If you're already Muslim, you could always convert to Christianity and change your name to Kevin Pryce.

3) CHANGE YOUR SEX – Possibly a touch drastic

The Many Many Names of Shihab Salim

Our mate Shihab is, as his name suggests, a Muslim. This means that, technically, his full name is Mohammad Shihab Salim, since in Islam all males bear the same first name. While at university, he used this fact to rip off several banks, opening accounts as Shihab Salim, Mohammad Salim, M.S. Salim, M. Shihab Salim, Mohammad S. Salim, etc. He managed to rip off the banks to the tune of several thousand pounds before they worked out what was going on. Unfortunately, when they did, he was blacklisted to the extent that his dad (who knew nothing of any of this) found himself refused credit when he tried to buy a car one day. Shihab currently lives in North Wales under the name of Colin Prendergast.

DON'T SUFFER IN SILENCE

If the bank are sending round a bloke called "Razors" for a "bit of a chat" and you're on first name terms with your credit card call-centre, it's time to seek help. Your initial gambit would be your University Finance Officer or, if you have one, a Union Finance Officer. All universities have a discretionary hardship fund for exceptional cases, and will try to help with planning a way out and mediating a solution for any student who asks. The key is, the earlier you go, the better. If that's not enough, for up-to-date information on grants, loans, budgeting and work advice, contact www.nusonline.co.uk.

FOOD

The popular notion of students' eating habits is that they subsist on a diet of pasta, baked beans, tuna, pizza and crisps. The other cliché is that many students haven't got the first idea of how to boil an egg, peel a potato or even make a cup of tea. Much as we would like to claim that students are in fact, a band of highly accomplished cooks with sophisticated palates, we have to admit that there is a grain of truth in these assertions. Ask any number of graduates what their most characteristic memory of university was, and they are bound to mention the time they tried to boil potatoes in the kettle or the week they lived off nothing but packet soup and Shredded Wheat because there was nothing else in the house*.

An article in The Sunday Times Magazine** averred that students these days (figuring that as they're going to be in debt anyway, they might as well throw caution to the wind) are blowing their cash on expensive food and fancy restaurants. This may be true in some cases — but even the most well-heeled gourmet is going to find him or herself short of cash at some point or other, and a clubbing bonanza one weekend is almost certain to leave you out of pocket, out of food, and lead to five days of eating nothing but pasta with tomato purée.

With this in mind, we offer below a thorough manual to university cooking — from the cheapest places to shop, easy recipes and basic food facts, to how to become a vegetarian without dying of cheese poisoning.

*(er..that was me — Ed) **March 10th 2002

man cannot live on beans alone.

es mondays 7pm @ the meeting house

MAKING THE BEST OF YOUR LOCAL SUPERMARKET

Cheap things: rice, pasta, pulses, grains, cheese, eggs, tinned tomatoes, bread, chicken, locally grown fruit, most veg, fish, breakfast cereals.
Expensive things: Quail's eggs, Pâté de fois gras, Caviar, Panda chops.

1. FIND THE CHEAPEST PLACE

These tend to be either Lidl, Kwik-Save or Aldi. If you draw a blank with these then try Morrisons, Somerfield and Asda. If you don't have any of these close by then just remember to avoid Waitrose and Harrods and you should be OK.

2. BUY THE SUPERMARKET'S OWN BRAND RANGE

Tesco's Own, Sainsbury's Own etc, tend to be exactly the same quality as the thing they're copying (Heinz, Kelloggs, Fender, Mercedes etc) but are usually significantly cheaper. Many supermarkets also do their own special Budget Value brand, which come in staunch, no nonsense packaging such as plain white labelled tins that just say things like:

1) Beans 7p
2) Peas 8p
3) Cornflakes 50p
4) Horse Meat 18p
5) Brown Stuff 24p

As a rule of thumb, the less processed the food, the less different in taste and quality it will be from its premium counterpart. A pack of Tesco Basics carrots isn't going to be much different from their Carrottes de Luxe range, whereas most Value Sausages taste of horror rather than meat and are made of the bits of dead cow/ pig/ dog that no-one else could find a use for.

3. LOOK FOR BARGAINS

Keep an eye open for 'two for the price of one' offers, avoid two for the price of three offers, and remember that you're unlikely to get arrested stealing the odd sweet from the pick 'n' mix section in the supermarket, so make the most of it.

And remember: you can also save money by using your local markets, independent butchers and green grocers for your basic foodstuff. It might take slightly more time than that all-in-one trip to the supermarket, but you'll be doing your bit in the fight against corporate globalisation. Markets particularly represent excellent value for money, especially if you go near the end of the day and are prepared, like in the haggling scene from the Life of Brian, to passionately argue your case for 20p off the last bag of avocados. Remember too that in-season local veg and fruit will be cheaper and much more nutritious than, say, a bunch of unripe bananas that have spent the last fortnight on boats, planes, trains and taxis, suffocating in cling-film.

General Shopping Tips

Set a weekly budget, see how much you can afford on food and try to build a nutritious menu round it.

Cook a big pot of something each week, like vegetable stew or lasagne, and freeze or chill the left overs. Then you can save yourself from those pizza urges and stick it in the microwave later on in the week. But beware of drunken fridge thieves.

Make sandwiches instead of shelling out for the food at the canteen every day. If you still want to hang out there to be with friends, bring a tea-bag, order a free cup of hot water and nibble your sandwiches under the table.

Make a list of meals you'd like to cook before you go shopping and stick to the ingredients. Whatever's left of your shopping budget you can spend on treats.

Base your meals around starchy foods; bread, potatoes, rice, pasta, cereals and pulses. They fill you up cheaply and give you energy.

Never shop when hungry! You will overspend and end up with eight thousand bags of crisps and biscuits.

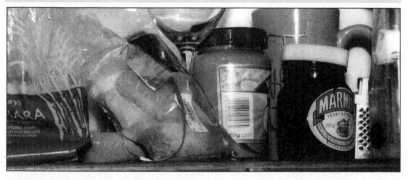

FRIDGE RULES

Adhere to the following rules and you can sneer at Salmonella, laugh in the face of botulism and steer clear of the Plague.

1) Never store raw meat on a shelf above cooked meat. If you don't know why, ask your mum.

2) Store fish away from vegetables and other products, as your flatmates will not thank you for that two-week old piece of haddock getting cosy with their defrosting pizza.

3) Check your fridge is cold enough. 5° C is the recommended safe temperature for chilled food storage. Anything much above this and bacteria will wake from their slumbers and throw a party on your turkey wings.

4) Defrost any meat thoroughly before cooking; particularly chicken, as it is often rife with Salmonella. (The best way to defrost food is to leave it in the fridge if you have time).

5) Defrost your fridge once a term and you won't have problems closing the door owing to the ever-growing blob of ice from the freezer department. This involves taking all the food out (which can be stored in a coolbox if you have one, and you should as they are ideal for beer at festivals) unplugging it, and letting all the ice from the freezer compartment melt away into the trays and newspapers that you should have put around the bottom but forgot. Leave the ice monster untouched and, like the Blob, it will grow to gigantic proportions, eventually filling the fridge, kitchen and whole house, and before you know it there'll be woolly mammoths in your garden, and you don't want that.

6) Every couple of weeks, try to clear the fridge of abandoned foodstuffs. This can be a fraught process, for if left unchecked, you may well be on your way to finding new forms of life growing in there. If you do, find a pair of rubber gloves for protection, and come back armed. Of, course, not everyone will necessarily be happy if you do choose to give the fridge a good clear out. Throw away that five-week old half-can of frankfurters, and your Art student flatmate will no doubt denounce you, claiming that he was saving them to use in his 3D food sculpture. But rest assured, you have done him, and the art world, a big favour.

'It's a pity that no-one in my corridor realises that it's not a good idea to eat mayonnaise once it starts to smell funny…' First year student at Portsmouth University

A CRASH COURSE IN NUTRITION FOR THE UNENLIGHTENED FISH FINGER FIEND

By State Registered Dietitian and King's College University Graduate Katie Clarke

If you want to stay healthy and not die of scurvy it is necessary to pay some attention to your diet. Eat foods from the following 5 food groups every day and you can't go far wrong.

CARBOHYDRATES (Bread, cereal, potatoes, pasta, rice etc)

Contrary to the misinformed views of multitalented singer and yoga expert Geri Halliwell, these foods are not the root of all evil. Actually they should make up the main part of your diet and are very filling and cheap, with the added bonus of containing important vitamins and fibre.

FRUIT AND VEGETABLES

Try and eat at least five portions of fruit and vegetables each day, fresh, frozen or canned, as they are essential sources of many minerals and vitamins. Interestingly, frozen veg often contains higher amounts of vitamins and minerals as they are picked when ripe, whereas fresh stuff is often picked whilst unripe, stripping it of much of its goodness. But do check you've got room for it in the microscopic freezer space where the ice-monster lives.

PROTEIN

This group includes meat (beef, pork, bacon, lamb), poultry, fish, eggs, pulses (baked beans, chick-peas, lentils, mung beans etc.), nuts, Quorn and bogies.

CALCIUM

Milk, cheese, yoghurt and fromage frais are all good sources of calcium, which is good for teeth and bones. If you're trying to watch your weight, lower fat versions (semi-skimmed milk, half fat cheese etc.) have the same amount of calcium as full-fat. If you don't eat dairy products make sure you choose Soya milk or Soya products fortified with calcium.

FATS AND SUGARS

These should be eaten sparingly, especially if your calorie intake is doubled by your increased alcohol consumption and/or an addiction to Kit-Kats. Use butter or margarine sparingly and try not to fry too often.

LIQUID INTAKE

Dehydration is a growing health problem in the west, owing to the fact that so many of the things we now drink are diuretic (i.e. dehydrating). Fizzy drinks, tea, coffee and alcohol all put a strain on your liver, requiring extra fluids to flush out the crap, so they actually deplete the water levels in your body. Try drinking more water (ideally 2 litres a day) favouring hot water/ herbal teas in winter. If you need any more encouragement, drinking lots of water is the secret to healthy skin, keeps your body toned and will almost inevitably mean you'll get a First.

The Student Caff

Starters

A fag whilst waiting for the main course:

Main Course

Pasta with tuna

Pasta with mushrooms

Pasta and pesto

Pasta with 'Chicken Tonight' curry sauce

Pasta with grated cheddar

Pasta with Dolmio Sauce

Pasta au naturel

Chef's Special

Frozen pizza

Spag Bog

Dessert

Coffee and a fag

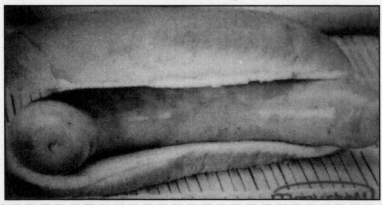

THE TOP FIVE MOST DEPRESSING MEALS

(WHEN YOU COME HOME FROM THE PUB AND THE CUPBOARD IS BARE)

1. Cornflakes with water
2. Tomato purée on toast
3. A tin of pears
4. Smash with ketchup
5. The crusty bits stuck to the
   bottom of yesterday's pizza box

Brian's Baked Potatoes And Curried Beans

This meal has saved my life on many an occasion when I have been utterly broke and dispirited. It is very cheap to make (most of the ingredients can be scrounged from an understanding flat-mate without too much pleading) and is also quite substantial and satisfying.

YOU WILL NEED:

Two potatoes
Half an onion (from the back of the fridge)
A 7p tin of beans (Asda or Safeway)
A few mushrooms (from the back of the toilet)
2 pinches of salt
A tablespoon of oil
2 teaspoons of curry powder
A knob of butter

1 Scrub and pierce the potatoes, rub with half the oil and salt, and place in an oven, pre-heated to a high setting, for about an hour until golden brown. (Conversely, you could nuke them in the microwave and throw them in the oven for ten minutes to crisp up the skins.)

2 After about half an hour's cooking time, peel and finely chop the onion and fry gently in the remaining oil in a small pan.

3 Wash, and chop the mushrooms and add when the onion has started to soften.

4 When the onion has browned, stir in the curry powder until the onion and mushrooms are evenly coated. Then pour in the lovely, lovely beans.

5 Simmer until the watery tomato sauce has almost completely evaporated, and the ingredients have become an indistinct, gloopy mass of curried goodness.

6 Halve the potatoes, add a knob of butter, sprinkle with salt and then smother in the beans.

Joseph's Vegetarian Shepherd's Pie

This was the first proper dish I ever learnt to cook at university. My flatmate Claire told me how to do it, and I shall remain forever grateful to her. I'm still making it to this day. It's a meal that you can quickly whip up on your own after a night out clubbing, and you can produce it at a dinner party, and no one will complain. The perfect veggie repast.

YOU WILL NEED:

One onion
One packet of 'Beanfeast'
(Bolognese is best)
A tin of tomatoes
A tin of carrots
½ pint water
Five or six good-sized spuds
Oil
Milk
Butter or marg
A bit of cheese

1 Peel and chop the potatoes, and then put on to boil.

2 While they're simmering away (see how easily this chef-talk comes to me. I could be the next Gary Rhodes) peel and chop the onion and simmer in a little oil.

3 When the onion has softened, bung in the tomatoes and the carrots (do not drain the carrots of their brine. This adds much-needed flavour.)

4 Stick the Beanfeast and water in and stir.

5 Turn down the heat. Wait fifteen minutes and have a fag.

6 When the spuds are done, drain and mash with the milk and a knob of butter or marg.

7 Spoon the mince into a pan, stick the mash on top and shape lovingly using a fork.

8 Grate some cheese on, and finally bung in the oven at a medium heat for half an hour. Even hardened meat-eaters will love this dish.

David's Winter Warmer Soup
(aka Nutty Soup)

While I urge you not to scrimp on the bread (this meal will be ruined by that floppy, lifeless cardboard known as the cursed 'thin white sliced loaf') the rest of this meal can, pretty much be made up of stuff that's normally lurking in the back of the cupboard. What's more it's a doddle to make, is utterly delicious and will impress anyone you cook it for (despite what appears to be a rather lacklustre list of ingredients).

YOU WILL NEED:
Sunflower oil
One tin of chopped tomatoes.
A third of a jar of crunchy
peanut butter
One small onion
One small knob of Marmite
Salt
A good loaf of chunky bread
from a proper baker

1 Chop and fry the onion (amidst a torrent of blubbering).

2 Throw the cooked onion into a pan and add the chopped tomatoes.

3 As the mixture begins to get hot, begin to stir in big spoonfuls of peanut butter until the mixture turns the colour of diarrhea (or perhaps should I say the golden light of dawn). Add a teaspoon of Marmite and salt to taste.

4 Serve with heavily buttered thick slices of bread. Mmmmm…

That should read – 'Eat junk, become junk'

DINNER PARTIES

In your second year, when you're living off campus in a shared flat, you may well have the compunction, for the first time in your life, to 'have a few people round for dinner'. This may be motivated partly by your desire to display your new standing as a sophisticated man/woman about town, and partly just an excuse to try and make that Mediterranean vegetarian lasagne recipe in the latest Nigella Lawson book that you got for Christmas and which you haven't opened since.

One of the most important ingredients of a student dinner party is lots of cheap red wine. Get in at least six bottles yourself, and encourage your guests to bring one each. The key point about these occasions is nobody gives a damn about the food. Really. By the time it arrives (invariably two hours late) the assembled party will be so pissed that they would happily eat chilled monkey brains. Don't knock yourself out preparing an exquisite banquet as the barbarians you've invited will not appreciate it in the slightest. Aim for something old-fashioned, filling and hearty (cottage pie, pasta, risotto, paella, toad-in-the-hole). Failing that make a pizza.

Despite all the mythology surrounding whom one should invite, it's difficult to really cock up as long as you obey a few simple rules:

A) Tell your guests that it's *invitation* only (thus avoiding the inevitable gate-crashers and scavengers).

B) Don't invite any two guests whom you know to hold diametrically opposed views (i.e. a fox-hunter and an animal-rights activist, a rugby-player and anyone). They'll just spend the whole evening shouting at one another and breaking your plates.

C) Don't invite anyone who's recently split-up with someone as he/she'll just cry over the crème brulée and go on and on all night about what a bastard their 'ex' really was. This may sound a bit heartless but it will spoil the evening.

NB. The most successful dinner parties involve sitting around a table. Not only does this add a veneer of civilisation to the enterprise, but also prevents your guests having to sit about the floor cross-legged complaining of cramps and pins and needles after the first quarter of an hour.

One last tip – have an ace up your sleeve to whip out when the last chocolate has gone, and everybody's getting a bit restless. A video, a game, or a couple of joints will generally do the trick.

Remember, dinner parties will never again be this easy or this much fun. In later life they will be filled with banal conversations about mortgages, patios, divorce, stomach ulcers, the pros and cons of having babies, and how TV isn't as good as it used to be. So have fun, talk crap and make the most of it. "Bon Appetit!"

FOOD HORROR STORIES

During your time at university you will undoubtedly consume a meal that belongs in the food chamber of horrors. We have canvassed many students around the UK as to their culinary nightmares, and the best spine-chilling (and stomach churning) results are detailed below.

I SEE DEAD PEOPLE

"As a vegetarian, I was pleasantly surprised when my meat-eating flat-mate offered to cook a vegetable curry that night for dinner. An hour later it arrived and was rather good – potatoes, carrots, mushrooms, courgettes, cauliflower, and onion. Very nice.

'Thanks,' I said, 'that was great.'

At this point my flat-mate left the house to go to the pictures with his girlfriend. Half an hour later I began to get stomach cramps. I started shaking and broke into a cold sweat. I then vomited uncontrollably and shat out a stream of hot liquid like a mud spring. Crawling on my hands and knees into bed, I spent the next eight hours hallucinating that zombies were dancing around my room and crawling between the sheets with me.

I have taken acid, and magic mushrooms, but have never suffered a trip of this calibre before. Christ alone knows what he'd done with this curry. It's quite difficult, or so I believed, to get food poisoning from vegetables.

Until the day I die I will be haunted by this vision of animated, decaying corpses, courtesy of my flat-mate. Naturally, he was hardly affected, complaining merely of a slight pain in the belly. I still pray to god every night that the bastard gets Mad Cow Disease."

Third Year Engineering Student Hull University

THE WAY TO A WOMAN'S HEART IS NOT THROUGH HER STOMACH

"The first time my boyfriend cooked me a meal, he was obviously trying to impress me. 'Come round,' he said, 'I'll make dinner.'

I was actually rather touched by this, because we hadn't been going out for very long, and it seemed quite a gallant gesture. While in no way labouring under the delusion that he was Jamie Oliver, I thought he might at least provide something edible – even beans on toast.

What I got was this: a bed of noodles ('Supernoodles', but without the flavour sachet) with a fried egg on top and a generous portion of mango chutney on the side. This, he assured me, was his favourite meal. It wasn't mine. We're still going out. But, needless to say, I've never allowed him to cook for me again."

Third Year Medical Student Nottingham Trent University

MARMITE FINGERS

"The worst food crime I was ever subjected to was in my first year in halls. I went to visit a friend and she suggested we head to the communal kitchen to get a snack. On arriving, she spotted a piece of bread in the bin. To my astonishment, she fished it out. Without any suggestion that this was in any way unusual, she proceeded to poke her finger into some butter and use it to spread the butter on the bread. Then she opened another jar and with her buttery finger held aloft above it, turned to me and graciously offered: 'Marmite?'"

Joanna, Exeter University Graduate

LORD OF THE FLIES

"Everyone left our house one summer to travel. We disconnected everything, including the fridge. However, in true student houseshare style, no-one bothered to clean out all the left-over food from it. Consequently it had eight weeks to rot. Upon our return my boyfriend and myself wandered into the kitchen to find seven or eight flies buzzing around the fridge. My boyfriend opened the door and to our horror hundreds, perhaps thousands of large fat bluebottles flew out of the fridge, making a big, angry buzzing noise. I did the sensible thing; I ran out of the room, pushed my boyfriend back in, slammed the door shut on him and instructed him in a calm, screaming sort of way to "Get rid of them! GET RID OF THEM!!!" Fly spray was bought, and a killing field set up by the back door. We killed so many the floor was black and squelchy, and we were finding dead flies caught in blinds and the like for months. The fridge had to be taken into the back garden and sprayed from a distance. It was completely disgusting."

Lynn, Brighton University Graduate

COOK BOOKS / WEBSITES
Yumyum.com
This is a fantastic site specifically designed with students in mind. If you don't know the first thing about cooking and don't have much time, money or inclination towards becoming a gourmet chef, then this should be your first port of call. And of course it's free.

Most of the recipes can be prepared in an apartment, dorm, or house as long as there is some heat source (gas, electricity, Bunsen burner). In fact, one person mentioned on the site survived his third year with just a barbeque as his main cooking apparatus. We don't recommend this.

More Grub on Less Grant
by Cas Clarke
More Grub on Less Grant is an updated version of the student classic Grub on a Grant. Like its predecessor it's a small, fun, easy- to-use recipe book centered firmly on the culinary needs of students. This means cheap, quick, easy but tasty food. Quick and easy student food books are a dime-a-dozen (just have a trawl through Amazon.co.uk), but this one does have the advantage of being brutally road tested and improved "in the field" by students over many years, and has received critical acclaim from users. Its simple and organised layout allows you to plan and cook with minimum effort and time wasted. Comes highly recommended.

Student Vegetarian Cook Book
by Silvana Franco
Over 100 vegetarian recipes that don't include cheese on toast, Beanfeasts and pasta with pesto. And all aimed at those on a low income. A good port of call for the fledgling veggie.

Appetite
by Nigel Slater

Quite apart from the fact that Slater has an obvious, almost pornographic love of food, the main feature of this book is good, filling, comforting food that shows some real flair and élan, yet because he does stylish takes on things like bangers and mash, it's not really too difficult or expensive.

Any of the Naked Chef Books
by Jamie Oliver

OK, so he rides around thinking he's a cross between Phil Daniels and Guy Richie, and should probably be gunned down for his relentless Sainsbury's campaign, but he can cook. And he's pretty good at showing you how, too. None of your Robert Carrier/Delia Smith nonsense of having to make one thing three days before you cook and the final ingredient being a Polar Bear's kidney that costs £100 an ounce and is available only from Harvey Nic's. It is, by and large, fairly healthy, adaptable stuff, teaching you a lot of the principles of cooking that can be applied generally. And we know that some of you ladies only buy it for the close up pictures of his cheeky smile.

Other recommendations...

How to Boil An Egg
Author: Jan Arkess
Publisher: Right Way
ISBN 0-7160-2073-4

The Students' Vegetarian Cookbook
Jenny Baker
ISBN 0-571-19038-3

Student Grub
Alastair Williams
Summersdale
ISBN 1-840241853

Quick and Easy Students' Cookbook
Molly Perham
Foulsham
ISBN 0-572-01805-3

BECOMING A VEGETARIAN

A lot of students turn veggie at some point during their time at university. There are a number of reasons for this – making an ethical stand, exposure to pro-animal pressure groups, a desire to impress a member of the opposite sex, or simply to annoy their parents. For some, this meat-free stance will last all of three weeks, until they get trolleyed and gobble down three kebabs and a Bacon Double Cheeseburger on the way back from the pub. For others it is a decision that will stay with them for the rest of their lives.

FLATULENCE & PARANOIA

Vegetarians are more notorious for blowing off than any other species (with the possible exception of cows and Johnny Fart-Pants in Viz). The black museum of veggie foods that induce killer trouser-trumpets includes such notorious offenders as red kidney beans, Sosmix, chick peas, Beanfeast, soya chunks, baked beans and good old Brussel sprouts. In theory, this kind of friend-losing flatulence is said not to last very long, and that the gut will grow accustomed to the change in diet. In practice this is, however, utter cobblers.

Many veggies are also prone to an intense food-based psychopathy, whereby they suspect others – either accidentally or by design – of trying to taint their blameless meals with meaty substances. Expect long, pointless arguments with your meat-eating flatmates along the lines of '*You've used the same spatula for my egg as you used for those sausages, haven't you?*' and '*What's been fried in that oil? Is it chicken? IS IT?*'
    This can grow into a full-blown persecution complex, whereby you find yourself having the following discussion in a restaurant:-

> **YOU**:   *I ordered the vegetarian sausages.*
>
> **WAITER**:   Yes sir, There they are.
>
> **YOU**:   *They look suspiciously meaty to me.*
>
> **WAITER**:   I assure you, sir, they are 100% vegetarian.
>
> **YOU**:   *(CUTTING SAUSAGE OPEN) What's that?*
>   *That looks like a vein to me.*
>
> **WAITER**:   *(SIGH)* It's an onion.
>
> **YOU**:   *You're trying to get me to eat meat, aren't you?*
>   *All of you! Everybody!*
>
> **WAITER**:   But sir, this is a Vegan restaurant.
>
> **YOU**:   *Yes, a perfect cover for forcing meat on poor, unsuspecting*
>   *vegetarians. It's a conspiracy! You're all out to get me! Aghhhhh!*

Mmmm..bacon butties

GOING HOME

The first pitfall for the fledgling veggie tends to be when he or she pops back to the family home for Christmas. It's a good idea to let your parents know of your conversion beforehand – after slaving over a roast turkey, your mum won't take kindly to being informed abruptly that you don't eat that sort of thing anymore and that, moreover, she is worse than Hitler. Mothers do, on the whole, show love for their offspring by producing rich, warming, meat-based foods and the rejection of their lamb casserole can seem to be a personal slight. It's sensible to explain in advance what it is that you actually eat, and perhaps even provide a few recipes, unless you want to end up with a cheese sandwich at Christmas while everyone else wolfs down a full turkey dinner with all the trimmings.

There are, however, certain members of your family (usually the more elderly ones) who will be utterly in the dark as to what vegetarianism entails. A sample conversation follows:-

GRANDFATHER: Do you want a bit of this nice liver?

YOU: *No. I'm a vegetarian now.*

GRANDFATHER: Oh. Well have a sausage then. They're lovely, these are – full of pork.

YOU: *Er…no, I don't eat sausages either.*

GRANDFATHER: Oh. Well what about some bacon?

YOU: *I can't have bacon.*

GRANDFATHER: I'll cut the fat off.

YOU: *No, even without the fat, I can't have it.*

GRANDFATHER: How about some gravy?

YOU: *No. I can't have that.*

GRANDFATHER: It doesn't have meat in it.

YOU: *But it's made from meat.*

GRANDFATHER: Oh. (PAUSE) But you must eat chicken surely, that's not meat. etc.

FALLING OFF THE WAGON

One word – bacon. It's odd that the meat that lures most vegetarians back to full-fledged flesh-eating isn't rump steak or roll of topside – something you can really get your teeth into – but the humble slice of Danish. This is because of the smell – very few things smell as alluring as bacon sizzling on a griddle. It's a scent that instantly whisks one back to childhood, conjuring up memories of bacon butties eaten on cold September mornings before playing football in the park. In short, it reminds you of a time when life was simple, and you didn't have to worry about anything – like not eating meat, for example.

Like most vices, heartbreak or drunkenness render one more susceptible to its power. Stumbling home after being dumped by your partner, you'll almost certainly be unable to pass KFC without ordering everything on the menu. Twice. You'll hate yourself in the morning, and resolve never to do it again, or at least not until the next time you get chucked.

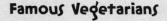

Famous Vegetarians

George Bernard Shaw
Lisa Simpson
Richard Wagner
Morrissey
Paul and Linda McCartney
Adolf Hitler

A BALANCED DIET FOR THE VEGETARIAN

By abstaining from eating meat, you need to ensure that you get your fair share of protein, iron, vitamin and calcium. Below we have listed various sources of these that mean you can vary your diet, keep healthy and not die of cheese poisoning…

Alternative sources of protein
Dairy products, seeds, nuts, Quorn, Textured Vegetable Protein (usually dried, but cheaper than Quorn), tofu (soya bean curd), Red/ green lentils, peas, chick peas, kidney beans, black eye beans, Sean Bean, Mr Bean etc etc

Good sources of iron
Breakfast cereal, dark green leafy vegetables, pulses & beans, dried fruit and eggs (Unfortunately Guinness is no longer a good source of iron since they stopped brewing it in iron casks. Now you'd have to drink something like 31 pints in a day to meet your iron requirements).

Vitamin B12
Eggs and milk, fortified soya milk, fortified breakfast cereal, vegemite.

Calcium
Milk and milk products. The best non-animal sources include tofu and fortified soya milk. Other sources include dark green leafy vegetables, bread, dried fruit and almonds.

For more information about being a vegetarian, the organisation Viva have some terrific information on the advantages of a meat-free diet, facts about the harm of intensive farming, excellent cooking tips and much more. Your first port of call should be their website: *www.Viva.org.uk*

Don't Suffer In Silence
With eating disorders and IBS worryingly on the increase among students, it is vitally important that you seek help immediately if you, or someone you know, has a problem. The first port of call should be the **University Health/Medical Centre**. After an initial chat they will be able to determine a course of action, be it medical, 'lifestyle related' or require a referral to counselling, welfare or therapeutic services. Don't feel embarrassed or afraid; these people would be out of job if it weren't for you, and they tend to be very supportive and understanding.

ALCOHOL

Alcohol by now should be an old, familiar friend. And unless you have been cursed with a face that could pass for Ron Weasley or Hermione Granger, your local pubs and clubs back home will no doubt have been your preferred address for the past couple of years, allowing you the opportunity to experiment, learn your alcohol limit and discover what a truly disgusting drink Pernod and Black really is.

However, one new experience that university does offer (for better or for worse) is the opportunity for excessive drinking. With so many parties, club-nights and endless evenings out (particularly during your first year), unless you go on to become an actor/pop star/ Paul Gasgoigne after university, such heavy indulgences in the devil's brew may never be repeated again.

It is with this in mind that we have dedicated this chapter not only to the pleasures of drinking but also to money-saving tips, hangover cures, drinks to avoid and how to make a new liver out of only flour and water.

DRINKING GAMES
#1 COIN GAMES

9 HEADS

Each person around the table must flip a coin once in turn. The person who gets the third head has to order the most disgusting drinks combination he/she can think of (whiskey and Advocaat, Baileys and lime??). The one who gets the sixth has to purchase it and the one who gets the ninth has to drink the bloody thing.

DRUNKENNESS RATING: 6/10

BURN THE NAPKIN

A tissue is secured over a full pint glass, and a coin is placed on top. The players have to take turns burning holes in the tissue with a lighted cigarette. The one who causes the coin to fall through has to sink the brew. This works equally well with the top layer of a beer mat, if carefully peeled off.

DRUNKENNESS RATING: 4/10

FLIP, SIP OR STRIP

Each player tosses a coin in the air and has to call heads or tails; if he is correct he passes the coin to his right, if wrong, to his left while either removing an article of clothing or drinking a shot. The catch is that you can't do the same thing (i.e. sip or strip) more than twice in a row.

DRUNKENNESS RATING 8/10 (or total nudity)

TRUTH, DARE, OR DRINK

Like 'Flip, Sip, or Strip', this game involves flipping and calling a coin – if you're wrong you must choose between Truth (revealing an embarrassing fact thought up by the other players), Dare (doing something stupid in public) or Drink (downing a double of your favourite beverage). Once again, you can't do the same thing more than twice in a row.

DRUNKENNESS RATING: 8/10 plus the chance to learn a few scandalous facts / lies about your friends.

#2 WORD GAMES

A.B.C.

Player one says, for example, 'A is for Aphex Twin, player two says 'A is for Aphex Twin, B is for Britney Spears, and so on through the alphabet until someone, inevitably, forgets some part of the ever-growing list (the subject matter is of your choosing). This person then has to drink a shot and the game goes back again to A.
DRUNKENNESS RATING: 5/10

CHEDDAR GORGE

Each player mentions one word in turn; the words should keep forming a proper sentence. The player who either renders the sentence gibberish or completes it must drink three fingers of spirits.
DRUNKENNESS RATING: 9/10

CONNECTIONS

An old classic. Player one says, for example, 'Dog', player two says something not associated with dogs, e.g. 'bricks', player three then mentions a word not associated with bricks, e.g. 'Priest', and so on in rapid succession. If someone hesitates then he/she has to drink, or if any player can prove a connection between the last two words, then the last player has to drink e.g. you might challenge and say 'In the film The Exorcist, the priest's surname was Bricks' (it wasn't, but you get the idea).
DRUNKENNESS RATING: 8/10

The Grand old Duke Of York

This game is a real no-brainer, but very funny.
Basically everyone has to sing, in unison:

Oh the grand old duke of York,
He had ten thousand men,
He marched them up to the top of the hill,
And he marched them down again.
And when they were up they were up,
And when they were down they were down,
And when they were only halfway up,
They were neither up nor down.

Everyone then repeats the song, omitting the word 'up', then again omitting the word 'down', and then finally omitting both. Anybody who cocks up has to take a drink and the process starts all over again.
DRUNKENNESS RATING: 10/10

#3 MOVIE / TV GAMES

These games are played in the comfort of your own home. All you need is a TV, a video, some alcohol and a film of your choice. There are two species of movie/TV drinking game…

MATCH THE ALCOHOL CONSUMPTION

This involves matching characters in a movie or TV show drink for drink. It's important to choose your film/show wisely, otherwise everyone could be on the floor within fifteen minutes if you pick Barfly, or stone cold sober if it's Sound of Music. Recommended films/TV to choose are: Withnail and I, The Sweeney, Inspector Morse, Harvey, Arthur, The Big Lebowski, The Big Sleep.

SPOT THE CATCHPHRASE

Probably the most popular drinking game of the moment, this involves having a drink each time a character utters his or her peculiar catchphrase or cliché, e.g. Captain Kirk saying 'Beam me up Scotty', Homer Simpson saying 'Doh!' or Joe Pesci saying 'Fuck.'

A variant of this game includes the spotting of mannerisms, e.g. Giles from 'Buffy' removing his spectacles thoughtfully, or every time Joey gives an Italianate shrug in 'Friends'.

If you want to be fancy you can allocate a different drink for each catchphrase or mannerism, i.e. a gin and tonic for 'That's illogical captain', a whiskey sour for 'He's dead, Jim', and a bloody Mary for 'She cannae take it! She's gonnae blow.' This will ensure you get incredibly drunk in a very short space of time. Here are a few good ones to start you off…

ANY JAMES BOND FILM

A dry martini for any of the following clichés – 'The name's Bond…', 'Shaken, not stirred', 'For God's sake 007', and 'So Mr. Bond, we meet at last.' An even drier Martini for Bond making a bad pun after offing a bad guy, or seducing a ridiculously-monikered female. A specially dry double one for Q getting testy and blowing something up with a briefcase.

FRASIER

A drink whenever you hear 'I'm listening', 'Wishing you good mental health', 'I'll have a half-fat latte' or whenever Eddie performs a trick/Martin puts Frasier down/Niles suffers a panic attack/ reference is made to Roz's sexual promiscuity/Daphne mentions her family in England.

NB All these games can be played with joints, instead of alcohol, but don't expect the games to last longer than 20 minutes. Beyond this time your party of friends will naturally divide into two groups: one will transform into a silent zombified mass, reeling in a void of paranoia, while the other will have forgotten the game and be laughing their tits off for hours over something someone said five minutes ago, even though no-one can remember what it was that was actually said.

STRANGE BREW
(OR: Drinks to Approach With Extreme Caution)

TEQUILA

Originally made by South American natives, as a form of revenge on the invading Spanish, Tequila is available in white spirit or the superior and more deadly Mezcal (named after the Cactus it is brewed from). This version contains the infamous Mescal worm, which lives in the Mescal Cactus, and so traditionally ended up in Tequila, presumably because everyone at the distillery was too blitzed to think of fitting a sieve to the end of a pipe. It is said that eating the worm will induce a mild hallucinatory state. No one has been able to prove or disprove this, as eating the worm tends to happen when the whole of the bottle has been drunk and ingesting a pickled grub seems like a splendid idea. You might have a trip, but who knows? You're too busy trying to moon passing Police Cars to notice.

In fact, no drink can reduce the intelligence and moral rectitude of the average human quicker and more viciously than a few rounds of Tequila slammers. Just ask yourself – how good for you can a drink be, that requires a lick of salt followed by a wedge of lemon just to stop you gagging?

Rest assured, you will be upchucking at some point, or (as happened to a friend), being rushed to hospital to have shards of broken glass removed from your wrists after an over-zealous slam…

OUZO

Although not readily available in this country, Ouzo seems to crop up every now and again at parties, owing to the fact that some bright spark has lugged four crates of the stuff back from a package holiday in Rhodes, where it 'only cost 30p a bottle'. There are however, several problems commonly associated with this sweet, sickly aniseed based spirit. Nauseating taste aside, it is lousy as a cocktail mixer and has the ability to quickly reduce you to a frenzied Jekyl and Hyde character, curled up in the corner of the room with the bottle under your arm, snarling at any passers-by who stop to stare in amazement at your hairy hands and tail.

OUZO

But the stinger really comes the morning after. An Ouzo hangover is something special; for after awakening bleary-eyed at 7am to down three pints of water in a desperate attempt to drown the rats that are trying to gnaw their way out of your head, you find yourself getting unexpectedly and disconcertingly drunk all over again, as your body re-activates this malign spirit. Utter hell.

ABSINTHE

A Central European drink of incredible strength (good Absinthe should be about 70% vol), this Czech moonshine is a noxious green brew that resembles fairy liquid, tastes like cough medicine and is traditionally made with a blend of herbs, including wormwood; (a poisonous plant capable of sending you mad or, worse still, making you want to study Geography).

The Parisians, at the turn of the 20th Century certainly found it such a harmful and toxic brew that as a consequence it was banned from France and other sensible parts of Europe, and replaced with the more innocuous Pastis.

Having made a recent comeback (thanks to the pretensions of a few louche popstars), Absinthe is now all over the place again though not quite the original bad boy it once was, as some of the strength and original active ingredients have been reduced or removed (the real thing is only available in little shacks up the hills in the Czech Republic).

To drink Absinthe correctly, get a spoon of brown sugar, dip it in the spirit, light it, allow the sugar to melt, put the flaming sugar into the glass of spirit and, while stirring, pour in water to douse the flame. If you're not on to this sharpish it's bye-bye flat, and of course, the more absinthe you have, the more slapdash and carefree you're bound to become about the process. After only a few glasses of the stuff, you will be rendered numb, deeply stupid and, if you drink enough of the stuff, temporarily amnesic. Which brings to mind that old W.C. Fields joke, where, in one of his films, he rushes into his local bar early one morning with no recollection of the night before and a look of concern on his face, and says to the barman:

'Hey Charlie, did I spend $20 in here last night?'

'Yes,' the barman replies.

'Oh, thank god for that,' replies Fields, *'I thought I'd lost it.'*

SCRUMPY

It's hard to get real, full on Scrumpy outside of Devon, Cornwall and Gloucestershire, as they still keep the best stuff for themselves. It's just the same with their cheese, their Pasties and their lax rules on inbreeding. A proper dry farmhouse Scrumpy, bought out of big barrels from a farm, will have you playing the banjo and saying *"boy, you sure do have a pretty mouth"* within three pints and after four, have you banging your flagon on the table shouting – *"Burn the Witch! Burn the Witch!"*. Sadly though, the real stuff is on the decline, even in the West Country. With farming in such a sorry state that it is, the old boys who would come first thing every morning and load up with a gallon of Scrumpy on the back of the tractor are almost extinct. Though perhaps this explains why they all died out in the first place.

OVERPROOF RUM

Exactly the same as ordinary strength white rum, only twice as potent and utterly disgusting. Never be deluded into thinking that an alluringly high alcohol volume makes a drink cool and dangerous, in this case you'd be far better off trying to drink lighter fuel. Just opening the bottle induces retching, skin rashes and temporary blindness, while nothing can disguise its nauseating taste and smell – however skilful your cocktail prowess. Rum is a fine and honourable drink, even Bacardi has its place, but this is bad Jamaican voodoo. You've seen "Live and Let Die"? You've seen the Zombies? Now you know.

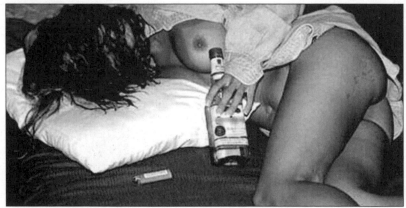

If you're often in a state like this, it's probably time to switch to Horlicks

Girls just wanna have rum…

LOST WEEKENDS

Lost weekends are so dubbed because they are periods in which, due to overindulgence, one loses everything – money, sense, dignity, memory, coordination, and bowel control. They are not necessarily limited to a weekend, and can last as long as a month, depending on how hedonistic and out of balance your life has become.

University may be your first chance to experience the dubious pleasures of the lost weekend, as either living with your parents or having to yield to the rigours of the workplace severely curtail such expeditions.

There are three main causes of the lost weekend: boredom, heartbreak, or a disreputable old mate coming to visit...

BOREDOM

After slaving away on your essays all term, you begin to feel as though you're stuck in a rut. Dissatisfied with your lot, you decide to go along to that vodka n' champagne party in room 375. The next thing you know, you wake up four days later in a field in Hampshire, wearing nothing but waders and a sombrero and with the word 'TWAT' painted on your forehead. You get back to university to find that your friends think you are dead, and that your parents have notified the police, who are dragging all the nearby rivers for your body.

HEARTBREAK

The heartbreak lost weekend differs from the boredom one in that it is planned. Having been blown out by that history student you've fancied since the first term, you decide that you're going to spend the next few days getting absolutely trollied. Like a spy about to drop into enemy territory you assemble your kit meticulously – booze, fags and handkerchiefs, and hurl yourself into a vortex of debauchery that would have Keith Moon reaching for the Alka Seltzer.

The next thing you know, you wake up four weeks later in a field in Dorset, wearing nothing but a surgeon's mask, a pair of comedy breasts/ strap on dildo, and the message 'SATAN WAS HERE' painted on your stomach in somebody else's blood. You get back to university to find that somebody else has moved into your room and that your parents have left the country. But at least you've gotten over your lost love.

AN OLD MATE COMING DOWN TO VISIT

Having your wayward (and possibly psychotic) old drinking partner from sixth form pay you a flying visit will end in oblivion for both of you. Be prepared to wake up with him or her four years later in a field in South Korea, one of you dressed as Bungle from Rainbow, the other as Hitler, with the words 'ANTICHRIST and 'LONG LIVE THE WELSH' tattooed onto your foreheads. You return to university to find that it has closed down.

Try to limit your lost weekends to a maximum of one a term.

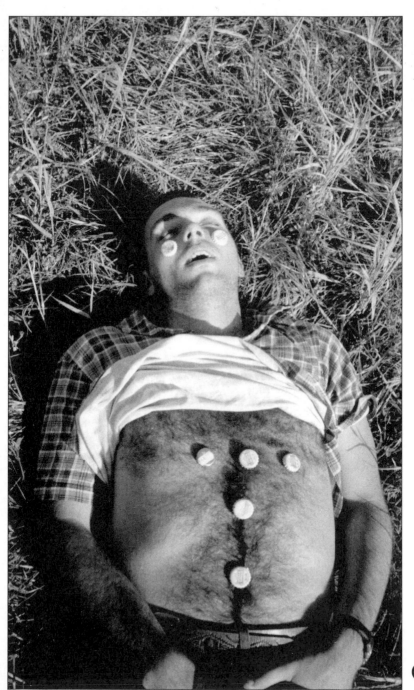

GETTING DRUNK ON THE CHEAP

1. CARRYING A HIPFLASK

One of the best pieces of advice we can offer for saving money on your drinks bill at uni is to take one of these whenever you go out. Trust us, nothing will sap your meagre finances better than 500 Red Bull and vodkas, so unless you are a strict pint-lover or fashion victim to bottled designer drinks, this simple trick will save you hundreds and hundreds of pounds every year.

When in a pub/ nightclub, simply order your mixer in a bottle/can (and a glass to go with it), then, when you're sat down, discreetly pour yourself a generous triple under the table from the hipflask, and have a toast to an honourable life of crime. And considering the vulgar profits of most clubs and pubs, and the grossly inflated prices they charge for alcohol, you shouldn't have too much guilt on your conscience about cheating them out of a few quid.

2. SEEK OUT THE HOUSE DOUBLES

3. CHECK THE ABV ON LAGERS AND BEERS

Go for anything over 4 percent. The stronger beer may even be the cheapest!

4. AVOID BOTTLED PRE-MIXERS AND BOTTLED BEERS

Try and get away from paying over the odds purely because of branding. A typical nightclub will charge roughly £3 for a bottle of Becks, meaning you're paying nearly six quid for a pint of lager, never mind the hideous prices of pre-mixed drinks.

Hiding Boozy Breath

Should you sink a couple of pints before your tutorial with Dr Nicholaus (a Christian, tee-total, pudding of a man whom you desperately need a good grade from) and go in with a breath like a distillery, you're not going to fare well. Mint sweets help to some degree, though you could just end up smelling like you've been at the crème de menthe. Instead, try the Philip Marlowe method (from the detective novels of Raymond Chandler) and carry a handful of cardamom seeds in your pocket at all times. Chew on these after you've been at the booze and when you walk into that tutorial you'll feel like an extra from a mouthwash ad.

HANGOVERS

Medically speaking, the hangover is actually a form of food poisoning. (This is good to remember, since 'I had food-poisoning' is a better excuse for missing a lecture than 'I drank fifteen Tequila slammers the night before and couldn't get out of bed the next morning without throwing up.')

Basically, when you drink, your liver metabolises the alcohol, producing a nasty little poison called acetaldehyde. This, along with several other toxic by-products, is what gives you an irritable stomach, makes you vomit, and gives you worse diarrhoea than a sitcom-character on a Spanish holiday.

Coupled with this is dehydration. You actually lose fluid when you drink booze, since your body needs more water than usual to help flush out the toxins. It is dehydration that gives you a monstrous headache, eyes like raisins, and a mouth as dry as an Angus Deaton one-liner.

So, if you want to avoid the sort of hangovers that will leave you looking and feeling like Gollum from Lord of the Rings, there are certain preventative measures you can take.

HOW TO AVOID A HANGOVER

A) Choose your drink carefully

A general rule-of-thumb is 'the darker the drink, the worse it will leave you feeling.' This is because the hue is, generally speaking, a reliable indicator of the number of impurities the drink contains. The only exception to this being lager, which possesses a lethal mixture of chemicals, pesticides and washing up liquid. (Should this be your preferred tipple, the purer European beers such as Becks or Grolsch will be much kinder on your liver). Champers is the favoured tipple of the upper-classes, not simply because of its taste but also because one can drink seemingly limitless quantities without suffering any after-affects (besides driving your Bentley into a lamppost).

The good guys:

Vodka, Tequila, Gin, Martini, White Rum, White Wine, Champagne, Schnapps.

The villains of the piece:

Red Wine, Whiskey, Brandy, Dark Rum, Port, Sherry, Cheap lager*

*Guinness and bitter don't quite fit the bill, as they are brewed more naturally than lagers. Excessive boozing from these will not give you such a stinking hangover as say, whiskey, but do have the power to torment your bowels for days.

B) Line Your Stomach

This is an age-old technique involving eating a hearty meal, or imbibing a good quantity of some soothing liquid prior to going out on the raz, thus protecting the stomach from the alcohol's ravages. Popular stomach-liners include; a pint of milk, a spoon of olive oil (sounds revolting, but really does the trick), anything with a lot of fats and carbohydrates, (i.e. steak and kidney pie and chips).

But for God's sake don't do this the wrong way round; it's no good drinking thirteen pints of lager, and then belatedly lining your stomach at the nearest curry house. A belly already agitated by alcohol does not take kindly to a prawn Vindaloo, four poppadums with lime pickle, and a Sag Aloo, as the decorated pavements around curry houses every weekend go to prove.

C) Don't go straight to sleep

There is, on returning home after a drunken night out, a tiny window of time in which certain measures can be taken to avoid a hangover if you can only collect your wits for a minute or two. Before succumbing to a death-like slumber, it is advisable to get one or more of the following down you:

1) Water. (Drink as much of this as you possibly can – preferably matching your alcohol intake pint for pint. You may feel like a human water bed when you eventually lay down, and have to get up every five minutes to pee, but you'll thank yourself in the morning).

2) Sports drinks. (Non-carbonated are better) The combination of liquids and sugars works a treat.

3) Pepto-Bismol

But avoid caffeine (as this will continue to dehydrate you) and anything acidic (such as orange juice, as it can further upset your stomach).

girls like trollied, boys like girls...

HANGOVER CURES

OK, so it all went awry and you woke up feeling like someone weed in your mouth while you were sleeping, played pinball with your head and injected seawater into your stomach. Now medical science holds that there is no such thing as a hangover cure, but there are certain aids that can speed this process along, or at least make the ride less bumpy.

Hair-Of-The-Dog

While not recommended by most doctors, this genuinely works for some of our friends (though I suspect because they are actually alcoholics and this merely stops their hands from shaking). Advice on what specifically to drink ranges from a nip of whatever you had the night before to a pint of Guinness with a raw egg in it (yuk!), but if in doubt, a large Bloody Mary should hit the spot.

The Full English Breakfast

This really shouldn't work, but it does. It may only be psychological, but it's the number one, solid-gold cure of choice for all hardened boozers. Go to a café (no-one's suggesting you cook this yourself) and order a gut-buster – eggs, bacon, sausages, black pudding, fried bread, plum tomatoes, baked beans, mushrooms, bubble and squeak, hash browns and chips. Plus a round of toast and bread and butter on the side and seventy-two cups of tea.

A third of the way through, you will start to feel nauseous, but don't turn back – persevere. Trust us – this cure only works if you manage to polish it all off.

Painkillers

The scientist who invents a pill that genuinely banishes the hangover will instantly be elevated to the status of a god. Be they Aspirin, Paracetamol or Ibuprofen, painkillers enjoy only limited success for the hangover-sufferer. A common problem associated with them is that, while clearing the head, they can further irritate the stomach, so it's a bit of a Catch 22.

The Cold Shower

It is, we are reliably informed, refreshing and invigorating, and also has the effect of sobering you up. An actor friend tells us that Art Malik (the baddie in 'True Lies') recommends a slightly more elaborate method, involving placing the head under a shower, and running the water as hot, and then as cold as you can stand, in short bursts, repeating this action six times. Sweet Jesus…

Exercise

Many drinkers subscribe to the theory of sweating the alcohol out of the system, either by jogging, going to the gym, swimming, or playing tennis. If you can face getting the bus down to the gym, or visiting the university sports centre for a game of squash when your head is pounding and you're minutes away from throwing up on the cat, then you are a nutcase.

Sleep

Even the mildest of hangovers is exacerbated by having to rise at 8.30am for a tutorial. A bad hangover requires you to cancel all appointments, draw the curtains, and return to bed for the rest of the day. The obvious pros of this method are, of course, that you don't need to be conscious and (therefore) have to face the pain and torment of your hangover. The cons are that if you stay in bed for more than a week you may get thrown off your course.

TO HURL OR NOT TO HURL?

Throughout the ages, philosophers have pondered the question "Is it better to throw up and get it over and done with, or keep it down and weather the storm?" While regular vomiting is actually physically rather bad for you (it harms the stomach, can damage the oesophagus, and plays havoc with the teeth), the occasional Technicolour yawn is better than keeping all those poisons in your system. Throwing up at bedtime can make you feel a hell of a lot better, since you'll be expelling alcohol that hasn't been fully digested yet, thus preventing it from working its mischief while you slumber. Be sure to drink a great deal of water afterwards though, to make up the lost fluid.

If the desire to be sick doesn't come until the morning, it will be of little use to you, as the booze by then will be in your veins, but it will probably still help you feel a bit better and make space in your stomach for that breakfast hangover cure.

Some people are horrified at the idea of being sick and would rather gnaw off their own legs than have to kneel in front of the toilet waiting for their stomach contents to say hello. To avoid the dreaded thing, try the following:

Fresh air
(Take a walk around the block. If you don't feel better – do it again)
Suck a sweet
(A polo or extra-strong mint can work wonders)
Focus on something else
(i.e. watching the telly, although this is probably not a good plan if 'Titanic' is on)
Cold water on the face
(or a shower, but remember to get undressed first)
Stop drinking
(Seems obvious advice, but nothing's obvious when you've sunk a bottle of brandy)

RECOMMENDED WEBSITES

ALL ABOUT HANGOVERS
www.all-about-hangovers.com
Information on hangover cures, symptoms and preventions, plus a cocktail guide and histories of your favourite tipples.

HANGOVERS: PREVENTION, INTERVENTION & CURES
www.estronaut.com/a/hangovers.htm
Useful advice for the female drinker.

DRINKEASE.COM
www.drinkease.com
Contains 'Wild 'n Wacky' cures from around the world. In Haiti, for example, they stick thirteen black pins in the cork of the drink that gave them the hangover.

HUNGOVER.NET
www.hungover.net/home.asp
Good cure ideas, and esoteric info on booze and hangovers.

HAIRY TONGUE.COM
www.hairytongue.com/thecure/index.php3
Some rather fantastical hangover cures (including masturbating and crying).

Don't Suffer in Silence

While social drinking and the occasional excesses are the norm at university, alcohol dependency is not. As with other social drugs, alcohol tends to be misused by a minority of students particularly those seeking to block out anxieties and/ or personal problems. If you or someone you know has a problem with alcohol, don't let it fester. Contact the university doctor/ welfare officer as soon as possible and try and get some counselling to find out the reasons for the excessive drinking in the first place. Alcohol addiction is a terrible and debilitating thing, and withdrawal for long-term addicts a long, painful and frightening experience. Don't ever let it come to that.

SMOKING

While by no means wishing to encourage smoking, there's no denying that students get through more fags than any other section of the population (with the possible exception of doctors and nurses) and therefore it would be simply perverse not to devote an enormous chapter to it.

If you want to know more about the evils of tobacco, consult your fag packet, doctor or nearest cemetery. All the information you need is there. Instead, this chapter details the customs, mores and pitfalls of this much-maligned habit.

A CULTURAL ANALYSIS OF THE STUDENTS' FAVOURITE BRANDS

Marlboro lights*

Personality: Ubiquitous, contemporary, a smooth sociable little number. One for the ladies.

Pros: Easy on the throat, undemanding, popular.

Cons: Bland, conformist and characterless; the Jamie Theakston of cigarettes. Not only that, they're also dried over Mercury, adding even more unnecessary carcinogens.

Benson and Hedges

Personality: Manly, no-nonsense, staunch and patriotic. As horse-racing is the sport of kings and wide boys, so B&H is their fag of choice. As favoured by the Queen and Noel Gallagher.

Pros: Patriotic. Smoke these and think of England.

Cons: Naff, nouveau-riche packaging. And Noel Gallagher smokes them.

Silk Cut

Personality: Feeble and dull. The Anthea Turner of Cigs.

Pros: Standard introduction for the fledgling smoker.

Cons: Utterly unsatisfying. You might as well just stand next to a smoker and inhale deeply.

Rollies

Personality: Bohemian, shabby, vagrant and chic. The Charles Bukowski/ Johnny Depp in 'Chocolat' of tabs.

Pros: Contain less carcinogens that straight ciggies, they're dead cheap and make smoking into a DIY experience. You can even flavour them with Liquorice Rizlas.

Cons: A an absolute bugger to keep lit and depressingly difficult to assemble whilst on the move, never mind in a high wind/ storm. You'll also have to get used to nicotine stains the colour of a Van Gogh sunflower on your fingers and be prepared for forever pulling stray bits of tobacco off your bottom lip (or stray bits of bottom lip off your tobacco).

Lucky Strikes

Personality: Wild, unpredictable ride. Rock'n'roll of cigarettes.

Pros: Legendary American brand, Retro chic packaging granting instant access to Marlon Brando-esque mystique.

Cons: High tar; early death. Plus there are few retail outlets that sell them. Run out on Sunday evening and it's back to the Marlboro Lights for you Sunny Jim.

*if you live north of the border or in Wales, substitute Regal for Marlboro lights throughout this book

Economy Smokes

Personality: Cheap and cheerful imitation of the fags listed above. Think Robbie Williams does Frank Sinatra.

Pros: Half the price of normal fags

Cons: Made of the floor sweepings at the local B&H factory. Rough as a badger's arse.

NB. It is a well-observed phenomenon that the cheaper the cigarette, the more regal the name eg. Mayfair, Royals, Dorchester, Sovereign, Golden Buddha. Interestingly , this applies in a similar way to vodka, in that, the cheaper the brand, the more eminent the writer it is named after. So avoid Checkov, Tolstoy and Dostoyevski, and plump instead for Ostrovsky and Solzhenitzen. Exactly, we've never heard of them either.

UK DUTY PAID
ROYALS
KING SIZE

20
SMOKING CAUSES CANCER

Foreign Muck

Whether they be Ducados, Linda or the Indian twig-like Bhinis which crackle like sparklers when you light them, some mate is bound to turn up with a box of these buggers at some time while your at uni, proudly boasting that they only cost 50p for 600.

Personality: Pungent, foul-tasting and aggressive. Taste like the exhaust pipe of a tractor.

Pros: The packet is a good conversation starter, lending one the air of being a seasoned traveller. And what's more, one pack will last forever as no sod will actually want to smoke them, not even you.

Cons: Ludicrously high tar. One puff will hospitalise you.

The Healthy Option

Native American Spirit claim to be one of the few, if not the only, brand currently on sale in the UK that makes its cigarettes with just 100% tobacco and no harmful additives. The reason that the majority of cigarettes manufacturers add extra poisonous chemicals (so we're led to believe) is to keep them lit, but Native American Spirit claim to have avoided this by packing more tobacco into their ciggies. So, not only do you avoid all those horrible extra toxins, but you also get a longer smoke for your money. If you happen to be that unhappy and paradoxical creature known as the health-conscious smoker, this is the brand for you. *(For more info on additives in tobacco: www.sfntc.co.uk)*

N A T U R A L
AMERICAN
$PIRIT
100% ADDITIVE-FREE NATURAL TOBACCOS
LIGHT FILTER CIGARETTES

TOBACCO SERIOUSLY DAMAGES HEALTH

The Ashtray Shimmy

(AKA butt-mining, cigarette reincarnation, raising the dead)

The Ashtray Shimmy is a form of occidental origami that involves harvesting the bits of tobacco left at the end of a bunch of dog-ends, and rolling them up to form a reconstituted cigarette. Needless to say, shimmying should be reserved for those desperate moments when you're on your own, the shops are closed, and you're totally skint. It's not the most sophisticated of habits, and is seldom indulged in by chic, urbane high-fliers. You almost never see James Bond, for example, grubbing around in an ashtray of stubs in a casino, in search of a quick nicotine hit.

There is, however, an almost Frankensteinian feeling in shimmying, in that you are creating a new being from the parts of extinct ones. Indeed, many seasoned shimmiers find themselves yelling 'It's alive!' as they bring the finished product to their lips.

For the eternally penniless student smoker, the biggest catastrophe is when your flatmate throws out the overflowing ashtray of butts you've been keeping for an emergency. *'But I was saving those!'* you wail, heartbroken, as if your dearest treasure had been disposed of (which indeed it has).

As regards taste, the shimmy is not a dainty smoke. Since the tar from the entire cigarette collects in the half-centimetre of tobacco nearest the filter, inhaling the accumulated detritus from half a dozen finished bifters can be a heady experience, akin to French-kissing a dead tramp. It is, however, better than nothing. But only just. N.B. – If you find yourself shimmying shimmies, it's probably time to give up.

A Cheeky Tale

"One of my closest friends at university was a mature student known to us as 'Veggie Andy'. A 26-year old hippy with a 40 a day habit, he was what you might call a professional smoker, and the only person I knew to have a permanently full ashtray in his toilet. One fateful night, at two in the morning, with no dog-ends on hand, and miles from the nearest 24-hour shop, he ran out of smokes.

I still recall the horror, as, beside himself with desperation, he lunged into the kitchen and began banging cupboard doors and drawers in search of inspiration. Ten minutes later, I detected a noxious smoky odour emanating from the kitchen. He emerged, sucking heavily on a rolled-up tube of newspaper stuffed with tealeaves..."

Keele University Graduate

THE KU KLUX KLAN/ MARLBORO CONSPIRACY

Do Marlboro donate funds to the Ku Klux Klan? Some people think so and believe the proof to be right there on the packets themselves. To judge for yourself take any Marlboro packet and you'll discover the existence of three subliminal K's located on different sides of the carton.

(BACK COVER)   **(FRONT COVER)**   **(BOTTOM)**

Not only this, but focus on the shape found between the horse's legs, dot a couple of eyes in and you have a Ku Klux Klan member carrying a weapon.

 Proof enough or just another 'Paul is Dead*' conspiracy? Well of course it's just a rather intriguing urban myth, but then we would have to say that wouldn't we, if we didn't want to be sued by an all-powerful tobacco company?

*In the late 1960s a rumour ran that Paul McCartney had died and been replaced by an impostor, but the Beatles had left clues to his death on their album covers. Evidence included the subliminal message 'Paul?' written in flowers on the cover of Sergeant Peppers, the backward message 'Paul is dead' at the end of the same album and the fact that the real Paul McCartney would never have gone on to write such tripe as 'Pipes of Peace', 'No More Lonely Nights' and 'The Frog Chorus'. There's even a book been written recently to support this conspiracy, which, while utterly unconvincing, makes a fantastic read.

STYLES OF SMOKING

The manner in which a person puffs on his/her cigarettes can speak volumes about them. Below is a brief summary of some of the more easily observable traits, offering a chance for the dedicated smoker to adopt an entirely new personality whilst at university.

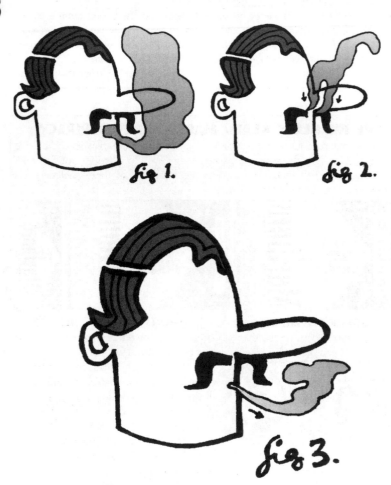

fig 1.

fig 2.

fig 3.

"THE FRENCH INHALE"

This involves exhaling the smoke from the mouth without taking it into the lungs, and then dramatically drawing it up the nostrils.

USED BY: Marlene Dietrich, poseurs and the French.

"THE SQUADDIE"

The standard working-class method. Traditionally the cigarette is shielded by the hand, so that it can be easily concealed or discarded should the boss hover into view. *USED BY:* Nick Cotton, gangsters in Sixties Britflicks, and anyone pretentious enough to want to adopt an air of proletarian left-wing chic (ie the Union President).

"THE KENNETH TYNAN"

Popularised by the famous theatre critic, the 'Tynan' involves holding the cigarette between the second and third fingers, while pontificating about the state of the English theatre.

USED BY: Luvvies and people so affected that you can't believe they're real. Can come in useful if you fancy your chances in the Drama Soc.

"THE HOLDER"

Cigarette holders are hardly ever used any more, except by people in fancy dress attending 'Cabaret'-themed parties, and would-be Oxbridge eccentrics, sporting mustard-coloured waistcoats, monocle and spats.

USED BY: Aspiring vamps, old flamboyant gay actors, Holly Go-Lightly in Breakfast at Tiffany's, Margot (The Good Life) and the Pink Panther.

"THE DOT COTTON"

In the 'Cotton', the fag dangles constantly from the corner of the mouth, as if glued there. It remains in place whatever the smoker is doing — talking, eating, kissing, making love, skydiving, etc.
USED BY: Roadies, shabby Seventies TV detectives, car mechanics, Sid the Sexist (Viz).

"THE SOPHISTICATE"

Invented in the 1920s, this truly bizarre smoking method consists of holding the cig the wrong way round, with the back of the hand towards the face.
USED BY: The camp playwright, Noel Coward, and people who labour under the delusion that they are the camp playwright Noel Coward.

CONCEALING YOUR
SMOKING HABIT FROM YOUR PARENTS

If you've developed the habit at university, and are due home for a weekend or holiday period, you will doubtless want to conceal from your parents that their sweet, angel-faced child is now on forty a day. This is nothing to be ashamed of, there are fifty-year-old men who still have to nip behind the shed for a sly fag when their parents come to visit. There are, however, certain cunning strategies you can adopt in order to hide the fact that you smoke like an Eastbourne crematorium:

THE HIGH-SPEED SMOKE

People whose parents don't know they are smokers manage to develop the amazing ability to light up, smoke, and discard an entire silk cut in approximately 1.2 seconds.

You will, with practise, develop the art of 'the quick fag out the window', 'the quick fag in the bog' (if out at a restaurant with your parents), 'the quick fag in the garden,' and, if really desperate, 'the quick fag under the duvet.'

THE CUNNING EXCUSE

'I'm just going for a walk.' is, of course, a classic ruse and you will, doubtless, find yourself uttering these words time and time again to your parents, despite the fact that:

> **A)** You've never, ever, ever gone for a walk on your own before.
> **B)** It's 1.30 in the morning.

Other classic excuses include *'I'm just popping down the shops', 'I though I'd just go and have a look at the garden',* and *'I'm just popping down the shops again.'*

BLAMING SOMEONE ELSE

Pipe-smoking granddads, and uncles who are fond of cigars are always good for explaining away the heady aroma of tobacco in the living room. Having a mate who smokes is also a must, as the eight thousand fag ends in an old saucer in the corner of your bedroom can be blamed on him/her. If you haven't got a friend who smokes, pay one to take it up.

HIDING THE SMELL

Chewing gum, mints and fisherman's friends are time-honoured favourites for the discreet smoker, but be warned, parents are not as naive as they might seem. They'll soon cotton on, if, every time they go in your bedroom, the window is wide open, the room stinks of Brut and you've got a full pack of Polos in your mouth.

NOT TELLING ANYONE

Beware younger siblings. If your brother or sister finds out about your habit, he or she will either blackmail you for the rest of your life, or blurt it out at the nearest opportunity. One of this book's writers was grassed-up by his six-year-old niece, who piped sweetly to his mum *'Uncle Brian smokes. I saw him.'* He has still not forgiven her.

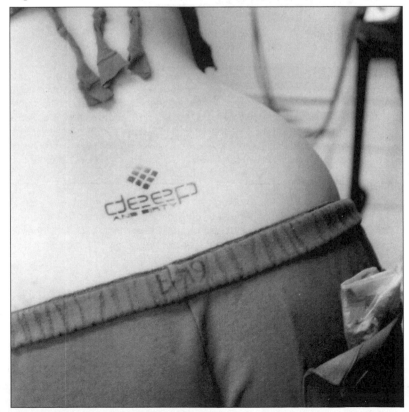

GIVING UP

So, you've flirted with decadence, deceived your parents, stained your fingers, damaged your lungs and chucked away tons of money to insidious multinationals (a lifetime smoker spends an average of £40, 000 on cigarettes) and now you've had enough and want to kick this filthy habit. That's easier said than done, nicotine is one of the most addictive substances known to man. But don't despair; there are, nowadays, a multitude of crutches available to soften the blows of cold turkey.

GUM

Available from pharmacists, nicotine gum is supposed to help wean you off cigarettes by providing the nicotine your body craves in a less harmful form, while also giving you something to do with your mouth. The only drawback is that it tastes exactly like gum that's been chewed and spat out by a smoker. Maybe people who are addicted to gum have to smoke gum-flavoured cigarettes.

PATCHES

Also available from pharmacists, these are supposed to be the discreet way of quitting smoking while gradually decreasing your nicotine intake. Merely affix an adhesive patch to your arm under your shirt and get high as a kite, with no-one any the wiser. Some lunatics go out wearing a patch, get drunk, and smoke a pack of Marlboro in half-an-hour, thereby experiencing a nicotine hit akin to giving mouth-to-mouth resuscitation to Liam and Noel. Well-favoured amongst seasoned quitters.

SELF-HELP BOOKS

In the vast and annoying world of self-help books, the most popular one we've come across seems to be Alan Carr's 'Easy Way to Stop Smoking'.

To be fair, if you can swallow the cheap pop-psychological tricks then they're probably quite useful (Alan Carr's book, for example, has a section entitled 'Reasons For Smoking' which is simply a blank page. Oh very clever). If, however, you possess one iota more self-knowledge and insight than the average Cornish Pasty, you will throw the book aside with a cry of 'What a load of crap!' and later tear out the pages to use as roaches for the next joint.

NICORETTE INHALERS

Of all the gimmicks available, these are probably the closest thing to providing a re-assuring nicotine hit when withdrawal is kicking in, combined with the luxury of having something to stick in your mouth. Take it down the pub and when you feel a moment of weakness coming on, whip it out and give a good suck (insert Carry-On style joke here). No doubt your friends will relentlessly take the piss out of you for 'smoking' what looks like a white plastic tampon, but this embarrassment will in turn help wean you off the inhaler.

HERBAL CIGARETTES

Ever snapped a cigarette by accident and still attempted to smoke it by holding it together or trying to tape it with a Rizla? Remember the frustration, as you couldn't get any hit off it? Combine that experience with, say, the smell of a burning tyre factory, and you have the perfect reason why herbal ciggies are an utter waste of time.

ACUPUNCTURE

This can be extremely helpful in giving up, if you don't mind having needles inserted into your ear. Actually, revolting as it sounds, this practise is painless and significantly reduces cravings as well as helping detoxify the body after quitting. Treatments tend to be once a day for 30-40 minutes for the first few days after giving up. Thing is, you'll need a very progressive campus doctor to have this facility on hand, as it can be quite costly getting it done privately. Of course you could try getting your mates to stick a few pins randomly into your ears but all that's likely to achieve is septicaemia.

Cold Turkey Reconsidered

As with most things in life, the hardest path is usually the most direct route to success. If you can muster the almost superhuman will to lay off the fags without recourse to any of the gimmicks listed above, then you probably stand a better chance of staying off them for good. Try and avoid places/ habits that you associate with smoking (e.g. drinking coffee/ the pub/ your bed) for a short while at least, and keep reminding yourself that rather than missing out on a pleasurable habit, you are liberating yourself from an addiction.

The Futility Of Giving Up The Ciggies (But Not The Dope)

"In my second year at university, fed up with waking up with a hacking cough and bright yellow fingers, I made the brave decision to finally quit. Scared at the thought of never tasting creamy warm smoke in my lungs ever again, I convinced myself that I'd still be able to smoke the occasional joint without being weaned back onto the nicotine...

At the end of day one, pleased with my newfound abstinence, I allowed myself one modest joint before bedtime and went to bed happy. On day two, I had several joints, including one at lunchtime but still seemed to be holding out pretty well.

By day five I was wandering around college in a state of permanently stoned bliss, brought about by my new, 20-a-day spliff habit. On day six I 'disappeared', and by day seven was discovered, by my friend Claire, standing outside the Natwest bank in Coventry High Street, at 9am, clutching a bag of table-tennis balls, barely able to stand or speak and with absolutely no notion of why I was there, who I was waiting for, or what the 100 plastic balls in my hand were for. After carrying me home and sobering me up, we both decided the experiment had failed. I returned, gratefully, to the blessed roll-ups."

Third Year Geography Student, Coventry University

For the hardened smoker, determined to quit, nothing has greater potential for getting you back onto the evil weed faster than smoking spliffs. If you really can't live without the odd J, try rolling them with herbal tobacco, or smoke the stuff straight from a pipe.

Don't Suffer In Silence

If you want to quit but need help, your best bet is still to take a visit to the university doctor, who will happily fill you in with horrifying statistics. More importantly, you should be able to wangle a prescription for any of the Nicorette products, saving you a bundle of cash.

DRUGS

'Drugs are a one person birthday party – you don't get any presents you didn't already bring.'

Author, P.J. O'Rourke

Like religion, prostitution and Terry Wogan, drugs have been around since the dawn of civilisation. From the ingestion of peyote cacti by Native Americans to the widespread use of ecstasy in the west, the use of drugs has been, and probably always will be, an important force in shaping society.

But although people's desires to experiment with drugs have altered very little in the last few thousand years, what has changed is the way drugs are used. History denotes that narcotic substances were at one time used almost exclusively in the name of religious experience. Like dancing, fasting and meditation, drug rituals had the power to transport the user to the 'realm of the gods', to experience the universe in its infinite glory and develop an insight into ones own psychological make-up, rather than merely acting like an arsehole at parties. In the last twenty years in the west however, the rise of the 'chemical generation' has meant that pills and powder are now the preferred choice, overshadowing the psychedelics and opiates of the past and reflecting the faster pace of society and the rise in club culture and hedonism, not to mention a rapid increase in nose surgery.

The government and the tabloid press tend to use 'drugs' as a blanket term, which is highly misleading since it encompasses many different substances (including the 'legal drugs', alcohol and tobacco) some of which are reasonably healthy if indulged in moderation, and some that should be avoided like the plague. It is also important to realise that the prohibition of 'recreational' drugs is something that has only been imposed by the West in the last fifty years of civilisation; drugs such as opium, cocaine and cannabis were once freely available at markets and local chemists in the UK, and as America's attempt to prohibit alcohol in the Thirties was a disastrous failure, the same can be said of the drug laws today: make a drug illegal and the price rockets, the quality falls, criminal gangs become interested in the high profit margins and users become ostracised and despised. Authorities then react by clamping down even harder, and round and round it goes.

But while the evils of drugs are often exaggerated, the same goes for their benefits. The ecstasy comedown can leave you more miserable than a Joy Division record, cocaine can demonstrate to the world what an egocentric arse you really are, and cannabis can eat away all your ambition and energy, leaving you hoping for nothing more in life except more repeats of Star Trek.

'Treat drugs with respect, moderation and common sense, for most of the time they are stronger than you are."

William Powell, author of 'The Anarchist Cookbook'

CANNABIS

Dope, Draw, Blow, Weed, Ganja, Shit

Probably the most widely-taken recreational drug in the country, cannabis comes from the 'Cannabis Sativa' plant. Recently demoted to Class C, this means that although the police will usually turn a blind eye to possession of small amounts, growing acres of the stuff in your back garden is still very much frowned upon.

It is generally sold as either 'resin' – a dark brown lump that looks like (and sometimes is) Oxo – or as 'grass', the dried leaves and stalks of the plant. Much less common is the very strong 'cannabis oil'. Cannabis is either smoked (in spliff, pipe or bong), or eaten, generally in the form of a cake, biscuit or Vindaloo.

THE EFFECTS

Dope tends to make the user feel happy, relaxed, talkative and yet unable to string a sentence together. It also provides one with a heightened sense of colour and sound, making even the most jaded rubbish from the likes of Phil Collins sound like the best music you've ever heard. If smoked enough, it can bring on mild and even strong hallucinations, leaving one (from experience) staring in wonder at the un-tuned TV set as giant birds, pixies and Mars bars fly out of the screen and whirl around the room.

It is worth noting that first time users often profess to feeling no effect from dope, to which only perseverance will pay off. Cannabis can however, have the very unsettling effect of making the user feel immensely paranoid, which can be a frightening experience, leading you into believing that either:

Everyone in the room hates you
Everyone in the room thinks that you hate them
Everyone in the room thinks that you think that they hate you
Everyone in the room thinks that you think that they think that you hate them
etc, etc…

If you find that smoking cannabis does regularly leave you in a paranoid frame of mind or feeling nauseous, try smoking another variety. In the same way that different types of alcohol affect people in different ways (eg whiskey can bring out aggression), cannabis can be the same. If resin makes you feel unsettled, try skunk. Skunk is a much lighter, friendlier hit than resin, somewhat akin to champagne. If you still feel lousy after all this, don't smoke the damn stuff.

POPULAR WITH
Hippies, Rastas, slackers, surfers, musicians, Trekkies, computer buffs, students.

FAMOUS USERS
The Beatles, Bob Dylan, Bob Marley, Cheech and Chong, The Fabulous Furry Freak Brothers, Queen Victoria (for her period pains), Howard Marks, MS sufferers, George Washington (who used to grow it in the White House!) and pretty much anyone who doesn't read the Daily Mail/ Daily Express.

UPS
Can make absolutely everything, from old episodes of 'Happy Days' to 'Changing Rooms' completely hilarious.

DOWNS
Can cause nausea, paranoia, and short-term memory loss. Can also cause short-term memory loss.

CONTRIBUTION TO CULTURE
Nearly always a side dish to a more potent narcotic main course, dope has however played a major role in the following…

Howard Marks' career, every Reggae album ever made, The Small Faces – 'Ogden's Nut Gone Flake', Bob Dylan 'Blonde on Blonde', Cypress Hill, the Cheech and Chong film – 'Up in Smoke', and the Alice B. Toklas Cookbook (for inventing the hash brownie). The Beatles too, after being introduced to dope by Dylan took to it like ducks to water and made many well-documented references to various drugs in their songs. Have you ever considered – 'Roll up, Roll up for the Magical Mystery Tour' ??

GOOD TIMES TO GET STONED
- Sitting with your mates in the living room, surrounded by Kettle-chips, a huge tin of Quality Street and watching 'Sex and the City'
- Lying naked on the floor of your bedroom with headphones on, listening to your favourite album.

The Munchies
The favoured topic of stand-up comics everywhere, the munchies is the increased appetite that comes from smoking dope. (In the U.S. medicinal cannabis is prescribed to cancer and AIDS patients as an appetite stimulant.) Rather than smoked salmon and lobster, the munchies make you crave the sort of food you haven't eaten since the age of six – Monster Munch, Smarties, Maltesers, Midget Gems etc. You can always identify a hardened toker by the number of empty packets of Pringles and Wine Gums littered around his or her room.

Rolling your

THE BEATLES

INGREDIENTS
Bag of hash
Matches / lighter
Rizlas (preferably red)
Pack of low tar ciggies (e.g. Silk Cut)
Biscuits / cakes / chocolate bars / crisps
An old vinyl cover (preferably a pale one with psychedelic
overtones; the Beatles White album is perfect)
**A copy of Star Wars / some old Simpsons episodes / Buffy
the Vampire Slayer series 1-6 / 2001: A Space Odyssey
A few mates**

1) Take your album cover and rest it on your knee. (This is to be your rolling mat
   for the operation – the pale cover will help you notice any cannabis strands that
   may go astray during the proceedings.)

2) Take two Rizlas. Lick down half the gummy side of one, and stick it
   perpendicular to the other making an 'L' shape, with the gum running down the
   inside of the 'L'.

3) Take your lump of hash and heat it under a flame until you get a nice crumbly
   texture to gently layer in the base of the rizla.
   !!!A note of caution – underburning will cause big lumps to fall into your joint
   causing blims*. Overcook it and the lump will start to burn up in your hand!!!
   If you have grass / skunk, there's no need for heating. Simply pull off small
   amounts and crumble them into the joint.

4) Take a cigarette, lick down one side. Wait a few seconds, then peel the wet strip
   away and add about two thirds of the tobacco into the joint.

5) Tear off a 15mm strip of the cardboard flap from the pack of rizlas, thus creating
   a 'roach'. Shape the roach into a small cylinder, diameter approximately 2.94mm.

*Also known as whinnetts, this is a smokers term for a burning oversized lump of hash that falls out of a lit
joint, making a perfectly sized burnt hole in your T shirt. This is to be avoided. Heavy dope smokers can be
spotted a mile off, owing to numerous blim burns in the upper half of their T-shirts / jumpers / kaftans…

first joint

6) Insert the roach at the far end of the joint, and then hold up the joint as if the letter 'L' were backwards.

7) Roll the joint, gently tweaking the thumbs up and down along it to create a nice tight, even sausage.

8) Keeping it tight, lick both lines of the gum, keeping the left tightly round the roach, roll it around and seal.

9) Take a match and poke down the end of the joint to avoid stray fallout.

10) Twist the end.

11) Insert video.

12) Sit back on the sofa surrounded by friends, confectionary, ashtrays and drink.

13) Light the joint, inhale deeply….

He's caned off his head, help him Obi-Wan…

Hash Brownies

The most popular of all the narcotic confectionaries (since the withdrawal of the original 'Space Dust' from British sweet stores in the early Eighties), the hash brownie was invented by the lesbian chef Alice B. Toklas, and first featured in her celebrated cookbook. A more civilised and less pungent alternative to spliffs and bongs, the hash brownie lends an air of respectability to cannabis and should ideally be served in formal evening wear.

YOU WILL NEED:

- Half a teaspoon salt
- Three quarters of a cup of baking flour
- 1 cup sugar
- 3 oz. Cooking chocolate (if you don't have any, get a bar of dark chocolate such as Bournville. Failing that, sling in a Milky Way and hope for the best)
- Half a teaspoon baking powder
- 3 eggs
- Half a cup of sweet butter
- 5 grams powdered hash

1 Melt the chocolate and butter together, then add the sugar and hash.

2 Beat the mixture until creamy.

3 Sift the flour, baking powder and salt together, and then add to mixture.

4 Pour the mixture into a cookie tray and bake for 30 minutes at 375 degrees.

5 When cool, cut brownies into small squares and garnish with chopped nuts, 'Hundreds and Thousands', raisins or raw chilli.

Note. Under no circumstances leave them lying around when your parents are visiting or your dad may inadvertently take a nibble and spend the next 2 hours giggling at the stray hair on your mother's chin.

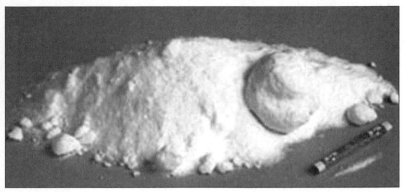

COCAINE

Charlie, Coke, Snow, Peruvian Marching Powder
Derived from the leaf of the coca plant, cocaine is a white powder, commonly sniffed up the nose, smoked or rubbed on the gums (or even the genitals for the pure hedonist). More highly purified forms of cocaine are Crack, Ice and Freebase.

THE EFFECTS

Cocaine is a stimulant, making the user feel 'wired', euphoric and energised; it has the power to keep you up all night talking crap to whoever will listen, provided you can afford to keep shovelling the stuff up your nose every 45 minutes. In the form of crack cocaine, the effects are further intensified, giving an intensely euphoric physical 'rush' that makes you feel like God for 3-5 minutes, followed by Gollum out of Lord of the Rings until you can get some more.

POPULAR WITH

Once the province of millionaires, pop stars, Wall Street types and various members of the glitterati, coke is these days taken by virtually anyone who likes the sound of their own voice and can afford the stuff. In 1999 a random analysis of bank notes in London found that 99% showed traces of cocaine.

FAMOUS USERS

Just about every pop star who's ever lived; most notably Elton John, Noel Gallagher, and Freddie Mercury (who famously served it at parties in bowls strapped to the heads of dwarfs), Daniella 'no nose' Westbrook, author Martin Amis, Steve Tyler out of Aerosmith, Richard Bacon, Queen Victoria (again), Sigmund Freud, Sherlock Holmes and the entire staff of the BBC (allegedly).

UPS
Coke gives the user an almost superhuman feeling of self-importance and an overwhelming desire to write songs using recycled Beatles riffs. Good for long and sustained amounts of partying.

DOWNS
The effects only last half an hour before you realise what a bag of shite you've been talking. Although not classically addictive in the physical sense, cocaine (especially crack cocaine) can quickly create a strong psychological addiction, making it increasingly difficult to imagine having any fun not involving cocaine. Used heavily cocaine can cause a temporary condition very much like paranoid schizophrenia known as 'amphetamine psychosis', symptoms of which include hallucinations, paranoid delusions, and bizarre and compulsive behaviour. Sufferers of a less serious but more common side-effect of frequent cocaine use are known on the street as 'arrogant self-obsessed jerks', victims of a syndrome which develops when users start to believe they really are as cool and interesting as the drug makes them feel. It can't be denied that prudent amounts of cocaine can make the dullest parties fun, but in the long run, regular snorting will lead to depression, dependency, anxiety, an empty bank account and a hole where your nose used to be.

CONTRIBUTIONS TO CULTURE
'What's the Story (Morning Glory)?', 'Cocaine' (Eric Clapton), all the Seventies Bowie albums, the novels 'Less Than Zero' (Brett Easton Ellis) and 'Bright Lights, Big City' (Jay McInerney), 'Boogie Nights', 'Scarface', 'Casino' and the collected works of Sigmund Freud.

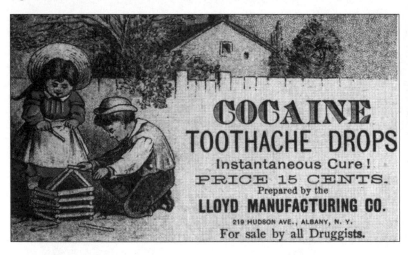

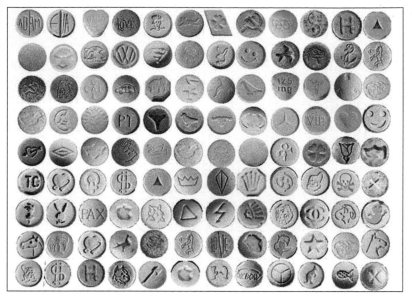

ECSTASY

E, Pills, MDMA, XTC

A natural ingredient found in nutmeg, Ecstasy was originally developed by the Germans as a diet pill! Sold as a white, yellow, pink or brown tablet, ecstasy is extremely popular amongst students, particularly the clubbing fraternity.

THE EFFECTS

Ecstasy causes a profound and unstoppable desire to dance to everything from Steps to the sound of a mobile phone. Along with this comes a 'loved up' feeling, in which the user finds everyone in the human race absolutely delightful, even Anne Robinson. Ecstasy works by stimulating the release of a flood of seratonin – a chemical that exists naturally in the body – into your brain. Seratonin is normally only generated in those sorts of quantities when you do something particularly splendid and laudable, like saving the world from alien invasion or inadvertently wiping out the entire cast of Hollyoaks.

UPS

It's rather nice to love humanity unconditionally for a couple of hours, even if the feeling is chemically assisted. Taken sensibly in the right circumstances, Ecstasy can be a useful reminder of what it actually feels like to be perfectly happy and contented – which can be a revelation for those stuck in a melancholic rut. It also breaks through that British reserve and allows you to express your open-hearted love and affection for partners, friends, mild acquaintances, complete strangers, alcoholic vagrants, feral cats and road signs.

DOWNS

If you have epilepsy, high blood pressure or a heart condition, stay well clear: taking ecstasy would be akin to your grandparents having a three hour game of squash. It can also bring on dehydration and overheating (caused by dancing like a maniac without taking any fluids) which is extremely dangerous and very unpleasant. Paradoxically though, some deaths have been caused by people dancing for hours while swilling down pints and pints of water to make sure they didn't dehydrate. This unfortunately flushes all the electrolytes (salts) out of the body, disabling the body's natural osmosis and causing major organ failure. The general rule is to drink a pint of water an hour, take regular rests to cool down, and replenish your salts with packets of crisps or nuts or an isotonic soft drink.

Although there have been plenty of reported deaths in the papers over the years, the number is still very small (less than 100). A bigger problem with this drug is that you never know what's actually in the pill you're taking, as it is regularly mixed with everything from speed, heroin, laxatives, muscle relaxants, animal tranquilisers and household cleaning products, leading to an acute addiction to Mr Muscle. In Holland they have the good sense to provide special 'labs' in clubs where you can have your pill tested before you take it.

CONTRIBUTIONS TO CULTURE

'Ebenezer Goode' (The Shamen), 'Pills and Thrills and Bellyaches' (Happy Mondays), Eighties/ Nineties Dance music, 'Human Traffic' and 'Go'.

The 'E' Comedown

The Ecstasy comedown is a curious one – the day after you'll probably feel fine, but two days after that you'll suddenly burst into tears upon discovering that you've run out of cornflakes. Sometimes known as 'Terrible Tuesday' it's the flip-side of artificially stimulating your seratonin levels, giving a 'peak' during the Ecstasy trip and a 'trough' a day or two later during which you'll feel depressed, irritable and occasionally panicky. Terrible Tuesday is best spent on the sofa under a duvet watching light romantic comedies.

SPEED
Sulphate, Whizz, Billy Whizz, Uppers

Amphetamines were at one time used in pill-form to treat depression or as an aid to dieting. In the days when they were known as 'mother's little helpers', doctors used to dole them out like sweets, as a cure for anything from lethargy to in-growing toenails. This probably explains why so many buildings were erected in this country between the years 1950 and 1970. Street speed however is a white or grey powder, which can be snorted, eaten or injected.

THE EFFECTS
As the name suggests, speed is a stimulant. It makes your heart race, makes you breathe like someone who's just done the London marathon, and gives you the energy to run, jump and dance around all night like a maniac. Speed stimulates the central nervous system and 'speeds' up the messages going from the brain to the body. It's an edgy, frantic high, which also for some reason appears to temporarily make one's penis shrink (although conversely they do say that if you can get an erection while on speed you're stuck with it for hours, even if you have to go round to your grandparents for tea).

POPULAR WITH
Mods, depressed Sixties housewives, long-distance lorry drivers, American Beat Poets from the Fifties, Pulp Fiction novelists.

FAMOUS USERS
Singer Judy Garland, Adolf Hitler, Pete Townshend, Phil Daniels in Quadrophenia, Harry Dean Stanton in the Eighties cult movie 'Repoman'.

UPS
Cheap, the high lasts longer than coke, and it certainly makes the housework more fun.

DOWNS

Speed contains more impurities than any other illegal drug (it's usually only about 10% pure). This possibly explains why a speed comedown is the worst of all, and can leave you feeling depressed, edgy, exhausted and with the desire to invade Poland.

Overdosing on speed can lead to strokes, heart failure, seizures and dangerously high body temperature ('speed kills', as the hippies used to say). Long-term use of any 'upper' is going to totally bugger up your sleep-patterns and make you grouchy, irritable, and unable to work. Heavy users sometimes resort to using downers such as alcohol, tranquillisers or heroin to counter the effects of a binge and finally get some sleep.

Plus, it's pretty hard to have a conversation with people who are on speed, as they tend to talk in a rapid stream-of-consciousness that goes something like:-

'HithereyoumustbeJackyeahI'mDaveyeahI'mafriendofHelen'syeahshe'sagreatgirlwowIwa swatchingThePrisonerlastnightonDVDyouknowthatepisodewheretheydrughimandgethise xactdoubletoimpersonatehimgodthat'sweirdimagineifthathappenedtoyouImeanwhatwo uldyoudothatwouldreallyfreakyououtwouldn'tit?what'sthatpictureonthewallovertthere?isitV anGough?noit'swhat'shisnamedon'ttellmeit'sonthetipofmytongueGoyanonotGoyawhat'shi sbloodyname?Gauginthat'sitGauginhe'stheguywhoSomersetMaughambasedthatnovelon youknowthemoonandsixpencewasn'tit?wedidthatatschoolalongwiththegrapesofwrathanda streetcarnameddesiregodIreallyfanciedmyenglishteacheratschoolMissPlumweusedtocallh erlittleplumafterthatcharacterwhousedtobeinthebeanoyouknowtheindianoneornativeam ericanasyou'vegottosaythesedaysgoddoyourememberrogerthedodger?whataboutthebash streetkids?fantasticeh?ohyou'vegottogotothetoiletokayI'llseeyoulateryeahgreatniceonesee youlater.'

CONTRIBUTIONS TO CULTURE

Sixties Mod Culture, 'Quadrophenia' and the first four Rolling Stones albums. And it did help Jack Kerouac finish 'On The Road', and Sci-Fi novelist Philip K Dick churn out fifty odd masterpieces in the space of only a few years (though he did eventually commit suicide).

Jack Kerouac

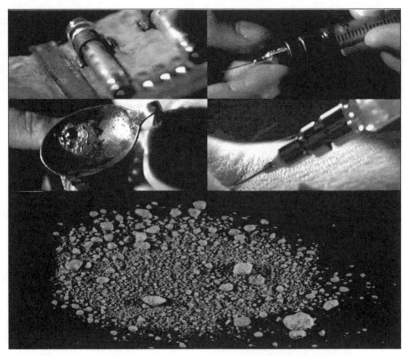

HEROIN
Smack, Horse, Junk, Skag

Heroin is derived from morphine, the pain-killing drug named after the Greek God of Dreams, which is itself derived from Opium, the product of the Opium Poppy. A white or brown powder, heroin can be snorted, injected, or smoked ('chasing the dragon').

Heroin is actually a brand-name created by the German pharmaceutical company which first invented and marketed it. Ironically it was originally promoted as a non-addictive alternative to morphine, which had created thousands of addicts among the soldiers prescribed it for battle injuries.

THE EFFECTS
Heroin gives the user an unsurpassed sense of warmth, peace, relaxation, and well-being, but excessive use can result in coma and death. It produces a trance-like dreamy euphoria which is sometimes hallucinatory in the way thoughts and images float through the mind. Large enough doses bring about a complete insensibility to pain, so that soldiers on the battlefield can be made comfortable and carefree even if their legs are five yards away and their genitals are dangling from a nearby tree.

POPULAR WITH
Characters in Irvine Welsh novels.

FAMOUS USERS
Lou Reed, Sid Vicious,* William Burroughs, Janis Joplin,* Billie Holiday,* John Belushi,* Tim Buckley*.

UPS
Few. 'Monging out' can be dreamy and hallucinogenic as the user drifts in a half-asleep twilight, but staring at a space on the wall for five hours like this isn't exactly going to make you a hit at parties. Not that you'd care though.

DOWNS
Lots. Although heroin in controlled dosages is not toxic or harmful to the body and you could theoretically use it all your life without harm, it rarely works out that way in reality. Heroin is viciously addictive, both physically and psychologically, and although casual users do exist, heavy and constant use is the norm. Without the seriously large amounts of cash necessary to feed a habit, addicts are forced to switch from smoking to injecting (with all the attendant health issues) to make the drug last longer and hit harder, and also commonly turn to crime to finance the addiction. Degradation, squalor and intense self-loathing usually follow close behind, although it's worth noting that much of the dire criminal and social problems associated with heroin would not be an issue if it was cheap and legal.

CONTRIBUTIONS TO CULTURE
The first three Velvet Underground albums, Punk Rock, William Burroughs 'Naked Lunch', 'Symphonie Fantastique' (Berlioz) and the films 'Drugstore Cowboy', 'Sid and Nancy', 'Man with the Golden Arm', 'Christiana F' and 'Panic in Needle Park'.

*RIP (they all died from overdoses)

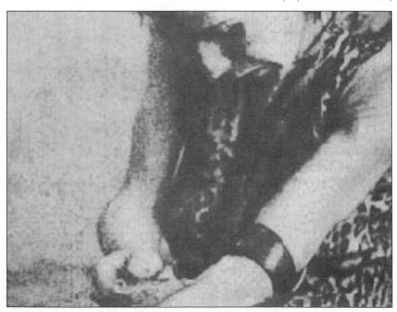

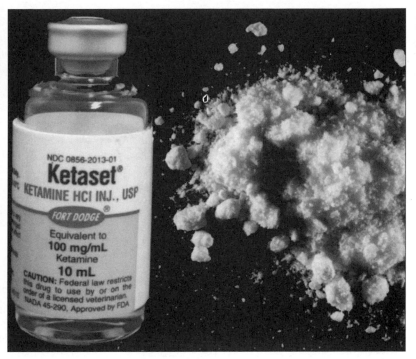

KETAMINE

K, Special K, Vitamin K

Ketamine is, bizarrely enough, an animal anaesthetic used by vets, although it was originally developed for use on humans. It is chemically related to nitrous oxide (laughing gas) and PCP (Angel Dust). In its legal form it is a liquid which is injected into muscle tissue, but street Ketamine usually comes in pill form or as a powder snorted like cocaine.

THE EFFECTS

Ketamine is fast-acting, causing a speedy rush followed very quickly by an anaesthetic effect which, depending on the dosage, causes anything from heavy limbs to full-scale paralysis. It is a 'disassociative anaesthetic' which appears to shut down the parts of the brain involved in physical movement and sensation, and amplify the imagination and the 'inner mind', leading to powerful and vivid hallucinations. Users often report mystical out-of-body experiences. Atheist household pets are frequently seized with a deep conviction of the existence of God.

FAMOUS USERS

The Cheshire Cat, Godzilla, Babe the Pig, Badger (but not Bodger), Fiver out of Watership Down, Scooby Doo (and Shaggy), Red Rum, Mr Ed, Lassie, King Kong, Skippy, Huckleberry Hound, the entire cast of Rolf's Animal Hospital.

UPS

The anaesthetic qualities of Ketamine seem to remove the fear and panic that often come with powerful hallucinogenics, so users are left free to experience any amount of psychedelic weirdness. The full-on out-of-body nature of a major Ketamine experience is known as the 'K-hole', and often leaves users with the conviction that they have contacted non-human or alien entities and intelligences. Famous psychonaut Dr John Lilly performed many experiments involving Ketamine and isolation tanks, and concluded amongst other things that a major television network was trying to conquer the world, and that dolphins were our only hope of salvation.

DOWNS

Again due to the anaesthetic aspect, Ketamine can be lethal when mixed with downers such as alcohol, tranquilisers or barbiturates. Taken alone though, the fatal dose is very high – you are likely to pass out long before you can take enough to kill you (unless you try hard).

Ketamine can cause bouts of intense nausea and vomiting (although users report that it's possible to be 'distracted' out of these) and obviously paralysis AND vomiting are to be avoided should you wish to reach retirement age. In lesser doses, movement is possible (although haphazard) and the combination of feeling entirely care-free and being impervious to pain is a dangerous mix.

Although not classically addictive like cigarettes and alcohol, Ketamine can create powerful psychological addictions: the blissed out weirdness of the 'K-hole' has for some users proved much more attractive than everyday life (and for this reason, along with its paralysing and disorientating effects, its use as a "date rape" drug is worryingly, on the increase).

Because Ketamine is a relatively new drug (it's only been used as a street drug for about ten years) very little is known about the long term effects of its use, although they almost certainly include barking, running after sticks, and pissing against lamp posts (that's enough animal jokes – Ed.).

CONTRIBUTIONS TO CULTURE

The experiences with Ketamine of the aforementioned Dr John Lilly were immortalised in the excellent Ken Russell film 'Altered States', not to mention an episode of Rolf's Animal Hospital in which Rolf was accidentally injected with Ketamine during a struggle with a dangerously constipated orang-utang and subsequently made psychic contact with the Venusian High Command. Sadly, this was never broadcast.

THE U.F.O. EXPERIENCE

A lot of people who take Ketamine report basically the same visionary experiences: meeting with or being kidnapped by extraterrestrials. This suggests one of two things:

1) Human brains react to certain chemical stimuli in the same way, regardless of cultural differences.

2) There's some sort of 'contact embargo' on planet Earth that means aliens are only allowed to communicate with people who are tripping their tits off on drugs and who, therefore, no one will ever believe.

POPPERS

Amyl /Butyl Nitrate

Poppers are a clear or gold-coloured liquid (usually contained in a small jar), which is inhaled through the nose. They are popular in clubs, especially gay clubs. Trade names of Amyl include such dead giveaways as Thrust, Ram, and Rock Hard, also called Snappers, Rush, Liquid gold, Locker room, TNT.

THE EFFECTS

Snorting poppers causes a 'head rush' that lasts for 5 – 10 seconds, with a milder effect lasting a few minutes. Poppers cause blood vessels to dilate, resulting in a sudden drop in blood pressure and a drastic acceleration in heart rate as it tries to compensate. As a result, it's not uncommon to temporarily faint or 'swoon' after a good sniff. Users experience a brief period of 'heightened reality' in which sounds, colours, and feelings appear to increase in strength. Amyl Nitrate is also a muscle relaxant – it famously relaxes the sphincter, which explains its popularity with those fond of anal high jinks.

POPULAR WITH

Clubbers, gays, gay clubbers. Sometimes smuggled into school by trainee drug users and sniffed behind the biology lab.

FAMOUS USERS

Waylon Smithers
C3PO from Star Wars

UPS

It's cheap 'n' cheerful. One jar lasts (almost) forever. You'll still have it when you're 75 years old (when you'll probably need it in order to have a bowel movement).

DOWNS

A whole smorgasbord of damaging effects. One sniff trounces hundreds of thousands of brain cells and may result in you joining a cult. Due to the racing-heart effect, it is terribly dangerous to those with heart problems. It is also damaging to the immune system and carcinogenic (cancer causing). Over-use can cause rashes around the mouth and nose.

Poppers can also cause truly awful headaches, especially if used when drunk.

CONTRIBUTIONS TO CULTURE

None, as far as we know. A film based on an amyl experience would only last for five seconds and be absolutely incomprehensible (so it would probably win the jury prize at Cannes).

The terrible side-effects of inhaling poppers

DRUG DEALERS

Should you choose to enter into the twilight world of scoring, there are a few situations to avoid at all costs:

1) NEVER BUY FROM A STRANGER

2) NEVER FRONT MONEY

If a dealer asks for your cash in advance, claiming he is going up to his apartment to get you your stuff, you could be waiting a looonnnggg time.

3) NEVER BUY A LARGE QUANTITY OF ANY DRUG WITHOUT FIRST SAMPLING IT

You could end up with £100 worth of washing powder/ Oxo cubes.

If you do get into the drugs scene at uni, the chances are, you are going to meet some seriously shady and disturbing characters, particularly if you live in Manchester. Over the following 12 pages, we cover some of the unsavoury types of dealers who may cross your path…

#1 THE SCARY DEALER

He may be the mildest-mannered fellow in the world, but it is impossible to relax in his presence – this is largely because he keeps receiving calls on his microscopic mobile which imply that he is heavily involved in murder, international bank robbery and snuff porn. Occasionally, when you pop round to score you'll find him seated with several terse, besuited men, whom you would swear you saw on 'Crimewatch', and whom he will introduce as 'Mr Fucker', 'Razor Eric' and 'The Torturer'.

On no account complain should you feel this dealer has ripped you off if you want to keep your thumbs where they currently reside. Dealers like this only remind you that the drugs you revere for their 'loved up' qualities are actually supplied and controlled by thick-necked sociopaths who would gladly sell their grandmas for a pony.

NP/ 091643

#2 THE THROWBACK

It's a miracle that this man hasn't been nicked more often, as his general appearance suggests the caricature of the classic hippy that Nigel Planer brilliantly portrayed in Neil from the Young Ones. He wears a poncho, sandals, has hair down to his arse, and refers to everyone as 'man'. You can never work out how old he is – his wizened visage suggests any age from 25 to 60 – so you never know if he's actually a leftover from Woodstock or would merely like to be. His blatant lack of regard for the law causes him to produce enormous bags of grass with a cavalier attitude directly below police cameras, thus making you shit your pants.

#3 THE UNLIKELY CANDIDATE

This dealer has short hair, wears a tie, and looks like he might be the manager of a small chain of electrical goods retailers. You would never in a million years guess that he'd smoke a joint let alone sell you one. He's obviously not a copper in disguise though, because no copper, however ill-informed would choose this persona as cover.

#4 THE NARC

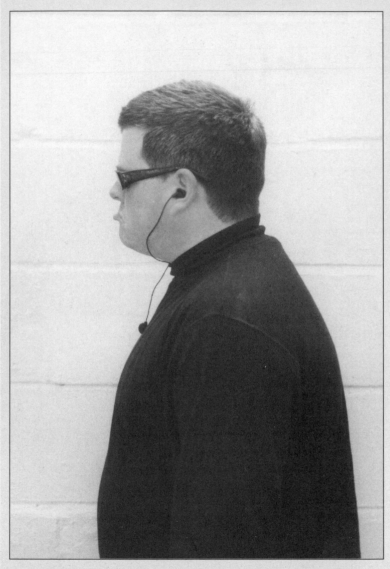

The narc is an undercover copper who sidles up to you in the pub and says, *'Ello 'ello 'ello, you want to score some marijuanas, daddio?'* A further giveaway is his dress sense (C&A trainers, combat trousers, and a mac) as well as his quoting of 1978 prices. If you are taken in by his act then you deserve everything you get.

NP/ 7129584

#5 STARK RAVING MADMAN

You can buy any drug you want from this man as long as it's speed. He himself has clearly taken far, far too much of this, as he will only invite you into his tiny, unheated flat after looking up and down the street in a paranoid fashion for ten minutes, and then spend an hour and a half telling you about the radio the C.I.A. have put in his head. Periodically, his serial-killer-like friends will turn up and they will cheerily discuss death camps or the best way of disposing of a human head. This man is the best advertisement yet for 'just saying no'.

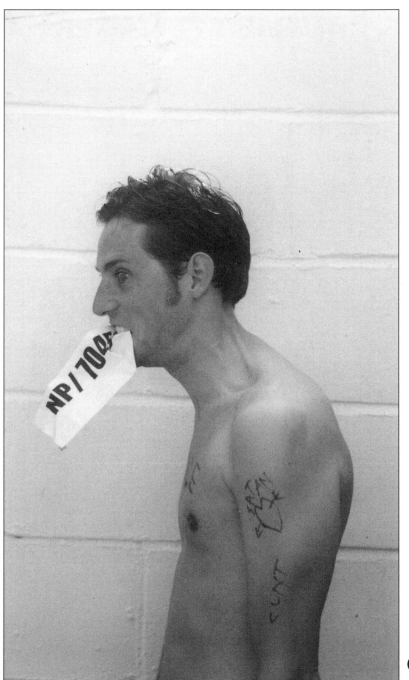

#6 THE TEENAGER

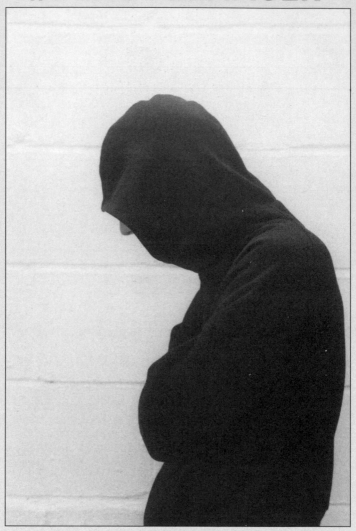

Nihilistic, inarticulate, gangly and barely human, the 'streetwise' teenage dealer is possibly the most dangerous of the lot, displaying little concern for his fellow beings as he happily touts heroin at the gates of the local Primary School. Life to him is cheap, except when it comes to his customised Escort with in-house sound system and his collection of designer trainers. He is a sad freak of nature in a hooded top, and under no circumstances conduct any business with him unless he pulls a gun on you.

A BRIEF HISTORY OF PSYCHEDELICS

Psychedelics have actually existed for millennia and their use has been entwined with human spirituality since the very beginning of civilisation. By far the oldest expression of human spiritual activity is the practise of shamanism. Part of the shaman's role was to undertake the 'soul journey' to the underworld to encounter gods and demons where he/she would gain power and wisdom, and the employment of psychedelic compounds was usually the primary method of producing such visionary awareness.

Shamans the world over have shown particular skill in both preparing hallucinogenic drugs and inventing novel ways to take them. In Northern Europe, the Fly Agaric mushroom – the classic red-with-white-spots Enid Blyton fairy mushroom (which contains several poisons) was made safe by feeding it to reindeer and then collecting and drinking the reindeer urine. If you think that's revolting, there are accounts from Russia in the Middle Ages of whole chains of people drinking the urine of others who'd drunk the reindeer piss. Your position in the queue depended on how much you could pay.

Similarly, the old legend of witches 'flying' on broomsticks is thought to derive from the practice of smearing an hallucinogenic unguent onto a broomstick and then inserting the stick into the vagina or anus so that the thin-walled blood-rich membranes of these orifices could absorb the active ingredients (but we're not suggesting you need to do this should you wish to experiment with these substances).

One element that crops up often in literature and demonstrates the seriousness with which the psychedelic experience was approached in older cultures, is the sheer noxious and vile nature of the powders, potions and mashed-up gunge that devotees were prepared to imbibe. Forgetting the reindeer urine for a moment, read Carlos Castaneda's accounts of the extraordinary bitterness of the peyote cactus and his struggle not to immediately throw it back up. Similarly (and from experience) the Ayahuasca potion can offend the digestive system to such an extent that all orifices can open-fire at random, leaving one confronting the Eternal Mysteries and the Great Spirit of the Cosmos in dire need of fresh trousers. Such purgative effects were however, often deliberately sought after and formed part of the preparation for the spiritual journey that was to follow.

What is to be realised from all this therefore, is that in older cultures the use of psychedelics was deeply immersed in ritual, myths and cosmologies that defined, guided and gave meaning to the experience. As Sixties LSD guru Timothy Leary pointed out, 'Set' (your expectations and attitude to the psychedelic experience) and 'Setting' (the environment you're in) are all-important, and strongly influence whether you have a wondrous soul-enriching glimpse of Heaven or a hellish schizoid freak-out. Ancient cultures feared and respected their spirits and deities and the purifications, rituals and mythologies were as important as the drug experience.

With all this in mind, it's important to realise that psychedelics are not 'fun' drugs. Unlike Ecstasy, which is designed to make you feel fantastic and loved up, psychedelics are both subtler, more intense and much more unpredictable. If you're keen to try LSD or magic mushrooms, doing so carelessly or impulsively could be a big mistake, and dropping an LSD tab in a club on a Saturday night after five pints and a line of speed can tempt the Wrath of the Gods.

These substances are potent, unpredictable, strange, life-altering, magical and much more powerful than you. Handle them with caution and respect.

WHAT IS IT LIKE TO TAKE PSYCHEDELICS?

'Well, blimey, it's just ...amazing, it's really weird, like your mind gets turned inside-out... no, it's more like your skull turns transparent and you can see through it... everything is so strange and vivid, and time goes kind of curved and it's as you're in a library where the books are reading you and it's just like totally freaking awesome... kind of like... sort of......' – etc.

The experience of altered states of consciousness has always been strangely resistant to being captured in words, and literary accounts of deep visions and cosmic revelations are often obscure poetic mixes of metaphor, symbolism and poetry; or if you prefer; mad ranting nonsense. This may be because the experience is so unusual that there's no shared language to describe it, or perhaps because psychedelics bring to the surface a deep part of your consciousness that is non-verbal or symbolic in nature, so that as with intense dreams, the impact and intensity of the experience is very difficult to grasp and convey.

Some common elements of the psychedelic experience are agreed upon though, and include: distortions in one's sense of passing time (it takes approx 17 days to go to the loo), enhanced perception of colour and shape making everyday objects appear strange and new, a visual 'rippling' effect that can make walls appear to be breathing and objects to shimmer; uncontrollable outbreaks of mass giggling followed by long enigmatic silences, peculiar physical sensations, instances of intense reverie in which thoughts become like waking dreams, greater sensitivity to sound and touch, and general high suggestibility (i.e. if someone shouts 'The umbrella stand has turned into a bucket of flamingos!' you'll probably believe them, even after close inspection of the umbrellas).

Some Tripping Tips

1) Frequency

Not often. As a rough rule of thumb, you can't trip unless you've been sensible for a few weeks, otherwise you've got nothing to trip with. See?

2) Environment

Go out in the countryside and bliss-out on nature, or at least use a house with a big garden: nature is astonishingly beautiful when tripping; towns and cities aren't. Have something fun and physical to do to focus your mind – Frisbee is perfect, but any kind of light and undemanding game will do. Be with people you know, like and trust, and ensure there's at least one person who is sober and straight to play 'mother' and make cups of tea when you've developed an irrational fear of the kettle. Make sure your environment is 'secure' and there's no chance of fifteen loud and drunk people turning up uninvited after the pubs close. It's a foolhardy individual who chooses Glastonbury or round at a stranger's house watching the Blair Witch Project as the environment for their first trip.

3) Fear and Loathing

The infamous 'bad trip' seems to have no single cause. It can be a specific event, or just too many damned events at once, or it can be an underlying anxiety about something completely unrelated that suddenly comes to the surface. Sometimes there are causeless moments of sheer terror, which then disappear like a popped bubble. There's no certain way of ensuring a bad trip won't happen, but it's more likely if:

        A) You are tripping without due care or attention.
        B) You're taking too much and too often.

There is no quick way of stopping a trip. There's some evidence however, that it can be smoothed out by taking niacin (in the form of vitamin B-3 or nicotinic acid). Also vitamin C (orange juice etc) has been shown to reduce the incidence of paranoia and prevent depletion of the vitamin from the body during LSD trips. Sugar levels can be an important factor too, and anything that brings them up is good, such as a sweet drink and a biscuit or three. Panic often takes the form of hypochondria – 'I feel weird, I must be ill, I'm dying!' – and it's not wholly unknown for stricken trippers to demand to be taken to hospital where usually they'll be fed charcoal pills (which marginally speeds up the absorption of the drug) and possibly a tranquiliser of some kind, put into a darkened room and left to sweat it out while nurses regularly pop in and out making sarcastic comments.

In most cases it's usually best to take panickers outside for a stroll or put them in a dimly lit room with quiet, gentle music and away from other people and too many stimuli. Panic can disappear as mysteriously as it arrives, so be calm and reassuring and attempt to distract the sufferer with interesting small objects and trivial showbiz gossip. Under no circumstances say things like: 'I just heard on the telly that the world is about to end', 'you know that everybody hates you, don't you?' or 'oh, I think your parents have just arrived.'

THE MAJOR PSYCHEDELICS

In the UK the two major hallucinogens you're likely to come across are LSD and Magic Mushrooms. The effects of both are classically psychedelic but there are some differences.

LSD (Lysergic Acid Diethylamide)
Acid, Tab, Trip

LSD ('acid') was discovered by the Swiss Chemist Albert Hoffman, who pioneered the first trip and had probably the most extraordinary cycle ride home in human history, after accidentally absorbing some through his skin at work. LSD is extremely potent: the average amount required to profoundly effect consciousness is 200-250 microgrammes, which is equivalent to a twentieth of the size of a grain of salt. That amount will generate a trip lasting between 8 – 12 hours. An important consideration if you drunkenly decide at three in the morning that you fancy a 'quick' trip.

LSD usually comes as small pieces of paper ('tabs') impregnated with the drug with a picture (invariably of Zippy, Bungle, or Jeffrey from Rainbow) on one side; although also in very small (but notoriously strong) pills known as microdots. Although you may hear that some acid tabs contain strychnine, the tiny amounts of the drug involved make it highly unlikely that any harmful adulterants are present in anything approaching dangerous amounts.

There are still wildly contradictory reports on the effect of LSD on the mind and body, and although as far as can be ascertained, LSD causes no physiological or neurological damage, (i.e. physical damage) to the body or brain; psychological damage is another question.

Some LSD users can experience 'flashbacks': moments when a user can re-experience intense memories from a trip that happened weeks, months or even years ago. Urban folklore says this is due to tiny LSD crystals left floating around the brain, but this is nonsense, and flashbacks are better seen as an example of the natural human process whereby any intense emotional experiences can reoccur in this way, for example in post-traumatic stress disorder. Flashbacks can be compared to the way events from last night's partying can suddenly float up into consciousness the next morning (often to one's intense embarrassment).

POPULAR WITH
Hippies.

FAMOUS USERS
Timothy Leary, Aldous Huxley, Syd Barrett, Peter Green of Fleetwood Mac, Jim Morrison, Po out of the TeleTubbies.

UPS
A good trip can (users claim) 'sort you out', psychologically speaking, putting you in tune with your feelings about yourself and the universe.

DOWNS
Regular use, or one bad trip too many can bring on insomnia, paranoia, anxiety attacks and can lead to you (in the case of Syd Barrett, ex-singer of Pink Floyd) spending the next 35 years living with your mother in Cambridge.

Syd Barrett

GOOD TIMES TO TAKE
Watching a sunset, seated by a babbling brook, surrounded by the myriad hues of nature at her most bountiful.
Watching the stars sparkle in the clear night sky.
Watching '2001: A Space Odyssey'.

BAD TIMES TO TAKE
Your mother's funeral.
While on trial at the Old Bailey
At Alton Towers.

CONTRIBUTIONS TO CULTURE
Too numerous to mention but here's a few highlights: 'Sergeant Peppers', 'Pet Sounds', 'Easy Rider', the novel 'Electric Kool-Aid Acid Test', The Psychedelic Experience (Tim Leary), Woodstock, 'In C' (Terry Riley), Pink Floyd (up to Syd leaving), The Monkees' film 'Head'.

The Most Boring Trip Ever
A friend once dropped acid and saw…a fish tank. That's it. Just a fish tank. With fish in it. The fish didn't talk, or sing, the fish tank didn't transform into a spacecraft or a hovercraft or anything. It just stayed there in the corner of his room for six hours.

MAGIC MUSHROOMS
*(the Liberty Cap mushroom
Psilocibe Semilanceata)*

There are innumerable other hallucinogens that grow around the world, but magic mushrooms are the only 'friendly' hallucinogens that grow naturally in Great Britain. They can be picked between mid-September and mid-October, and are most common in fields which have been recently grazed by cows or sheep (which explains all those people you've seen wandering around fields the morning after a rainstorm – and you thought they were bird watchers). The joy of Magic Mushrooms is that they're organic and free range, and also completely legal as long as you don't prepare them in any way (i.e. dry them or make tea with them).

THE EFFECTS
An L.S.D.-like trip, although mushrooms are generally somewhat kinder and smoother than acid. The effect usually lasts between 4 – 6 hours, with insane pointless giggling being a common feature.

UPS
They're wholesome, indigenous and free if you can be bothered to hunt them down.

DOWNS
The usual risks of taking any psychedelic, plus the small but possibly lethal risk of picking and eating the wrong type of mushroom. Liberty Caps don't taste great and some people do experience mild stomach upsets or diarrhoea after ingestion.
For a picture of the Liberty Cap mushroom try www.sporeworks.com/semilan.html

DRUG MYTHS AND HOUSEHOLD HIGHS

'Nothing gets you stoned quicker than a banana chopped up and smoked in a loo roll.' Or so says the rather ill-looking stranger standing next to you at the house party, moments before he runs off in search of the toilet. Tales of getting high on the cheap seem to do the rounds every year at university, in particular if they involve everyday stuff you can find in the kitchen. 'Household highs' unfortunately, rarely work, and can be rather dangerous if you start experimenting willy-nilly with smoking, snorting and injecting whatever you find lingering at the back of the fridge. Drug dealers may cut their speed with Ajax, but certainly won't waste their time trying to fob off clients with the filling from custard creams.

The following concoctions have all been tried at some time by over-zealous students in need of a hit, but we do strongly advise against these domestic science experiments, as they will only end in misery and loss of bowel control…

BANANA PEEL

Method. Scrape the goo off the peel, dry it on the radiator until brown, then smoke.
Result. Vomiting and diarrhoea.

NUTMEG

Method. Place several whole nutmegs in a coffee grinder, then pulverise with mortar and pestle. Ingest 10-15 grams.
Result. Vomiting and diarrhoea.

COKE AND ASPIRIN

Method. Based on the legend that one of the 'secret' ingredients of coca-cola is derived from the coca leaf (the source of cocaine), the idea here is, as our mate Mark Boucher from 5F explained – *'You see, the bubbles, like react with the chemicals in the aspirin and make cocaine. Honest, it's true. I swear to God.'*

In response to the cocaine allegations (not from Mark Boucher but other, more reputable sources) Coca-Cola admitted that while it had once been part of the ingredients (to give the drink that stimulating effect), it had for the last fifty years been replaced by caffeine. Of, course that doesn't totally denigrate Mark Boucher's claims as, through some bizarre alchemical process that drug dealers have kept secret for the last hundred years, dropping a couple of aspirins into a glass of pepsi might still produce 20 grams of pure coke, but we somewhat doubt it.

Results. No hit whatsoever. But, some would proclaim, a great hangover cure.

COFFEE GRANULES

Method. Smoking these is meant to simulate the effects of speed. Again, according to Mark Boucher from 5F, *'The caffeine goes straight into your brain and makes you go crazy.'* (Doesn't just drinking the stuff have exactly the same effect?)
Result. Vomiting and diarrhoea.

THE FLAVOUR SACHET FROM POT NOODLES

If snorted, this one actually works, but produces a psychedelic experience akin to watching Hollyoaks through the bottom of an empty beer glass, while someone nails planks of wood to your face. Not recommended.

HERBAL HIGHS

These days you can buy the herbal equivalent of most drugs – herbal marijuana, herbal hallucinogens, herbal stimulants, and even herbal Viagra. For some people these would seem to have the same appeal as no-caffeine coffee, or alcohol-free beer, but owing to increasing concerns about how long-term drug-use affects the health of the body (try anxiety, depression, low sex drive and insomnia for starters) herbal alternatives are well worth trying out for anyone who wants to get high without all the risks involved.

The manufacturers claim their stimulants to be 'totally safe, healthy and legal.' So what's the catch? Well, if you're expecting the full-on experience you'll be disappointed. Most admit that their products aren't effective one hundred percent of the time, but then this is true of all drugs (as anyone who's ever been ripped off by buying an aspirin, a tic-tac, or a piece of brown Play Dough will tell you).

The main drawback with herbal highs is the utterly stupid names that many of the manufacturers have called them in a misplaced bid to make them appear 'cool'.

Invariably called things like 'Merlin's Blend', 'Spirit Walk', 'Gandalf's Beard', and 'Druid's Fantasy*', going into a shop and requesting these is going to make you sound rather humiliatingly like a hobbit with learning difficulties, so it's probably best to buy via a website.

To purchase a whole variety of herbal highs, including ones that are claimed to increase your brain-power (and thus guarantee you a First), try:

www.naturalhighshop.com   www.naturallyhigh.co.uk

For further information on herbal highs contact: www.herbalhighs.co.uk

*What would a druid's fantasy be? Getting a fork-lift truck to help build Stonehenge? Gold lamé robes?

RECOMMENDED READING
The Doors of Perception
By Aldous Huxley

Taking its name from a line by William Blake, and in turn inspiring the band name of The Doors, Huxley's book is a candid and insightful essay on his experiments with the drug mescaline. Still pertinent today, his writing is coloured with fascinating insights into the mind and how we perceive the world around us. (There's a wonderful bit where he goes into raptures about the creases in his trousers whilst under the influence of the drug.)

A respected and celebrated author (Brave New World, The Island) Huxley demonstrated that not only could the psychedelic experience be a valid one, but also of extreme importance in re-conditioning the human soul. In fact, he valued the experience so much, he requested his wife to fetch him one last acid tab as, in his final hours, he lay on his bed close to death.

True Hallucinations / Food of the Gods / The Archaic Revival
By Terrance MacKenna

From incredible insights about the evolution of the human race through DMT/ mushroom/ yaje experiences, to bizarre journeys into the Amazon Basin in search of mythical shamanic hallucinogens, McKenna, in his three books, single-handedly attempts to make sense of the history of the use of psychedelic plant, and, more importantly, how it can still help us.

Far from the naïve hippy nonsense of the Sixties, McKenna's work is thoroughly researched and warmly written, and throughout the three books, puts forward some very convincing arguments in favour of the need for psychedelic plants in society and even suggests that, through taking them, he has discovered the missing link in the development of human consciousness and language. Powerful stuff.

Comic visionary, Bill Hicks

RECOMMENDED COMEDY

Rants in E minor / Arizona Bay / Dangerous / Relentless
Bill Hicks

'If you don't think drugs have done any good things, do me a favour, go home get out all your albums and CDs, and burn them. Because you know what? All those musicians who made all that great music that's enhanced your life throughout the years? They were real fucking high on drugs. Man, the Beatles were so high they let Ringo sing a couple of tunes.'

No comedian past or present has ever delivered such savagely funny and yet painfully honest material on the subject of drugs. Hicks was nothing short of a genius when it came to showing up the hypocrisy of the American government, the stupidity of the public's attitude towards recreational drug use, and the endless misinformation provided by the press. Of course Hicks' subject matter extended far beyond this, and his diatribes against the media, George Bush and non-smokers are equally profound and hilarious.

Hicks though, is not to everyone's taste. If your idea of good comedy is the Chuckle Brothers or 'Last of the Summer Wine'; this isn't for you. (I tried playing his routine about 'sucking Satan's cock' to my parents and they didn't laugh once- Ed.) We cannot, however, praise the work of this man highly enough. Bill Hicks was a true comic visionary whose work deserves seeking out.

DON'T SUFFER IN SILENCE

Long term and regular use of ANY recreational drug carries with it a whole host of potential health risks from loss of appetite, paranoia, anxiety and insomnia to actual brain damage and, in some cases, death. If you, or someone you know, is suffering due to drug abuse, it's vitally important the situation is dealt with straight away. Some universities actually have student bodies within the union to deal with drug problems but if yours doesn't, your first port of call should be the Welfare Officer or doctor.

For confidential advice call the 24 hour UK drug help-line 0800 776600 or check out the website www.ndh.org.uk

Another useful website with an open mind to drug use is www.urban75.com/drugs, which includes everything from essential information to an interview with Howard Marks.

SEX, LOVE & RELATIONSHIPS

Universities have always had a reputation for being melting pots of lust, free love, and sexual experimentation, but this is hardly remarkable – put several thousand 18-21 year olds together for any length of time and you're going to get enough hormones in the air to stun sparrows at two hundred yards. And according to a recent survey that found sex and clubbing currently riding high as students' top motives for going to university in the first place, it appears that you've already got it all planned anyway. Not surprising then, that something like 25% of people who go to university end up marrying someone they met whilst there.

Of course we are not trying to imply that university is simply one long shagfest. Whilst there are plenty of students who are keen to go bed-hopping from day one, there are plenty more whom, dare we say it, still enjoy a bit of romance. It is with such considerations that this chapter is full of advice on topics as diverse as coping with unrequited love to spicing up your sexual CV, and even includes a few sex horror stories of our own.

To conclude, while you shouldn't be unduly alarmed if you don't find true love during your studies, remember that this could be the last time you'll have the opportunity to stay in bed with someone for an entire fortnight until you reach retirement…

263

GOOD SOCIETIES FOR SEX

An unsurprisingly large number of students choose their particular society with a view to getting laid. And, of course, many of the societies know this, and will often employ their most attractive members to run the stalls at Freshers' Fair. (This is a plum job, since it's a good vantage point from which to flirt with the crop of new first years, so try and volunteer in your second year if you're anywhere approaching presentable.) Beware though; many naive young things have been lured into the likes of the Stupidly Dangerous Sports Society by a pretty face, only to end up getting smashed to bits whilst abseiling down the north face of K2 with a gorilla on their back.

However, if you are in need of a mate, it makes sense to hunt on the grounds of common interest. Your conversational gambits are ready-made for you, and at least anyone you chance to meet won't deem your hobbies or interests ridiculous or boring. Some societies however, are a much safer bet than others. A brief assessment follows:-

DRAMA SOC

Actors of both sexes are a notoriously promiscuous bunch. There is little point denying this, as no-one would (not even an actor). There are a variety of reasons for this. Firstly, the staging of a play can be a very intense and intimate experience, with passions enflamed and an equal number of slanging matches and one night stands. Secondly, actors are a befuddled lot, who often confuse their public roles with their private ones. This is easily done; the girl giving her Juliet can also give one to her Romeo and pass it off as 'method acting' or research. Thirdly, actors by their very nature are remarkably vain: praise someone's Ophelia or Tarzan, and say how they brought out the nascent sensuality of the part, and they'll be all over you.

NB. The only downside of this is that actors are incurable gossips – sleep with one of them and you can bet that by the next rehearsal, everyone down the Union Bar will know whether you spit or swallow.

SPORTS

A common misconception of sports societies is that they are single-sex affairs, composed either of boorish rugger-buggers who far prefer singing about sex than actually doing it, or of hardened, vicious female hockey players who shrug off broken shin bones as you would a paper cut. However, these societies also generally attract the fittest and most body conscious, and come Wednesday night after a particularly tough match, and there'll be hoards of these horny buggers in the union bar (regular exercise is one of the best ways of increasing the body's sex drive). And if it's you being carried on the shoulders of your team for saving that last penalty, you're bound to be someone's catch that evening.

CLASSICAL MUSIC

Believe it or not, that willowy girl who looks like butter wouldn't melt in her mouth, playing the Bach cello sonata with metronomic precision, is a seething pit of writhing sexuality. And that bloke singing 'Comfort ye.' is packing a 27-incher. OK, we could be generalising on this one a bit.

POLITICAL SOCIETIES

Naked ambition and power are undoubted aphrodisiacs. Why else would Ffyon have ever married old muppet face William Hague??

LOUSY SOCIETIES FOR SEX

SCIENCE FICTION

Be it Star Trek, Star Wars, Dr. Who, Red Dwarf, or Babylon 5, you will be met by a legion of emotionally-stunted degenerates, shouting *'Make it so!'* at you, and all wearing Vulcan ears. Nobody in these societies has ever had sex or ever will. They might as well have their genitals surgically removed.

ROLE-PLAYING

Anyone who likes to pretend to be an elf that conjures magical sprites to win the favours of the three-breasted Orc-Princess and thereby gain the sacred orb of Oragon is unlikely to be able to deal with sex in the real world. Not that he/she'll ever get the opportunity to find out.

CHESS

Enough said.

Top Student Chat Up Lines

"Would you like me to help you with that essay?"
"Why not pop round to my room to watch 'Sex and the City'?"
"I noticed that you weren't in the lecture yesterday. Why don't we go for a coffee and I'll explain what you missed?"
"Do you want to be in my degree film? It's called 'Naked Ecstasy'."
"God, I was really impressed by that point you made in Professor Shirovski's tutorial. Maybe we can talk about it over a drink."
"Would you like me to teach you to juggle?"

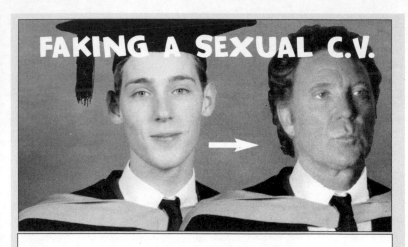

FAKING A SEXUAL C.V.

PHIL JACOBS
FIRST YEAR CHEMISTRY STUDENT.

REAL SEXUAL HISTORY:
Virgin. First kissed a girl at his 17th birthday party, but then passed out before things could go any further. Has never seen a woman's primary, or indeed secondary, sexual organs except on a porno video that his mate Danno nicked from his dad.

FAKE SEXUAL C.V.

1995
Aged 12, seduced by curvaceous, 18-year-old babysitter.
1996
Converted lesbian to heterosexuality with his sexual prowess.
1997
Aged 14, began affair with mum's sexy 34-year-old friend *("I'd just gone round to borrow a cup of sugar for me mum and she went upstairs, so I followed her and there she was, lying on the bed stark naked. It was fantastic – we did it all day")*.
1998
Aged 15, first proper girlfriend, Françoise, whom he met during a school holiday in France and who committed suicide when he left.
1999
Aged 16, first threesome with two Australian backpackers he met in the pub.
2000
Aged 17, travelled the world enjoying the erotic fruits of all lands. Starred in porn film in Indonesia to earn air-fare home.
2002
Left three girlfriends weeping behind at home and came to university.

With the exception of you, most people when they turn up at university, will have had limited sexual experience – the odd snog and a quick fumble in the toilets of the local pub being the high-point. This of course, won't impress anyone.

What you have to do of course is lie, lie like you've never done before, thus presenting yourself unashamedly as a sophisticated love god/goddess who has swum deep in the river of Eros.

Note: it is, however, important not to get your facts mixed up. People will get suspicious if the story where you claim to have lost your virginity keeps changing countries. So once you've carefully constructed your sexual C.V, ensure you commit it to memory. The following examples below should provide a few useful pointers…

CHARLOTTE ETHERINGTON
FIRST YEAR MUSIC STUDENT.

REAL SEXUAL HISTORY:
Chaste relationship with childhood sweetheart between ages of 12 and 16. Aged 17 – lost virginity in brief fling involving a local window cleaner with own motorbike.

FAKE SEXUAL C.V.

1995
Aged 15, ran off to London with famous poet and had tempestuous affair before being brought back by mum and dad.
1999
Aged 16, affair with Mr. Richards, her computer science teacher, which led to his dismissal. Cover-up prevented it from getting into the papers. Also had first lesbian experience with best friend from choir up in the organ loft.
2000
Affair with famous married rock star she refuses to name. Attended orgy with him in Beverly Hills.
2001
Passionate one night stand with famous married footballer she also refuses to name.
2002
Reason for current celibacy – actually conducting secret affair with famous married politician she refuses to name.

DITCHING YOUR CHILDHOOD SWEETHEART

Moving away to university can mean for some people, leaving behind a loved one. This can cause quite a bit of heartache, especially during the first term when you may be feeling more vulnerable and apprehensive about finding your feet. There will also no doubt, be concerns about fidelity – will your partner stay faithful? Will you? The stark reality is that few of these relationships survive long-term. For good or for worse, as one (or both) parties start new lives with new friends and new surroundings, that old relationship will start to wither. In many cases this is for the best, freeing both individuals and allowing them a new lease of life in their new environment. Of course, this doesn't apply to everyone, there are those rare occasions where the couple who started out throwing biscuits at each other in kindergarten actually end up marrying and living happily ever after, but on the whole you'll have to accept that your first term's correspondence may just read like this…

October 4th

Dearest Jason,

I have only been here for one day, but I already miss you so much. Everything seems so strange and new, and I long for the days when we would walk together by the river, arm in arm.

I haven't really got to know anyone here properly yet – I'm in halls with about ten other people on my corridor. The only one who seems really nice is Carol, the girl who lives next door to me. We had a chat this morning and I'm sure we're going to be great friends. The boy who lives down the end of my corridor is REALLY annoying – his name's Crispin or something and he's always playing his music really loudly, getting really drunk and singing along at the top of his voice. Someone set all the fire extinguishers off at 2am last night and I'm sure it was him. Carol says we should report him but I'm not sure. I don't want to make any enemies this early on!

Anyway PLEASE PLEASE PLEASE write back as soon as you can, and come to visit me. (I know it's a long way but PLEASE come and see me.) Not seeing you is driving me mad.

All my love forever my darling,

Sarah,
XXXXXXXXXXXXXXXXXXXX

October 9th

Dear Jason,

Thanks ever so much for your LOVELY LOVELY letter my little bunny. It made me cry (I know. I'm SO soppy.) I read it over and over again and it was just like you were here in my little room with me.

Gosh! What a week! I've been SO busy with all my lectures and tutorials and everything. I was worried that it would be too much work for me but Carol (the girl next door.) said that if you make a really detailed timetable and stick to it then you'll be okay. So thanks to Carol!

That idiot Crispin is in my sociology class, worse luck! He's such a pain! He's always making jokes (which aren't in the least bit funny) and making silly noises to distract Professor Shirovski when he's trying to speak. I hope he gets thrown off the course.

Anyway, I've got LOADS of work to do, so goodbye my lovely love.

Please write soon!

Love you loads and loads,

Sarah

XXX

October 26th

Dear Jason,

I'm so sorry I haven't written back sooner, but I've been so bloody busy. (I've got two essays to do by Thursday.) Thanks for your letter. It was so full of interesting news. I'm sorry you didn't get your promotion, but never mind.

Must dash now, as Carol and I are going to a party (!) on the third floor.

Will write again soon,

love you!

Sarah

X

November 10th,

Hi Jason,

God, I feel really bad for not writing back sooner. Crispin says that guilt is bourgeois but he says that about everything! I got to know Crispin really well at the party the other week and he's actually really good fun. I think you'd like him. Just shows what a bad judge of character I am!

Crispin and I played a great joke on Carol last night. We put little holes in all her eggs and then blew out the insides and then put the empty shells back in the fridge. It took hours but it was worth it when we saw her face this morning. I nearly pissed myself and I thought Crispin was going to have a heart attack. (Don't tell anyone it was us when you come down, but she deserved it the miserable cow.)

Anyway, write soon and tell me when you're going to come down. (I've had my hair cut really short so I hope you recognize me!)

Crispin sends his love,

yours,

Sarah

P.S. I was sorry to hear about you being made redundant.

November 15th

Jason,

I tried ringing your mum last night but no one was in. Listen - you CAN'T come down this Friday. I'm sorry, but I've got five essays to finish before the end of term and Professor Shirovski is going to put me on the sub-dean's list if I don't do them. (He's had it in for me ever since me and Crispin spiked his coffee with LSD.)

Sorry, sorry, sorry. I'll make it up to you when I see you at the end of term

Sarah,

P.S. STOP PRESS. Carol has dropped out of university with psychological problems. I always knew she was mental.

December 6th

Jason,

Phew! Finally got those sodding essays done. Crispin was a big help. I don't know what I'd have done without him. Going to your brother's party on the 15th would be great, it was so sweet of you to think of me, but I'm afraid I won't be back. Term ends on the eighth but Crispin has invited me to spend a week at his parents' house up in Shropshire with his friends Tristram, Toby, and Ben (they're great guys), so I probably won't be back until about the 18th.

Sorry to muck up your plans but will see you soon,

Sarah

December 17th

Jason,

God, this letter is difficult to write, so I'd better just go ahead and write it. I won't be back for Christmas - Crispin's parents have invited me to go to Monaco with them until the New Year. As you've probably guessed, me and Crisp are an item. I never meant for this to happen, but it did.

People say that it's difficult to have a relationship when you're living apart, and I guess they're right. Things hadn't been going well between us for some time, and I suppose it's because I've changed. When I look back to how I was when we were going out it's like I'm looking at someone else, a complete stranger.

I'm sorry to have done this to you but let's face it, it wouldn't have worked out. I'm sure you'll find someone else up in Mansfield. Try to forget about me.

Anyway, have a merry Christmas,

Sarah

P.S. Please don't ever write again.

TYPES OF STUDENT COUPLES

There are many different kinds of couples you can meet at university, and they are all, to some degree, dreadful. Learn to recognise their distinguishing features at a glance, and then, if at all possible, avoid them. At best they'll make you feel like a gooseberry and at worst you'll move in with them and they'll make your life an absolute, living, screaming hell. Here are just a few of the worst offenders…

The Siamese Twins

This couple move into the same room (usually the girl's) in the first week of the first term. From then on they work together, play together, cook together, go shopping together, and remain absolutely inseparable wherever they go. Their names merge (Janice and Steve become 'Janiceandsteve' for example) and they soon become dependent to the degree that neither can agree to do anything – even have a cup of tea – without at first consulting the other. To see one unaccompanied is as shocking as seeing an art student with a side-parting.

The Open Relationship

This couple spend all day every day telling everyone that they have a 'free and open' relationship and really wouldn't mind if the other slept around. Their arrangement works perfectly until one of them actually does get off with somebody else, whereupon all hell breaks loose and six months of pent-up jealousy and resentment are released. You are best avoiding both of them for a good few years after this.

The On-Off Couple

These are a nightmare. They split up and get back together again every fortnight, with all the attendant slanging matches, smashed crockery and hysterical crying fits. Invariably, you'll sit up until seven in the morning comforting one or other of them, only to have all your good advice instantly disregarded when they get back together again. Never share a house with an on-off couple, and never, never get involved with one of them during one of the brief periods when they are separated. Your heart will be crushed by the juggernaut of their blind obsession.

Noel and Meg

This couple met on drugs, organise their social and personal lives around drugs, and make love on drugs. If ever either of them stopped taking drugs for more than half an hour, he/she would realise that they have nothing whatsoever in common and the relationship would end.

The Tempestuous, Short-lived Relationship

The most common type of university couple. Students have the amazing ability to compress a forty-year affair into a week, especially in the first year, and especially if living in halls. Like some obscene version of Solomon Grundy they meet on Monday, declare undying love on Tuesday, break up bitterly on Wednesday, get back together on Thursday, have their second honeymoon period on Friday, have a cataclysmic row on Saturday, and finally say their last goodbyes on Sunday. On Monday they begin the process all over again again with other people. Consequently you will hear people complaining of how they've wasted their lives on another, to find they've only been going out for three days.

A Short Guide To Translating The Hidden Meanings Behind Being Given The Brush-off

"It's not you, it's me." – "It's not me, it's you."
"You're too nice." – "You're too dull."
"I just don't think of you in that way." – "You're ugly."
"I'm just not looking for a relationship at the moment." – "I am looking for a relationship at the moment, just not with you."
"I don't want to ruin our friendship." – "Can't you get it into your thick head that I just don't fancy you??"

The Odd Couple

UNREQUITED LOVE

"Never trust a guy who hasn't had his heart broken."
Author, Raymond Chandler

Unrequited love is a tricky one. Fancying someone who either doesn't reciprocate, or is – for various reasons – unattainable, is something that happens to most of us at least once or twice in our lives (not least at university) and it can cause a great deal of heartache and pain, not to mention buggering up your studies and turning you into a babbling wreck. And a great number of the problems that student counsellors deal with are to do with matters of the heart.

The usual nuggets of advice people give on how to cope with a broken heart will be of little comfort, and rarely work. Losing yourself in your course is a non-starter. It's hard enough to get the requisite work done as it is; and drowning your sorrows only leads to stupendous hangovers and eventually, alcoholism. As for avoiding all contact with the person, well that's not always possible, especially if it's your roommate. There are no golden solutions to your heartache and misery, but we present below a few pointers to help you weather the storm.

I. REMEMBER – THERE'S NO WAY YOU CAN MAKE SOMEONE FANCY YOU

The rules of sexual attraction are a mystery to everyone. However many funky dance moves you execute, or bunches of flowers you send, there's no way to force, cajole, or trick someone into liking you. You'll just end up indulging in increasingly ludicrous displays until you utterly alienate the person you were trying to woo.

2. TRY NOT TO BORE YOUR FRIENDS

While the subject of your tragic, doomed love may seem of immense importance to you, your mates may begin to tire of you recounting it after the 700th time. Friendship does have its unspoken limits, and if you bend too many ears too often you may end up not only unrequited but friendless too. If you must bore someone (and you probably need to) talk to your personal tutor, counsellor, or chaplain. Make them work for their wage-packets.

3. DON'T ROMANTICISE YOUR SITUATION

It's appealing to think that your situation is unbearably tragic, that no one has loved or suffered as you. Given time, you yourself will find how you built your fixation up into some sort of grand opera ridiculous. So think how it must appear to everyone else.

A Sorry Take of Unrequited Love from the Editor

In my first year at university, I had a huge crush on a girl called Vanessa. Looking back I find it utterly inconceivable and embarrassing, as she was a pompous blazer-wearing Thatcherite from Kidderminster. Sleeping with the enemy must have had some perverse appeal back then, (a bit like the coupling of Buffy and Spike), but whatever the case, I was totally smitten. And of course her complete lack of interest in me (except for us being 'just good friends'), only served to fuel the fire. In my infatuation, I managed to do just about all the wrong things- I got drunk one night and told her how I felt whilst climbing into her bed (which understandably freaked her out), I visited her at her parents home in Kidderminster over summer, which simply tugged more at my heartstrings, but the icing on the cake was introducing her to my best friend as inevitably, they ended up in bed together the next day.

As a consequence, I suffered emotional torment throughout my first year, and it wasn't until I moved out of my halls of residence that I managed to forget her. We lost touch after that, and I never saw her again until, by chance, years later in a pub in Brighton, I spotted her. It was really, really strange to see her again. She hadn't changed and was still wearing those godawful blazers. I realized that, had my former self got its way, I would probably have let her turn me into a blazer-wearing, right-wing yuppie like her. There's a lesson here I think we can all learn from.

Oh, but incidentally, if by any chance you happen to be reading this Vanessa, please get in touch. I still think of you every day…*(editor breaks down weeping into his ashtray, whisky glass and copy of The Communist Manifesto)*

INTERNATIONAL RELATIONSHIPS

One of the wonderful things about university is that you get to meet all sorts of interesting people from all over the world, without the hassle of having to get on a plane. And unlike being in the army, you don't have to kill them.

Foreign students can seem like exotic and fascinating creatures, especially if they speak with a lilting sexy accent, drive a scooter and dress in skimpy swim-wear during tutorials. Others just seem physically superior; Scandinavians and Americans especially seem to have been genetically modified to be bigger and better. Falling in love with a foreign student therefore can be very exciting; you have so much to learn about their country of origin, culture and habits, whilst they have the joy of being educated by you in the

catchphrases and theme tunes of tacky Eighties and Nineties TV shows. Being romantically involved with a foreign student can also afford you the prospect of international travel, and sex in a country where there's less chance of drizzle should you attempt to try it outdoors.

There can however be downsides. If you meet and fall in love with someone whilst on a year out/ placement, after the year they are here, or you there, what then? If you are serious, it's long terms of loneliness and desperately avoiding temptation while you work all hours to scrape together an airfare for the visits. Then if you are still serious, sooner or later someone has to leave his or her country and come and live with the other. Are you ready to give up expensive beer, bad weather and the NHS just so you can lead some frivolous, pleasure-laden existence in Barcelona or San Francisco? What if the lure of our splendid railways and beautiful shopping centres plays too heavily on your heartstrings? Remember, if you move to America for example, they make you jump through incredible hoops just so you can work. You have to naturalise after a certain period, which involves swearing allegiance to the flag!!

Of course, there are no easy answers. You will have to make some tough decisions if serious about wanting to continue an international relationship, but as the cliché goes, love will find a way. If you're truly devoted to someone, the mere fact that they live on a different part of the globe shouldn't be the end of the world. But never seeing them again just might be…

S█K HORROR STORI██

These tales of sexual miscreance are compiled from the annals of our own misspent years at university, mixed with stories that were recounted to us either via e-mail, or whilst visiting different universities around the UK. In some cases, the names have been changed to protect the terminally embarrassed.

TIE ME UP! TIE ME DOWN!

"I once had a deeply embarrassing incident whilst living with my American girlfriend in Boston during the summer holidays. We were in the front room of a big, clapperboard shared student house, with a large Walton's style verandah in front of our window that had a few steps up to it. Our bed was an old iron four-poster in front of the window.

One day, while feeling frisky and adventurous, I agreed to being tied up naked to this bed while my girlfriend did the business to me, as it were. We were having great fun, and I was in a state of some excitement when she decided to nip into the bathroom for some baby oil.

As I looked up I realized the Venetian blinds were not totally closed. Certainly, no-one from the road could catch a glimpse, but if you were on a ladder painting the front of the verandah, it would be possible to see directly in.

Unexpectedly someone was. An elderly American worker was staring down at me, with the kind of detached fascination people have on their face when watching snails mate in nature documentaries, his paintbrush paused in mid air. Our eyes met. We are not taught in England what the polite form of address is in this situation, but it would have been easy enough to say something as he was only four feet away and the window was open, it being blisteringly hot.

I was just clearing my throat to make an opening gambit about the weather when my naked, now oiled-up girlfriend walked into the room. This seemed to break the Great American Working Man from his reverie, and his face cracked into a broad, salacious grin. "You two kids havin' fun?" It was a statement of the obvious, but a 250-volt shock could not have had a greater effect upon my girlfriend, who screamed, ran for the blinds, and curled up in a ball of pure, whimpering, agonised embarrassment. It took me some minutes of whispered exhortation to even get her to untie me, and although within a short while we were laughing at the funny side, the moment had passed, and I did not get my exotic jollies that day".

Third year Leeds University student

NAKED LUNCH

"A mate studying at Leeds, was in a band that played Nottingham university. After the gig, and a bit drunk, he was chatted up by a girl who took him back to her room in halls. Halfway through some heavy petting he realised his bladder was bursting, so he reluctantly sneaked off to relieve himself. He returned some five minutes later to find the girl lying naked on her bed, smearing handfuls of her own shit over her breasts and laughing her head off. Not surprisingly, he freaked out, grabbed his clothes and made a run for it."

(As told to us by a second year student from Warwick University, though we suspect the story actually happened to him)

MISERY

"In my third year at university, I got to know a couple of very lovely Media Studies students, Clare and Lauren, who lived round the corner and possessed an overbearing streak of wicked humour that would have had Graham Norton running for cover.

One weekend, Clare invited down her ex-boyfriend Rob, down for a couple of days. Arriving quite late on the Friday, Rob claimed to be suffering a migraine and declined the offer to accompany the girls to the pub.

Halfway into the evening, Lauren, realising she'd forgotten her inhaler, headed back to the house to get it as her asthma was playing up.

Once in the house she entered her bedroom to discover the jaw-dropping sight of Rob, kneeling on the floor with a pair of her knickers held to his nose, and masturbating profusely.

Now Lauren had 3 choices ahead of her:
1) Scream in horror while running out of the room
2) Scream in disgust while trying to remove his gonads with a pair of scissors
3) Scream with laughter and run down the pub to tell everyone
That's right, she chose option three. The poor guy spent the next two days utterly shame-faced as the girls dragged him round the various bars of the university, giggling and laughing as they re-told the story to everyone they came across.
Women can be so cruel..."

Editor's own account from his four glorious years at Coventry University

THE MAN WHO KNEW TOO MUCH

"A second-year Geographer, Steve, was keen on a fellow student, (who, he had every reason to believe, was equally keen on him), and so went to visit her in her campus room one afternoon, where they chatted and discovered a mutual fondness for one another. At length, she offered Steve a cup of tea and he said yes. While she was making the tea in the kitchen, a repairman from Radio Rentals appeared and asked her the whereabouts of the girl who needed her stereo fixing.

'That's me' she replied, and directed him to her room. A minute later he reappeared, looking slightly disconcerted.

'Sorry Miss,' he said 'You did say room three, didn't you?'

'Yes.' she replied.

'The one with the naked bloke in it?' asked the repairman. She returned to her room to find our friend struggling hurriedly into his trousers."

Second Year student, Bretton Hall

THE JERK

"After his first couple of weeks at university, a friend of mine sat down to write two letters home, one to his parents and one to an old schoolmate. A few days later he received a call from his friend, who was perplexed both by the formality and tediousness of the missive, and by the fact that he had been addressed as 'mum and dad'. Seconds later, he received a call from his mother, demanding an explanation for the following:-

> Dear Arsehole,
>
> University's tops. I haven't done a stroke of work, I'm too busy drinking, popping pills and getting laid. I think my cock's going to fall off. You should come down here and get stuck in!
>
> Yours,
> Dan 'shagmaster' Monfeld

He managed to convince his mum that it was all a prank initiated by his friends.

Second Year student Sussex University

THE BOY WITH THE THORN IN HIS SIDE

"It is a very bad thing to be unfaithful. It is worse still to be caught doing it. But a very good friend of mine, who I shall call Rob, had an unusually embarrassing example of being caught cheating during our time at university. He had for some time had "a thing" for a very curvaceous young girl called Claire, but was stymied by the fact that she was very much taken.

One evening he contrived to get drunk with her, and got invited back to her place where more wine was supped and dope smoked. An early morning of illicit passion was joyfully embarked upon, and the next day, after a few more stolen kisses, he strolled home with a light heart.

After another twenty-four hours, Rob decided to ring his paramour to see if she would like more of the same. Instead of the whispered sweet nothings he was expecting, he got a total earful. How could he do something so dreadful? The fucker had ruined everything and he was never to ring again. After some frenzied ringing of mutual friends, a terrible reality emerged.

In the heat of the moment, somebody's extremity had pressed the record button on the stereo by the bed. This had faithfully documented the whole seedy event in Dolby B, then rewound itself to the start of the side. On his return, the boyfriend pressed play, and after five minutes of his favourite Smiths album, was rudely awoken from his relaxing mope by the bracing sounds of his girlfriend having loud and passionate sex with another man!'

From the sordid memoirs of our own Dave Mounfield

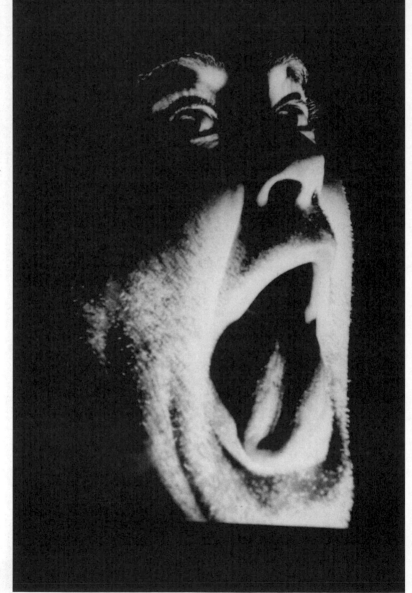

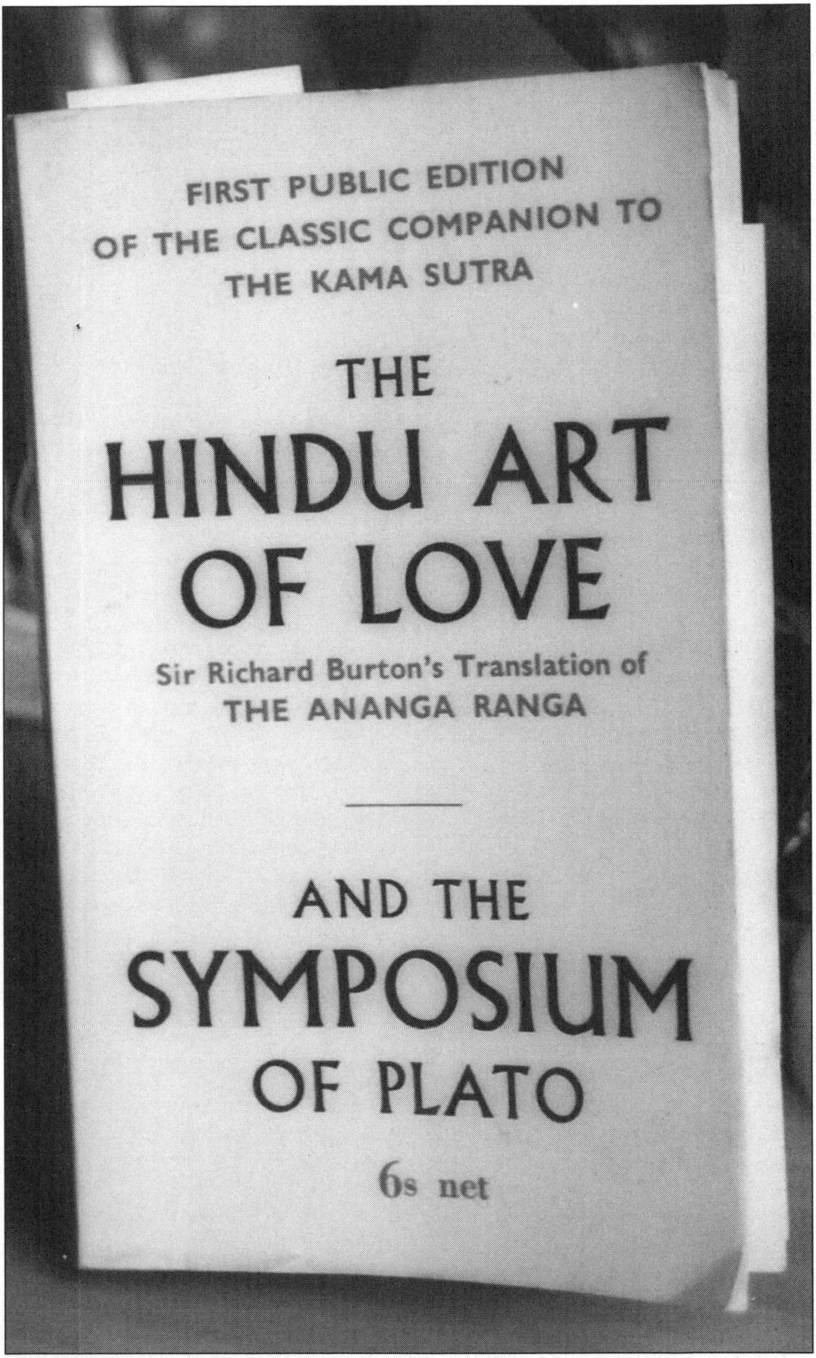

FIRST PUBLIC EDITION
OF THE CLASSIC COMPANION TO
THE KAMA SUTRA

THE
HINDU ART
OF LOVE

Sir Richard Burton's Translation of
THE ANANGA RANGA

AND THE
SYMPOSIUM
OF PLATO

6s net

COMING OUT

With an ever-growing number of lesbian, gay, bi and even tri-sexual students now, 'coming out' at University is an increasingly relevant issue to many.

It can however, be an intimidating affair, especially if you still fear the judgement of others (which is understandable) or, more importantly, fear that you'll be cut off from your vast family inheritance.

If, however, having arrived into a liberating and safe university environment, you feel confident enough to run screaming into every lecture that you're proud to be gay – that's cool. For the more apprehensive, our best advice is to go join the LGBT society and meet some like-minded souls, have a natter with your LGBT officer, or confide in a friend you can trust. But for goodness' sake, don't keep it locked away.

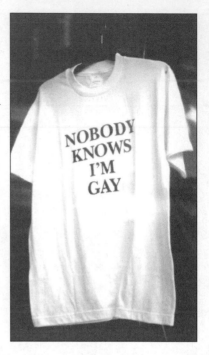

WHICH UNIVERSITY?

Your choice of university can play a crucial role in your happiness. Choosing somewhere with a large and supportive gay network is important. This usually means a large city. Pick somewhere small and relatively provincial like Oxford (with its one gay pub and one gay club-night) or, worse still, Royal Holloway near Staines and you could well find yourself feeling claustrophobic and frustrated by the end of it all. Below are a few recommendations as to where to find a good gay scene.

Birmingham Being the second largest city in the UK, it's not surprising that the gay scene is vibrant here. But can you cope with the accent?

Manchester One of the UK's largest cities, which, despite its reputation for nurturing knuckle scraping heteros like the Gallagher brothers and Sean Ryder, actually boasts its own gay village.

Brighton The gay capital of the UK, and far and away the best place to go to if you want to meet thousands of like-minded souls. There's everything there from clubs, pubs and shops to gay drama groups, annual parades and even the 'bushes' down on the seafront where unimaginable naughtiness goes on. (For full details get a copy of the Cheeky Guide to Brighton)

London Large city down south with the odd gay club.

While these three have, by a long way, the largest gay communities in the UK, it is generally true that the bigger the city, the better the scene. So even if you're off to Edinburgh, Bristol, Liverpool, Leeds, Cardiff or Sheffield for example, you can expect a thriving scene with enough club-nights and events to keep even the most rampant queen happy.

OUT OF THE FRYING PAN INTO THE FIRE?

By Daniel Menhinnitt, Sussex University Graduate

So, you find you've come to some conclusions about yourself. You have sexual feelings for someone of the same sex but just as you think the worst is over, you suddenly realise that you've got to find some way to express this to those around you; your friends and family. Unless, that is, you decide to stay in the closet for the rest of your days, and with your clothes already in there, I doubt it would be very comfortable.

'How will my straight friends react to the news? What will my family's attitude be? Will they be shocked? Disgusted? How do I tell them? Should I just let them find out?' I myself considered all these questions before coming out. One year on, I decided to tackle them by talking to the only people that could answer them, my straight friends and my family.

Those I asked told me they experienced a number of mixed feelings when they heard the news. Many were surprised, but at the same time felt that they should have known it all along. One friend said that everything fell into place, 'like walking through a door of realisation.' For some there was a degree of concern; how would this change the relationship? My family were in general, very accepting, so I was fortunate.

When coming out, you can't really expect your friends to be euphoric for you. While this might be a life changing moment for you, many of my friends will take it as just another part of life. Also, don't expect them to be accepting, or wholly relaxed about it immediately, after all it takes a long time – sometimes years – for people to come to terms with being gay, lesbian or bisexual themselves, so should we really expect our nearest and dearest to deal with it straight away? They may also feel unsure how to act around you. Should they turn it into a celebration and throw you an outrageous coming out party, or just consign it to the back of their mind and carry on as before?

Therefore, when coming out, the best advice I can give is to be patient. Whilst you may experience negativity from some (and you may wish to ask yourself if you are willing to accept bigots in your life) your (true) friends and family will come to terms with the news if given a little time.

Also it is probably better to tell them yourself rather than letting them find out, even though that might be the easier option for you. Telling them face-to-face gives them the opportunity to ask questions, to talk about it with you, and as a result, they are more likely to realise that it's not a joke, or rush decision.

While it is a tough challenge, and for many, a scary experience filled with fears or a complete upheaval in your life, ultimately it feels great to be honest about who you are.

Thanks to the USSU and Unisex for their help

SEX, LOVE & RELATIONSHIPS

Do's and Don'ts of 'Coming Out'

DON'T

- Expect immediate acceptance
- Get violent or depressive or vent your anger or frustration on somebody who is only trying to understand you
- Apologise (**NEVER** apologise)
- Be spiteful – don't come out just to hurt people

DO

- Judge the timing
- Evaluate the risks of telling someone
- Tell someone that you expect to be sympathetic first, be that a friend or person whose role is supportive
- Be honest and open with the people who care about you
- Get to know gay people who can support you

DON'T SUFFER IN SILENCE

Depressed? Lonely? Heartbroken? Worried that you might be pregnant and don't know where to turn for help?? Talking to friends can always help put things into perspective, though for more professional advice your Welfare Officer should nudge you in the right direction and provide you with the support you need. (For issues of pregnancy it is, of course, essential that you visit the Health Centre where they will be discreet and provide you with the facts you need, rather than you spending weeks needlessly worrying if your period is really late). If you are unfortunate enough to be the victim of a sexual assault, please, please report it. If you can't face going to the Police initially, then go to the Welfare Office. They can help you through. You owe it to yourself and the safety of the student population.

HEALTH & WELL-BEING

Every time you masturbate...
God kills a kitten
Please, think of the kittens

Unless you were raised by wolves, or Tubbs and Edward, you should have been nurtured by parents who, forever worried about your health, expressed their concern by enforcing such rules as: not sitting too close to the telly, not going out with your hair wet, not eating without washing your hands and not kissing the dog. Alongside this you were probably dragged, on occasions, to health clinics to be poked, measured, made to cough, bathed in radiation and injected with dead germs.

Having attained adulthood, you alone are now entirely responsible for your own well-being, and are likely to undo at least some of your parents' good work with your newfound but erratic lifestyle through irregular sleeping patterns, the stress of meeting deadlines, holding down a crappy job in the freezer department of Sainsbury's, living in a damp bedsit, eating sandwiches in the library canteen and never cleaning the kitchen. But a quick glance through the info below might save you some serious discomfort or even, conceivably, your life.

DEALING WITH DOCTORS

Any health treatment begins with a visit to your GP (General Practitioner), and most colleges and universities have some kind of Health Centre with which you should register (i.e. turn up and fill in a form) at an early opportunity, not least because access to other forms of NHS treatment such as eye and dental care require that you be registered with a GP first.

Doctors are an odd bunch and dealing with them can be tricky. They hold a position of authority and importance, and the high social esteem they command (possibly because we would all love to believe they really are infallible) can be daunting and unnerving. It's not an uncommon experience to arrive in a consulting room and immediately forget most of what you wanted to say, feel like an idiot and a time-waster and come away feeling bewildered and no better. (Come to think of it that may be a syndrome in its own right).

It's important to remember that the doctor is just an ordinary human being who is offering a public service. Your doctor may even be quite a crap one who needs you to explain in simple language why you're there, in which case it can be helpful to write down your reasons for visiting and refer to it during your consultation.

Although student Health Centres are generally well staffed, doctors can be busy people with heavy workloads and one can end up after a consultation feeling hurried, fobbed off and not taken seriously. This is the unfortunate result of many years of under-funding, and in some respects the NHS has become like the DSS: you sometimes have to make a real fuss for something to be done. If you are worried and don't feel like you are getting serious attention, remember that you have a right to proper treatment, so consider either asking to see a different doctor entirely, or bringing a friend or relative with you for support.

To emphasise this point, one student we met (who wished to remain anonymous) went to visit his doctor in the first year of term with recurring stomach cramps...

"I still remember the incident with horror; it was like some awful Monty Python sketch. The doctor, barely out of college himself, listened to my history of stomach troubles for about two minutes, then he nodded wisely, as if he'd figured out the problem, then asked me to bend over while he had a good prod around up my bottom with his finger! I have still to this day no idea at all what he was looking for (maybe he thought you'd nicked his pen? – Ed) and he certainly never told me. I left embarrassed and puzzled by the experience but learned to be much more demanding and forthright in future visits."

PRESCRIPTIONS, DENTAL CARE, EYE CARE, WIGS AND SURGICAL TRUSSES

The halcyon days when a student could claim a brand new set of colour-coordinated surgical support stockings and a Beatles wig are, sadly, long gone. You can still theoretically get all of the above things for nothing but only if:

· **you are pregnant**
· **you have had a baby within the last twelve months**
· **you are under 19 and in full-time education**
· **you are over 80 and in full-time education**

Otherwise it's well worth obtaining an HC11 from your medical centre or local DSS. This form is used to assess your eligibility by examining your financial incomings and outgoings. It's really long and dull and takes ages to fill out but could mean free prescriptions, eye and dental care. Make the most of it – once you're out of uni you could be paying up to £30 just to get someone to look at your teeth, never mind scraping off the green bits and polishing them.

Say, 'aaagggghhh!'

SEXUAL HEALTH
CONDOMS

As you are doubtless aware, the safe sex message, whether partaking in vaginal, oral or anal sex, is: CONDOMS! And along with the Femidom, they are still currently the only way to prevent bodily fluids from being swapped during sexual intercourse (unless you share the same perversions as a couple in Brighton we know who can both achieve orgasm simply by the girl throwing rubber rings over her boyfriend's penis from a distance of about 5 metres!?!).

For those who like to know such things, the first professional maker and seller of condoms was Mrs. Phillips of the Strand, London, a brothel keeper in the early 18th century who exported them all across Europe. At that time they were made from the intestines of various animals (much like the stuff sausages are wrapped in) but nowadays condoms are mostly made of latex rubber or polyurethane and come in a wide variety of size, colours, flavours, strengths, thicknesses and themes. Be aware however, that condoms still have their limitations. They are particularly vulnerable to Vaseline, oils and fats, which have the effect of weakening the latex almost instantly and making the condom much more likely to split. Oils and fats includes: ice-cream, chocolate, extra virgin olive oil, linseed oil and high-grade engine oil, so if you need extra lubrication for penetration, keep away from the fridge and stick instead to KY jelly, which you can buy in tubes at the chemist.

Useful tips for the Learner Driver

- Make sure your condom has a British Standard Kite Mark, and is not out of date or showing signs of mould.
- Always squeeze the tip of the condom before putting it on, as this helps release trapped air.
- After male orgasm, hold onto the base of the condom and withdraw gently.
- Without due care, the condom can get left inside the vagina, leaving the sperm you so carefully imprisoned, free to swim off and cause havoc.
- Standing on a used condom with bare feet and a hangover is a deeply unpleasant feeling – dispose of them as soon as possible, but not down the loo as they tend to float.
- Never blow up a condom and put it on your head, it's really not very funny.

HIV / AIDS

Although infection rates for HIV have been steadily dropping for some years, the number of cases in the UK of heterosexual transmission of the HIV virus, which leads to AIDS, have recently eclipsed those for gay sex. Sleeping around without protection is, as ever, the equivalent of playing Russian Roulette. And remember, HIV can lurk undetected in the system for years before manifesting itself, so often the carrier isn't aware they have been infected and you really can't tell who might have the virus, even if they look really nice. Your Health Centre or Union should have free condoms on offer. We strongly recommend you take advantage of this.

For more information on HIV/ AIDS try The Terrance Higgins trust www.tht.org.uk
Or the National AIDS helpline: 0800 567123 open 24 hours daily.

CHLAMYDIA

A nasty low-down sneaky fungal infection, Chalmydia is currently racing up the Pox Parade towards the number one 'most prevalent' position. This is partly because it's a relatively new sexually transmitted disease, and partly because 70% of women and 50% of men who have Chalmydia have no symptoms at all and remain blissfully unaware. When they do manifest, symptoms include:

* Pain when passing water.
* An unusual or unpleasant discharge from the vagina or penis (as opposed to pleasant ones).
* Pain in the tummy.
* Bleeding between periods or after sex in women.

If left untreated, Chlamydia can cause fertility problems in both men and women and long-term problems for women such as chronic pelvic inflammatory disease and damage to the Fallopian tubes. If you bear any of the above symptoms, stick on your cleanest pants/ knickers and go and see the doc.

THE 'MORNING AFTER' PILL

This is now available over-the-counter, so you don't have to endure the pursed lips and knitted brows of some frosty old nurse in order to get it, though it will set you back about twenty quid a shot. These pills can be taken up to 3 days after sex, but the earlier the better. Generally two pills are taken, one as soon as possible and the other 12 hours later. If first taken within 24 hours after sex the possibility of pregnancy is reduced by about 95%. But the 'Morning After Pill' is not something to be taken lightly. It is very powerful and its potentially harmful effects have been likened to ingesting a small nuclear bomb, meaning that you may experience abdominal pains, breast tenderness, headaches and nausea. If you should vomit within three hours of taking the pill you should speak to a doctor or pharmacist who may give you extra pills, or anti-vomiting drugs.

PENIS SIZE

While we know there are more important topics, the webmasters at www.studenthealth.co.uk say 'Penis Size' is their most accessed link. In short (oh, sorry) the average erect penis is 5 inches long, which is nowhere near as big as common myths would have you believe. And it's also not commonly realised that women's front-bottom dimensions vary too, so all you actually need is a rough genital match (though how to figure this out with a potential partner beforehand may be a tricky one).

If penis size is a critical issue for you then surgical intervention is a possibility, but the procedure is gruesome and the science imperfect, and you may end up with a partially-numb Frankenstein penis that points down when it's excited, like a dowsing rod, or one that bends in the middle like a clown's sad face. All things considered, it's probably best to leave it as nature intended.

MENTAL HEALTH

Increasingly these days, many students are suffering some form of mental illness, from depression to anorexia. And whether it's down to the long-term effects of living with overbearing parents, bullying at school, a lack of confidence, drug abuse, bad diet or the repeated anal probings from extraterrestrial abducters, the numbers are, worryingly, on the increase. Your student years are an especially likely time for these issues to arise owing to the stress and excesses often experienced during university, not to mention the fact that most students are, for the first time, managing their own lives without parental guidance and support, and are probably a long way from home too.

Hardly anyone leaves home perfectly well-adjusted and fully prepared for the world (and no one likes those who do, anyway). If your home life hasn't been happy and you've been counting the days until you can leave, you may find that escape isn't that simple, and old anxieties and problems have travelled with you. Despite the abundant social opportunities and activities and all the new acquaintances, many students go through painful periods of misery and loneliness, and although these will sometimes sort themselves out, there's no point in suffering needlessly – you don't need to be officially classed as 'mentally ill' to ask for help.

ANXIETY

If emotional problems were the menu of a greasy spoon café, anxiety would be the chips. Anxiety is a problem when bouts of worrying become habitual, and a pattern of negative thinking sets in so that even the most innocent and light-hearted of notions will transform itself into something to worry about.

Along with the usual 'butterflies' in the tummy sensation, symptoms of anxiety can include trembling, diarrhoea, insomnia, palpitations (racing heart) and headaches; also memory, decision-making and concentration are affected. The best anxiety-reducing strategies are lots of exercise and a healthy diet. Avoid excessive amounts of coffee and also heavy smoking and drinking, which might appear to help, but in the long term will just make it worse. To counteract negative thoughts consider a daily relaxation routine i.e. body stretches and slow deep breathing, but if it's really bugging you and you can't get a handle on it, find someone to talk to.

Social Anxiety support page – *www.phobics-society.org.uk/sa/supportpages*
www.patient.co.uk/illness/a/anxiety & *www.anxietycare.org.uk*

INSOMNIA

Insomnia can be brought on by any number of factors, from worry, physical discomfort due to a medical condition, environmental factors (such as not enough air in the room or uncomfortable mattresses or light or noise from outside), to an over-indulgence of caffeine or stimulants during the day (i.e. drinking coffee, Coke or energy drinks). It is also common among regular drug users, the major culprits being 'E', cocaine and speed.

Before seeking medical help you might try one of the following: herbal sleep aids; ear plugs or soft music to drown out other sounds; not napping during the day to make the lost sleep up; changing the mattress; taking more exercise (but not late in the day) so your body is more relaxed; having quiet time for an hour before bed, reading (but not studying!); and not having massive lie-ins. If you still can't sleep; don't panic! Half the purpose of sleep is to rest the body and as long as you lie still, at least you're getting physical rest. One time-honoured remedy is, in fact, drinking hot milk before bedtime, mixed with a pinch of cinnamon, nutmeg and cardamom. You might feel like someone's granddad/ grandma sipping this at night while your friends are still downing cups of coffee and having a fag but it can work wonders in helping you nod off.

If all this fails and the problem becomes critical, then talk to your doctor.

British Sleep Foundation – *www.britishsleepfoundation.org.uk*
Sleep Apnoea Trust Association – *www.sleepmatters.org*

DEPRESSION

Although people often use "I'm depressed" to describe low moods and bad days, proper depression, in which negative thoughts and feelings have become overpowering, is more than simply feeling miserable and unhappy. Signs of clinical depression include: an inability to feel pleasure, impaired concentration, fatigue, loss of appetite, suicidal thoughts, willful isolation, feelings of despair and helplessness, and constant self-critical and harshly negative thoughts.

Regular exercise is still one of the best ways to reduce anxiety, stress and depression, as this happy bunch demonstrate

Between 15-20% of us will experience clinical depression at some point in our lives. Counselling and psychotherapy can help, and temporary relief can be obtained relatively quickly through some of the more modern anti-depressants. Depression is rarely something you can just 'snap out of', so don't suffer in silence, talk to someone and get some help.

> *www.ability.org.uk/depression*
> *www.bi-polar.org.uk*
> *www.bbc.co.uk/health/mental/depression*

A good read is: 'Britain On the Couch' by Oliver James, which includes invaluable information on the anti-depressants debate and the depression epidemic in modern society.

EXAM NERVES

A certain amount of stress is inevitable and can be a useful motivational force, but the kind of high-adrenalin, racing-heart and loose-bowelled physical response that's appropriate to running away from a man-eating crocodile isn't going to help in the examination hall. Most universities offer courses in revision techniques and exam strategies, which can be immensely valuable, and you can bolster these through practising relaxation and getting some regular exercise to soak up some of the adrenalin.

Top Tip: a really good way to avoid extreme exam nerves and stress is not to leave all the crucial work/revision until the last minute…

SELF-HARM

Self-harm is thought to be surprisingly common, although accurate statistics are not available due to the secretiveness of self-harmers and the incomprehension of society-at-large. Although many of the actions of unhappy people can have a self-harm element, self-harm more specifically relates to self-mutilation: self-inflicted injury involving cutting, burning, scratching or gouging. Self-harm can be viewed as a symbolic way of expressing deep distress. Intolerable feelings are externalised and made real in the form of pain and physical wounds.

Many people have been successfully helped to reduce or stop this behaviour, so if you self-harm, or know someone who does, seek some advice from your doctor or from the counselling service.

www.myfriend-myenemy.com
www.selfharm.com www.selfinjury.freeserve.co.uk

ANOREXIA / BULIMIA

It's estimated that between 1-3% of college-aged students have anorexia nervosa, and 9 out of 10 of those are female (although male cases are increasing). Anorexia – the relentless pursuit of thinness at any cost can lead to death in extreme cases and, failing that, a host of health problems caused by malnutrition such as heart, liver and kidney damage, infertility and a severely weakened immune system. Bulimia Nervosa – the diet/binge/purge disorder – is far more common, estimates varying between 5-10% of college students. Bulimia in particular can go undetected for years as there is less outward evidence of its effects and people with bulimia are secretive, but it can still cause permanently impaired health.

Eating Disorders Association (EDA) Home Page – *www.edauk.com*
National Centre for Eating Disorders – *www.eating-disorders.org.uk*

COUNSELLING

Most universities have a counselling service. Don't be shy of making an appointment, as whatever worries or problems you may be carrying, they can easily become clearer and more manageable with the help of some professional and objective viewpoints. Talking about your difficulties, and bringing things to the surface this way can only be a good thing.

Never put off counselling on the grounds that you feel like you're just making a stupid fuss and won't be taken seriously. Everyone has different problems and concerns, and your justification for going is your unhappiness and distress, not the details of your problem.

A friend of ours (actually it was one of the writers of this book, ok it was Brian Mitchell) was late with a deadline for a dissertation for his finals, and hatched a fiendish plan to see a counsellor and get a time extension by faking terrible anxiety and depression. He prepared his story and booked an emergency appointment, but barely got into his tissue of lies before, to his own surprise, he burst into floods of tears. In the bar afterwards he was to be found nursing a pint, hands shaking and a shell-shocked expression, saying *'Bloody hell, I am depressed and anxious, I really am'*.

Samaritans *www.samaritans.org*
Open 24 hours daily, 0845 790 9090
Offer confidential advice, whatever your emotional problems

The Counselling Confessions
of a Mature Student

Contrary to the notion that all students have lots of fun is the experience of the feeble-minded, neurotic mature student….. i.e. me. Yes, I was a celibate, pseudo-philosophy undergrad with greying hair, IBS and shattered nerves. And I needed help.

Things came to a head when I found attending early morning lectures and seminars nearly impossible due to my anxiety and IBS. I would also leave all work preparation until the evening before it was due to be handed in and come over with brain fever when I discovered that I couldn't compound eight weeks' work into one seven-hour overnight sitting. Obviously I was in dire need of help, so I located the phone number of the 'Counselling and Psychiatric Services'. After an introductory meeting it was agreed that I would probably benefit from a short course of psychotherapy. Thus, strapped to a chair I was beaten with bags full of oranges until cured. Er, no, in fact my lovely analyst plied his trade; listening, observing and gently probing, searching for ambiguous responses whilst encouraging me to waffle on like a hairdresser on speed. It did the trick though, and six months later I felt like a new man, absolved of all guilt and able to talk like Woody Allen about my analyst's insights. In truth, counselling probably saved my degree from a somewhat ignominious end. And if you begin to feel out of your depth with work pressures, or anxiety in general, I'd recommend seeking advice like I did. My invisible six-foot rabbit happily agrees.

By Sussex University Graduate Gwyn Williams

ANTI-DEPRESSANTS

Many mental health issues stem from, or can lead to depression, and unless you have a specific form of illness, or are simply barking mad, the initial treatment can often be through the prescription of anti-depressants. While there are a number of different types of anti-depressants, the new generation of SSRIs (Selective Seratonin Re-Uptake Inhibitors) such as Prozac and Seroxat are an improvement on the older drugs, having fewer side-effects and little or no addictive potential. Millions of people have been prescribed SSRIs in the UK in the last decade.

Although they treat the symptoms and not necessarily the cause, anti-depressants can give great relief and create a valuable space in which to discover and address, often with the help of counselling or psychotherapy, the root of the problem.

www.depressiondepot.net
www.anti-depressants.net

BAD GUTS AND IBS

Wind, diarrhea, constipation and bloating may sound like a local firm of solicitors but they are, in fact, just some of the many symptoms of what doctors call "Irritable Bowel Syndrome". In the old days it was called gutrot, and people largely ignored it, safe in the knowledge they were going to die of TB or cholera in the next five years anyway. These days however, stomach related disorders are almost endemic amongst adults; and conventional medicine doesn't really know how to deal with a lot of them, partly because the symptoms are so numerous and varied and can be brought on to such varying degrees of severity by so many different stimuli. It is commonly perceived that stress is a dominant factor, and while it is certainly true that increased stress can often bring gut problems, it is probably because you are doing something else wrong in the first place. For example, consultant gastroenterologists estimate that some 60% of patients who make it into hospital with chronic stomach conditions such as ulcerative colitis and Chrones are there because they simply haven't been drinking enough water over a long period of time.

Bad diet, smoking, high alcohol intake, chocolate, tea, coffee, irregular sleeping patterns and recreational drugs (basically, everything that's enjoyable) can all contribute to gut related disorders. And few of these things will be completely alien to your lifestyle. But it is amazing how many students get up at two in the afternoon, go for a fry-up to get rid of the E/alcohol comedown, have five fags over three coffees, run to the loo, see the world fall out of their bottom, then come back to the table and say 'Jesus, my guts are a mess. I think I must be lactose intolerant or something. Better pay £100 for one of those food allergy tests and start eating tofu."

More enlightened health experts (i.e. not doctors) have suggested that IBS is on the increase owing to the sheer crap that we eat, together with the increasing number of additives in food, putting more pressure on the organs to flush out these unwanted toxins. Alternative medicine has many useful strategies of dealing with IBS, from acupuncture and herbal remedies to meditation and aromatherapy. Even ordinary medicine has useful anti-spasmodics such as Colofac, or fibre regulators such as Fybogel. But before you spend a lot of time and or money looking for that wheat allergy, just check that you're drinking plenty of water, getting regular sleep and eating a balanced diet. A couple of weeks of that can achieve wonders*.

*If the problem persists, consult your doctor but don't expect him/her to have the answer. Being fobbed off with tablets might ease the problem but won't explain why it's there in the first place. It will be up to you to experiment with changing your habits to find ways of improving the situation.

MENINGITIS

High-profile outbreaks of this killer disease, in halls of residence amongst new students during first term at university, have caused a number of deaths in recent years. The annual rates of meningitis infection in England and Wales are approximately 2000 cases causing 200 deaths. The early symptoms of meningitis are not easy to detect. It can begin with headaches, a temperature and feeling generally unwell, but more suspicious symptoms can then follow, including:

- Neck and back stiffness
- Over-sensitivity to light (photophobia)
- Severe headache
- Drowsiness
- Diarrhoea
- Fits and seizures
- A blotchy red rash

The most telling sign is the rash, which can be tested by pressing a clear glass cup bottle against the skin and seeing if the rash fades and no longer shows red when moderate pressure is applied. Sound the alarm if it doesn't.

A vaccination for meningococcus C is now freely available to students and it's highly recommended that you are immunised shortly after starting university, even if you've had the jab before. Group B however causes twice as many cases as C and is still out there.

The Meningitis Trust – *www.meningitis-trust.org.uk*
Meningitis Research Foundation – *www.meningitis.co.uk*
www.bath.ac.uk/students/meningitis*

For more info on Meningitis check the following websites or call the Meningitis 24 hour hotline on **0845 6000 800**

*There's even a downloadable 6 minute RealPlayer video from the University of Bath showing the tell-tale early sings on meningitis and septicaemia.

POLITICS

THE STUDENT UNION nus.org.uk

One of the biggest unions in the country, the NUS boats over four million members that have, in the past, included everyone from John Prescott to Rowan Atkinson. The union's role is to help and support your needs by providing services (such as shops, sporting facilities and advice centres) as well as representing you before the university (should you, for example, demand skateboarding access around campus).

The union also provides a variety of personnel to help run the show, including sabbatical officers. These are roles taken by students who receive a salary and one year out of their studies to take responsibility for a key area of student representation such as finance or welfare. Generally the six key roles for sabbatical officers are as follows:

THE PRESIDENT

The union figurehead and mouthpiece to the university, his/her job includes representing students on University committees and acting as the main point of contact for the union. They are also required, by law, to smoke rolling tobacco and read 'Living Marxism.'

VICE-PRESIDENT / COMMUNICATIONS OFFICER

The mouthpiece of the union, these are the guys who make public statements. Paid to be loud-mouthed and opinionated, they are destined for the London comedy circuit, parliament or driving a cab.

SPORTS / ACTIVITIES OFFICER

The Sports officer has a busy time of it, organising matches with other universities, representing the needs of students who play sports, and still finding time in his/her busy schedule, learning how to read and write.

EDUCATION OFFICER

Representing all things academic, this is the person to turn to for help if you've spent the last six months experimenting with the concept of human hibernation, awaking only to find the university has given you your marching orders.

FINANCE OFFICER

He/she is there to help you sort out your inevitable financial problems, and offer all manner of advise on money management. Worth talking to just to find out what kind of emergency funds the university has on offer to students who have financial problems.

WELFARE OFFICER

The super-heroes of the union body, these guys will offer advise on housing problems, deal with issues of homophobia and racism and help run the nightbus. They'll even write your essays for you if you're unable to meet your deadline and lend you the odd £50.

Not every student union, however, is able to provide all six sabbatical officers. Yours might be one where they are only able to offer these as voluntary rather than paid posts. Or you might have a very small, frugal union which can offer little more than an unpaid second year Biology student, who, in her spare time, sits in a cubicle in the girls' toilet for two hours a day trying to deal with everyone's problems.

On the other hand, the more affluent and organised union at Sussex University in Brighton boasts over 100 sabbatical officers including the: 'Oh dear you've lost your mobile phone, I'll help you look for it Officer,' Tattoos and Piercings Adviser, and 'I'll let you know what happened in Sex and the City last week in case you missed it Officer.' There are also, at each university, another 20 odd voluntary roles for executive members (e.g. women's officer/ overseas student officer) and also posts for course representatives, should you wish to be a voice for your course. For more information about these, and how to apply for the posts, see your student union.

AGM / UGM
These General Meetings are normally held in a big hall in the union building (if you have one). Chaired by representatives from the students' union and focusing on crucial student issues, the only thing that is usually missing from these meetings is students themselves.

HOW TO GET ELECTED AS A SABBATICAL OFFICER

There are many reasons why you would wish to run for office – an unquenchable lust for power, the chance to take a year out and laze around campus, the realisation that a union position would look really good on the C.V., or it could even be that you have a genuine wish to be a useful and productive member of university society and make some positive changes.

Actually, most students are motivated by a combination of the above. But how do you con your fellow undergraduates into giving you a ticket for this gravy-train? A brief guide follows:-

1) GO TO THE PROSPECTIVE CANDIDATES MEETING
(details of this will be available from your SU)
Choose what to stand for and why you want that post. A response of "Ooh, I don't know – What've you got?" when asked which post you're standing for will suggest you're not really very serious about all this. Play to your strengths. If you like helping people, go for Welfare. If you like the odd game of table football, go for Sports. If you don't have any strengths, run for President.

2) THINK OF A DESCRIPTION OR SLOGAN FOR YOUR CAMPAIGN
Try and avoid clichés ('Blair=Square'), alienating your voters ('You're all a bunch of bastards.') and flippancy ('Zippy is God')

3) FILL IN YOUR NOMINATIONS FORM, AVAILABLE FROM THE SU RECEPTION
You will need two friends to propose and second your candidacy. They must be students at your university who are also eligible to stand. (Bribe them if necessary with the promise of cushy jobs once you're elected.)

4) WRITE YOUR MANIFESTO
This is the fun part, since it allows you to make public all your ill-founded opinions, and empty promises.

5) RUN YOUR CAMPAIGN
Kiss babies, shake hands, mount the soap-box and generally bully, threaten and cajole people into giving you their votes, in the process making Charles Foster Kane look like a shrinking violet. Design and print a poster, and stick it on every surface that doesn't move (and some that do).

6) ONCE ELECTED, MAKE A GRACIOUS ACCEPTANCE SPEECH, DEMONSTRATING YOUR HUMILITY AND INTEGRITY
Then have your 'goons' round up and assassinate all candidates who put a slur on your good name, have the VC hung, drawn and quartered, plunder the university's gold supply, change your name to El Presidente and set about waging war with the nearest university…

VOTE ANDY COOMBS FOR PRESIDENT!
I PROMISE I WILL...

Sit on my arse in the union building all day, drinking coffee and smoking roll-ups

Lie, cheat, blackmail and backstab my way to a position of ultimate power within the university

Use my position to seduce impressionable first year students

Adopt an air of lofty superiority within the first five minutes of winning

Support whatever half-baked left-wing ideologies are in vogue this year

Re-name all the union buildings after the cast of DangerMouse

Sell-out and get a job with the Daily Mail as soon as I leave University

Crumble instantly when put under pressure by the vice-chancellor

VOTE COOMBS!
WITH THE UNION RENDERED POWERLESS BY A TOTALITARIAN CAPITALIST GOVERNMENT MASQUERADING UNDER THE GUISE OF A LEFT-WING PARTY ONCE LOVED AND CHERISHED BY THE VERY STUDENTS IT NOW DENIGRATES, IT DOESN'T REALLY MATTER WHO IS SU PRESIDENT, SO IT MIGHT AS WELL BE ME!!!!

POLITICS

A BRIEF HISTORY OF STUDENT ACTIVISM

Spontaneous surges of student protest have taken place in various pockets of the globe in different times throughout history, from the Paris riots to the 'Cannibal Happenings of 73' (a grizzly affair where a group of English Lit students, unhappy with their grades, responded by rising up and eating the entire faculty of Literary tutors at East Anglia Polytechnic).

It is the Sixties however that really mark the beginning of an historic upsurgence of student dissent. With the social climate in the West being what it was then, students for the first time became more organised, more political and prepared to stand up and do battle for social justice, civil rights and smaller queues at the library photocopier.

Whilst no means the first country to experience student unrest, the campaigns and marches in America's cities and campuses during the mid-to-late Sixties, showed the rest of the world what a powerful force students can be when dragged away from Eastenders. Mixed with the civil rights movement, race protests, hippy counterculture and Black Panthers, students helped spearhead fierce demonstrations all over the US, not least in protest against the war in Vietnam, where men their own age were being sent to their slaughter in the name of a war that most of the country didn't understand or care about. The government responded savagely to these uprisings, and in 1968 state troopers opened fire and killed several students on the Kent State University campus to quell an anti-Vietnam war protest.

In the same year in France, their Parisian counterparts decided to take things one step further and challenge the whole of French society, rising to fight long and bloody pitched street battles with police, in protestation over the quality of modern life in France. Such was the size and strength of this uprising that De Gaulle's government came perilously close to being overthrown, but was rescued by the support of the Trade Unions and Communist Party (though the students have always maintained it was because they ran out of Rizlas).

Also around the same time, Czechoslovakia (then under the icy cold grip of post-war Communism) experienced a similar uprising, where, for a while student-led artistic groups bravely challenged the dread force of Communist cultural control before the tanks rolled in and quashed all hope of revolution.

And on the subject of tanks, let's not forget the events in China in the Eighties. In 1986 students around the country began holding hunger strikes, demanding increased freedom of speech and greater democracy. By 1989, hundreds of thousands of Chinese people led by the students, chose to challenge the oppressive regime of the government by peacefully occupying Tiananmen Square in the capital Beijing. Many wrote their wills knowing what brutality the government was capable of. On June 3rd, troops and tanks were sent in to clear out the students and over two and a half thousand people were killed, with over sixty thousand injured.

But what of the UK?

Well, as you'd expect, student radicalism here has been earnest, largely non-violent and perhaps a bit shabby in comparison; but we've had our moments. In the Sixties, Nuclear Disarmament became high on the political agenda and if you didn't have a C.N.D. badge on your duffel coat back then, you weren't a student. In the seventies it was the turn of Women's Liberation and Women's Groups on campuses to take the message of equal rights for women to a wider population. Bras were burned. Men wondered how this was a punishment. It was the Eighties however, that brought the ultimate student hate figure; Margaret Thatcher. Like a right wing version of Hitler, she seemed to distrust all things academic and intellectual and decided to make the academics bow to her as she had quelled the Unions and the miners previously. Funding was cut, benefits were outlawed, Christmas was banned and small puppies were needlessly poked with sticks. The woman was a monster.

Life for UK students got tougher and tougher throughout the Eighties as grants were cut, and housing benefit and dole in the summer abolished. This led to many student marches, protests and sit-ins, this time not about something else that was happening 'out there', but actually about the brass tacks of education. What is really depressing is that since overthrowing the Tories in 1997, Labour has continued to do exactly the same. And with the very real worry of huge debts, the power of the union weakened and the two major parties occupying the same anodyne political middle ground, it is harder to know exactly how to fight back and who to trust. Consequently, demos and marches are a shadow of the past. It would be easy to think therefore, that students are now apolitical creatures, concerned more with their prospects, money problems and watching Hollyoaks than the affairs of the world, but this is not true.

Many students, ever one step ahead, have already realised that political change in the UK is relatively meaningless, as much of the world's real power is now in the hands of trans-global corporations and an illiterate baboon called George Bush, and as a consequence, student activism has shifted towards single issue campaigning. Free Tibet, the Environment, Third World Debt and anti-globalisation are all very popular student causes and do from time to time still mobilise large numbers of students. In fact, the anti-globalisation demonstrations in Genoa in 2001 showed that students are still prepared to take an active stance against corporate greed and political negligence. And yet again, another government was left with blood on its hands.

THE OXFORD STUDENT MASSACRE OF 1355

History denotes that the most horrific act of violence against English students, remembered as St Scholastica's Day, happened over 600 years ago in Oxford, then a small but celebrated university town.

The trouble all began, all rather innocently, in an alehouse in the city centre where an argument was brewing between a student and the landlord over the quality of a glass of wine, the student had been sold. Frayed tempers and perhaps a little intoxication lead to the student throwing the wine in the landlord's face and giving him a deadleg. A fight soon erupted between the two and before long a full scale brawl was underway, which soon emptied onto the streets where other students, townsfolk and the odd tourist came to join in. By the end of the day there were surprisingly few injuries (people were made of sturdier stuff back then) and as an uneasy truce between Town and Gown was agreed, the students believed that to be the end of it. This was far from the truth.

Tensions and hatred between Town and Gown had been a growing problem for years and the brawl opened up old wounds for many of the townspeople. The next morning, still feeling bloodthirsty for revenge, they enlisted the help of hundreds of other laymen from surrounding villages with the promise of 'giving the students a good kicking.' Woefully outnumbered this time, any students who didn't flee the city were massacred by the mob, and by the end of a two-day battle over 60 had been killed.

The king, having caught wind of this had the previous day, sent instructions for the massacre to stop, but his orders fell on deaf ears.

By way of punishment to the townsfolk he made them pay an annual fee to the students, giving the university cetain privileges, which even included their own police force.

Never again has the hatred of students been so venomous and brutal, though spend an evening in Colchester and you could be mistaken.

GRANTS NOT FEES!

LABOUR MAKE MILK-SNATCHING LOOK CHARITABLE!

STUDENT BENEFITS R.I.P.
1984-2002

It is an old cliché for parents, grandparents and hippies to go on and on about how things were 'so much better in the old days' but in the case of being a student, unfortunately they'd be right. There was once a time when students were entitled to grants, benefits, dole in summer, and even a small allowance for class B drugs. All that has since long gone and been replaced, as you know, with loans, overdrafts and crippling debt. To give you an idea as to the contempt both Tory and Labour governments share for higher education, we have (with the help of the lovely Nadya Kassam from the NUS) compiled below a brief history of the endless cutbacks and withdrawals of funding that have taken place in the last twenty years. Of course 'New Labour' insist a big change for the better is imminent. Anyone feel like holding their breath?

1984
Student Travel Costs Reimbursement abolished.

1985
Minimum Maintenance Grant abolished, leaving a 'fees only' minimum award.

1986
Special Equipment Grant abolished.

Sept 1986
Students entitlement to Supplementary Benefit and Unemployment Benefit during vacations withdrawn.

Oct 1986
Government withdraws Housing Benefit for students in Halls of Residence.

June 1987
Housing Benefit for accommodation left unoccupied during summer vacation withdrawn.

Nov 1989
Government introduces Education Bill (Student Loans).

Sept 1990
All forms of Unemployment Benefit, Income Support and Housing Benefit for full-time students are withdrawn.
Nov 1990
Government abolishes Vacation Hardship Allowance.

Nov 1993
Grants to be cut progressively by 10% each year over 3 years from 1994/95 to 1996/97 and loan increased.

Nov 1994
Grants cut by a further 8% and student loans increased correspondingly.
Students who take breaks from their studies are no longer entitled to claim benefits.

Nov 1995
Basic rate of grant cut by an average of 10%; student loans increase.

May 1997
The Labour Party replace the Conservatives and promise to 'make things better for students'.

July 1997
The Government announce plans to charge students for their Tuition Fees.

Sept 2000
Tuition Fees set at £1075.

Sept 2002
The Government announces plans that by 2004, all students will be required by law to donate one of their kidneys toward the cost of running the university library ....

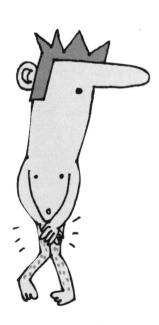

A sit-in is a form of protest, which, as the name clearly suggests, involves occupying a building to the maximum inconvenience of its owners. Unique amongst methods of dissent in that it doesn't involve marching, fighting, shouting, or anything remotely physically taxing, the sit-in naturally became the favoured tool of student activists the world over.

With the roots of the student sit-in probably originating from the Passive Resistance techniques developed by Mahatma Gandhi, they did not become a staple part of student life until the '60s, when they were all over American campuses like a rash. The most infamous site was Berkeley, the home of the University of California, which became a by-word for long-haired, pot-smoking, work-shy rebellion. At around the same time, British universities got in on the act, the most notorious examples being Sussex, The London School of Economics, and Essex (all of which continued this practice well into the late Eighties.) Sussex was so legendarily afflicted that Autumn Term became known as 'sit-in season'. In this country, the days of the great student occupations have long-gone. But that doesn't mean you shouldn't try to have a bash at organising one yourself. You never know, you might start a whole new revolution, man.

HOW TO ORGANISE A SIT-IN

1) FIND A CAUSE
Famous causes in the past have included the Vietnam War, Clause 28 and the legalisation of Cannabis. Nowadays you could try tuition fees, peace in the Middle East, or the public execution of Victoria Beckham.

2) TIME YOUR OCCUPATION WELL
Traditionally, very early in the Autumn Term (ideally after Freshers' week) has always been the most auspicious time for planning an occupation. This is helped by the fact that at this time Freshers tend to find it all awfully exciting, and can be enlisted to your cause, and second and third years can have their Summer vacations extended and put off the inevitable moment when they have to resume their studies.

3) PROPOSE YOUR SIT-IN OFFICIALLY
You do not have to be a member of the union to do this – in fact, it is a bonus if you are not, because you'll be less likely to be made an example of. However, it is a good idea to be affiliated with some kind of political organization, merely because a successful sit-in involves a deal of planning and manpower which you won't have access to yourself. Try if you can, to get a unanimous vote. Once passed, move instantly.

4) FIND A BUILDING TO OCCUPY
This should be chosen before the meeting. Make sure you choose a building that is big, important, and relatively close to the venue of the meeting (if it's somewhere on the other side of town, everyone will give up half-way there and go for a curry instead). Good places to occupy include the library, any science department, and the lecture halls. Never try to occupy the admin block, as this will merely get the V.C.'s dander up and you will either be fined or out on your ear.

5) TAKE PROVISIONS

When you attend the A.G.M., you and your political chums should have with you the following: sleeping bags/ inflatable pillows/ condoms/ food & water/ booze/ games/ reading matter/ several pairs of pants/ mobile phones and chargers This last item is particularly indispensable, as modern technology can improve the ease of negotiating, whilst also ensuring the smooth flow of supplies throughout the three weeks or so you intend to keep up this sorry charade.

5) KEEP SOMEONE POSTED AT THE DOOR

The entrances to the building, once occupied, must be closely guarded at all times. This is not only because of people trying to get in but also because you will almost certainly have to send out scouts (keeping their faces hidden) for supplies every day or so, and you want to make sure you're not ambushed when they return. Choose the most alert of your fellow revolutionaries for this task, and give them shifts so they can at least get stoned occasionally like everybody else. Don't pick anyone likely to admit a forty-five year old policeman wearing a "Smiley face"T-shirt and bandana.

6) AVOID THE LIMELIGHT

You may wish to have your mug on Newsnight, but it won't aid your cause and can get you into trouble. IfTV crews arrive wishing to relay your message to the world, refuse them – however much this may wound your vanity. In fact, make sure no-one, not even a close friend brings in any form of camera, as your photo falling into the wrong hands will get you into very hot water. Especially if it somehow ends up on the front of the Daily Express under the headline **'EVIL FIGUREHEAD OF LEFTY STUDENT SCUM.'** Instead nominate a spokesperson on the outside, keeping in constant touch with him/her by mobile phone. This person can give out any statement you wish to make and can distribute any literature or manifesto to the press.

7) HAVE FUN

Sit-ins are the most entertaining form of protest devised. Imagine it all as a great big camping holiday (or shagfest as some uni students of old demonstrated) with all your mates, plus the added frisson of illegality. Then simply hang around until either your demands are met, or they aren't. (If you get bored with the whole thing and the prospect of another game of Monopoly and a pot noodle with your cohorts is more than you can stomach, remember that this is why many other sit-ins in the past have failed – so be stoic!)

The Death Of The Sit-In

In the autumn of 1987, students at Sussex University successfully occupied 'Sussex House', the administration centre. This was something of a departure, as they had generally held their sit-ins at the school of molecular sciences. (This had become a yearly sport and no one, not even the head of that department seemed to mind.)

The sit-in lasted three weeks, during which time the students completely trashed the place, drank the VC's booze, nicked his robes, and went through all the important documents and confidential files. This effectively crippled the running of the university. The staff were utterly furious.

Unfortunately several protestors were caught on video outside the building, identified and, after the occupation, hauled up before the university board. The union was fined by the university who simply looked at the union's account and took back every single penny they had in it. This bankrupted the union and changed the face of Sussex student life forever. There have been no occupations at Sussex University, nor any major sit-ins at any other English university since.

The sat-on

THE ENVIRONMENT

Who remembers Swampy?

Environmentalism emerged as a serious political concern in the Sixties in response to scientific theories predicting dramatic devastation of the eco-system. It gained mass appeal in the late Eighties after increasing concern over the mass destruction of rain forests, and the discovery over Antarctica, of a huge hole in the ozone layer. Anxiety over the 'Greenhouse Effect', and a craze for re-cycling swept the nation, leading to the Green Party winning 15% of the vote in the 1989 European elections. Sadly, since then their profile seems to have waned somewhat, partly because the major parties have appropriated many of their policies, but more so because David Icke, their only spokesman with any charisma, went stark raving mad live on TV and started ranting about being the son of God and that the Queen Mum, Ronald Reagan and Country singer Boxcar Willy were all in fact…err….giant lizards. A set-back to any party – with the possible exception of the Conservatives.

In the Nineties the movement diversified in the UK into many single-issue groups, employing what became known as 'Direct Action' – occupying areas earmarked for 'development', such as the Newbury By-Pass and Twycross Down. With the introduction of such modern ills as G.M. crops, BSE and George Bush, Environmentalism will remain of enormous political concern amongst students who know that, as they are for the most part, young, they'll be left to deal with the mess everyone else makes of the planet.

HOW TO GET INVOLVED

GREENPEACE

Formed in 1971, Greenpeace is one of the largest and most effective environmentalist organisations. It campaigns on a whole raft of issues – stopping nuclear testing and dumping, renewable energy, the preservation of the rainforest, saving the whale, and dolphin-friendly tuna nets. Also very likely to have a local group in your area.

Greenpeace, Freepost ND944,
Northhampton, NN3 6BR
(Preferably including a donation)

FRIENDS OF THE EARTH

TEL: 020 7490 1555 www.foe.co.uk

One of the country's leading pressure groups, FOE is not aligned to any political party, but works with all of them, providing objective research on a wide range of environmental concerns. Its main aims are to encourage greater use of recycling, more efficient and renewable forms of energy, and to stop the waste and destruction of the natural habitat. Successes include securing a ban on CFCs, reducing trade in rainforest timber, and gaining political support for cleaner energy technologies. Recently it has been concentrating on GM crops, and energy-saving insulation for houses.

THE GREEN PARTY

The Green Party, Freepost Lon 6780, London, N19 5BR

www.greenparty.org.uk

Presently boasting over 30 members of major local councils, its current energies are focused on attacking GM farming, globalisation, and low-level radiation. Join up and stand as a local candidate, or give support to your local party.

MAGAZINES

Resurgence (Long established bi-monthly, with excellent features and philosophy of 'small is beautiful').

The Ecologist (Again, a well-established magazine on the environment, but with more of a political slant than Resurgence)

THE PEACE MOVEMENT

Pacifism only really became an organised political force in the early 1930s, under the banner of the Peace Pledge Union but its real boom time however, came in 1958 with the founding of the Campaign For Nuclear Disarmament (CND) in response to the alarming build up of the arms race.

Throughout the late Sixties, despite the ubiquity of its famous symbol, CND took a slight backseat, with anti-Vietnam protests at the forefront of student activism but enjoyed a new lease of life in the Eighties, under the directorship of Bruce Kent, with the infamous blockading of Greenham Common Nuclear Missile base by thousands of female protesters.

Each major conflict (Falklands, Gulf, Bosnia, Afghanistan) seems to give rise to its own anti-war movement – groups specifically concerned with that cause alone.

HOW TO GET INVOLVED

C.N.D.

www.cnduk.org/ TEL (0207) 700 2393

C.N.D. is a group dedicated to non-violent campaigning against all weapons of mass destruction. It aims to change government policies over the selling of weapons, the use of British nuclear power, and to stimulate public debate on alternatives to the use of nuclear energy. It is in favour of scrapping Trident submarines, opposing the 'star wars' anti-missile system, stopping the plutonium trade, and of the U.K. withdrawing from N.A.T.O.

CAMPAIGN AGAINST ARMS TRADE

C.A.A.T. want to bring an end to the international trade of weapons, and the UK's role as a major arms manufacturer and exporter. Its eventual aim is to base our economy on more peaceful means. C.A.A.T.'s methods include the 'naming and shaming' of corporations and institutions, such as political parties, the churches, health authorities, and banks that invest heavily in the arms export trade.

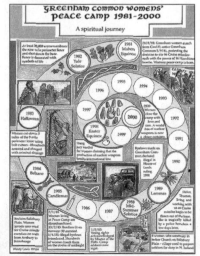

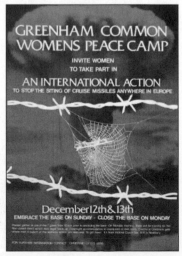

ANTI-GLOBALISATION

In recent years the meetings of international monetary, trade and environmental organizations, have drawn the attention of thousands of anti-globalisation activists. Representing a broad spectrum of groups, lobbyists, and overlapping networks, they share a mutual antipathy-that of multinational corporate power. This mistrust of multinational corporations stems largely from the obscene powers these companies wield (of the top hundred economies in the world, fifty-one are multinationals and only forty-nine are countries) for example, George Bush had his campaign bankrolled to the tune of 42 million dollars by Esso. He's not likely to tell them to stop polluting the planet is he?

Large corporations with international undertakings stand accused of social injustice, unfair labour practices (including slave labour wages, living and working conditions) as well as a lack of concern for the environment, mismanagement of natural resources, and ecological damage. Major brand names, among them Nike, Starbucks, McDonalds, and Shell Oil are popular targets as their brands are seen to represent corporate indifference and greed.

Protest objectives however extend beyond mere corporate impropriety. Multinational economic institutions, such as the World Trade Organization (WTO), the World Bank (WB), and the International Monetary Fund (IMF) are establishing, monitoring, and rendering judgments on global trade practices and are just as guilty of spearheading economic globalisation. They are servants of corporate interest, exercising more power than elected governments and interested only if it seems in the profit motive.

So why has this political tendency become so popular with students and the wider community? Partly it is due to the fact that a huge number of organisations and pressure groups share the same concern for the planet and economic justice. But it is also because traditional political parties that were the home of protest and championing the cause of the oppressed, are seen to have been 'bought off' and become corporate stooges. The world is in trouble, and even those responsible (in their less guarded moments) will admit as much....

"Where every prospect pleases, man is at his vilest when he erects a billboard. When I retire from Madison Avenue, I am going to start a secret society of masked vigilantes who will travel around the world on silent motor bicycles, chopping down posters at the dark of the moon. How many juries will convict us when we are caught in these acts of beneficent citizenship?"

David Ogilvy, founder of the Ogilvy & Mather advertising agency.

HOW TO GET INVOLVED

BOOKS AND MAGAZINES
Red Pepper
Aimed at raising the political temperature, this monthly magazine is insightful and provocative with regards to issues of world politics and corporate corruption.

No Logo
www.nologo.org
(Naomi Klein). This renowned book tracks the reasons behind the rise of anti-corporate activism and explains why this emerging movement is a force to be reckoned with. Not only a great source of information but persuasively and intelligently written.

SchNews
www.schnews.org.uk/
A radical weekly newsletter from Justice?, Brighton's direct action collective. Keeps you informed of campaigns, demos and much more around the UK.

For the best anarchist listing on the Internet try Spunk Press at **www.spunk.org**, or have a look at the 'Anarchist Timeline' or the 'Daily Bleed Calender'.

WEBSITES
Adbusters' Culture Jammer's Headquarters
www.adbusters.org
Designed to be an activist tool, this site allows culture jammers to learn about, and take steps to stop, the marketing pollutants in the mental environment.

Infoshop.org
www.infoshop.org
Offers links to anarchist organizations, information, and resources.

Reclaim the Streets.net
www.reclaimthestreets.net
Provides links to street-reclaiming direct action around the world.

To check out what groups exist near you, get a copy of the brilliant guide –
The Agitator c/o Haringey Solidarity Group, P.O. Box 2474, London N8 (send £1)
or on the net: *http://home.clara.net/hsg/agitator*

Seraph

Woman In Touch

Seraph are a group of like minded women, coming together to fight for human rights and women's rights around the globe. We also work on projects for the local, national and international communities. Our aim now is to join with other local organisations to tackle the growing problem of teenage pregnancy in the Brighton area.

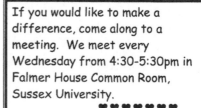

If you would like to make a difference, come along to a meeting. We meet every Wednesday from 4:30-5:30pm in Falmer House Common Room, Sussex University.
♥♥♥♥♥♥♥

Contact Vicci Stratton for Seraph (affiliated to Soroptimist):
✉ viccist@hotmail.com or ☎ 07787537274

ANIMAL RIGHTS

The welfare of animals in this country and abroad is an emotive issue (as anyone who's witnessed the fists flying in a 'discussion' between a vegetarian and a fox hunter will testify) and an issue for those who take up the cause that usually comes out much more clear-cut than the usual troubling moral complexities that much of political activism entails.

Along with this, it is something that you can get involved in on any level. For the casually concerned, it might mean for example, buying/ avoiding certain products, not eating meat except at Christmas or promising to stop making the family dog wear a Tartan waistcoat in Winter. Other students however, choose to go the whole hog (excuse the inappropriate metaphor), embracing vegetarianism/ Veganism and joining Hunt Sabs / pressure groups.

Incidentally, there is a group who manage to go 'beyond the hog' and become Fruitarians. These pious individuals choose only to eat things which have made the conscious choice to fall on the ground (rather than be picked) and go around with the intent of not causing any harm whatsoever to all forms of life. This is of course impossible folly, as even the simple act of washing your armpits, cleaning your teeth and hoovering the floor regularly wipes out millions of microscopic bugs in an instant, but it does explain why these people rarely get invited to parties.

HOW TO GET INVOLVED

VIVA

Tel: 01273 777688 *www.viva.org.uk/*

Viva is an organisation dedicated to the promotion of a vegetarian/vegan lifestyle, and various animal rights causes. Amongst their concerns are factory farming, the export of horse-meat, and saving the kangaroo (no, really!). Viva stages many rallies and marches all over the country. What's more, their website is packed with useful information that ranges from advice on how to maintain a healthy veggie diet, to all the latest campaigns and issues. For more information or a free veggie pack, contact Viva! (01273) 777688 info@viva.org.uk **www.viva.org.uk**

A.L.F.

www.animalliberationfront.com

The Animal Liberation Front is a non-violent 'direct action' organisation devoted to the rescuing of abused animals, and the damaging of property or equipment belonging to those who exploit animals. It is also against the law. Because of this their activists work anonymously in small groups.

THE PEOPLE FOR THE ETHICAL TREATMENT OF ANIMALS (P.E.T.A)

www.peta-online.org

Probably the most high-profile animal welfare group, P.E.T.A.'s concerns range from lab animals and bullfighting to the treatment of circus animals. They are particularly well known for their prominent celebrity supporters, and their anti-fur advertising campaigns.

HUNT SABS
0845 4500727 *www.huntsabs.org.uk*
Hunt saboteurs try to disrupt foxhunts with the use of disinfectants, misdirection and general…well…sabotage. There are many local groups, which you can find out about by accessing the website above.
The cops really don't like hunt sabs though, so be careful.

NATIONAL ANTI-VIVISECTION LEAGUE
Tel: 020 8846 9777
www.navs.org.uk/homepage.html

THE BODY SHOP
www.the-body-shop.com/uk

HUMAN RIGHTS

AMNESTY INTERNATIONAL
www.amnesty.org.uk
Amnesty is one of the biggest and most successful voluntary movements in the fight against human rights abuses worldwide, from the oppression of the Tibetan people to the use of the death penalty in the US. Those who they help not only include political prisoners, but gays, children and students themselves (Amnesty have identified over 70 countries where students and young people suffer state detention, torture and unlawful killing).

PEOPLE AND PLANET
www.pepleandplanet.org
Large student charity aimed at tackling world poverty, human rights and the environment.

SERAPH – WOMEN IN TOUCH
This is a group of like-minded women coming together to fight for human rights and women's rights around the globe. Initially set up at Sussex University, Seraph are affiliated to Soroptimists and co-operate with inter-governmental and other organisations to advance international understanding, goodwill and peace.
If you are interested in finding out more, or wish to set up your own group at a different university, contact either Mary Stratton, Extension and Membership Officer (S.E. Region) on 4strattons@supanet.com or Vicci Stratton, President of Seraph (Sussex Uni) on viccist@hotmail.com.

FREE TIBET
www.freetibet.org
Pretty self-explanatory.

TRADITIONS

RAG WEEK

Rag week is a tradition that dates back approximately 200 years. Its main purpose is to raise money for local or national charities (Rag is an acronym for Raising And Giving) but you'd be forgiven for thinking that it was just a flimsy excuse for loads of people to dress up as gorillas and schoolgirls, sit in baths of baked beans and get legless.

Once upon a time rag week could be relied upon to consist of a limited number of somewhat predictable events, such as pram races, three-legged pub crawls, slave auctions, jelly eating competitions, and any premise for mass transvesticism. In recent years however, rag organisers have branched out and current high-octane jinks now include sponsored bungee jumps, fashion shows, casinos, and film festivals.

The timing differs widely from university to university, but generally rag week falls in the Spring term, somewhere between February and April, so you probably want to hope it's as near Summer as possible when you're stumbling drunkenly about town at three in the morning, wearing only a pair of bikini briefs and a deerstalker.

Popular Rag Events: -

PUB CRAWLS

These are what students do anyway, so Lord knows how they persuade people to give them money for it. In the olden days, sponsored pub crawls were very, very basic, but have since transmogrified into a many-headed Hydra of nude pub crawls, transvestite pub crawls, Star Wars pub crawls, etc. If you go to the University of Essex it's probably not a good idea to try these in the pubs in Colchester.

HITCHES

The sponsored hitch involves getting to an out-of-the-way location under somebody else's steam, i.e. cadging a lift from some bored lorry driver. There's sometimes a race element, with the first person arriving at a specified youth hostel somewhere in Munich winning both the most cash, and all the glory. Thames Valley University used to run an annual hitch to Amsterdam until they realised three years down the line that no one ever bothered coming back.

FANCY DRESS EVENTS

Usually themed, e.g. James Bond, Vicars and Tarts, Seventies, pets in Eastenders, etc. Whatever the theme, you are guaranteed to spot:-

     A) A bloke dressed as a gorilla.
     B) A bloke dressed as Ali. G
     C) A woman dressed in a PVC catsuit.
     D) Eighteen rugby players in little cocktail dresses.

SLAVE AUCTIONS AND BLIND DATES

Slave auctions consist of a bunch of rugby players who think they're on to a good thing, getting up, taking off their shirts, and being 'sold' to any woman prepared to stump up cash for them. Be wary however of volunteering yourself for auction; a friend of ours was over the moon when a woman he fancied bought his services and kept him up all night – copying out her missed lecture notes.

The appeal of dressing up and getting drunk being what it is, rag societies are often the largest in the N.U.S. and are often assigned their own sabbatical officers. These are the guys to see if you fancy organizing an event yourself, or merely participating in one. Signing up shouldn't be difficult – the only criterion is a willingness to be ridiculed in public.

RAG MAGS

Rag Mags have somewhat bizarrely remained unchanged since time immemorial. And bearing in mind the almost oppressive regime of Political Correctness, which governed most universities during the late eighties and early nineties, they were (and still are) crammed with jokes so sexist, racist and homophobic they would make Jim Davidson blush.

Below is a spoof page from a Rag Mag complete with a random selection of tasteless jokes. Can you tell which one actually appeared in a student Rag Mag?

What do elephants use as vibrators?
Epileptic pigs.

What do you call a lesbian with long fingers?
Well-hung.

Did you hear about the two gay Irishmen?
Patrick Fitzwilliam and William Fitzpatrick.

Did you hear about the two gay Scotsmen?
Ben Dover and Phil McCrack.

A man walked into a shoe shop and flopped his cock out on the counter.
'That's not a foot.' said the sales assistant.
'No,' said the bloke, *'but it's a good ten inches.'*

A young girl goes to a tattoo artist and asks for a tattoo.
'Where do you want it?'
The girl takes her knickers down, spreads her legs, and points.
'Down there.' she says.
The artist tells her he will have to numb it first.
'Okay.' she says.
So the artist buries his head between her legs and goes *'Num num num num num num num.'*

ANSWER: Did you work it out? That's right – it was all of them.

STUDENT BALLS

Usually held once in Freshers' Week and once at the end of the final term, the student ball has hardly changed in the last 20 years, and is still comprised of bland buffet food, a cheesy tribute band, a bouncy castle, jugglers, drunken rugby players with their trousers down, watery beer that runs out by 11pm, couples doing coke in the toilets and a lame performance from some one-hit wonder, who had a hit single 6 months ago but is now destined for obscurity.

Over-priced and uninspired they may be, but worth attending just once, if only for the unique experience of seeing your mates in tuxedos and slinky dresses.

Having sneaked into St John's College Ball in Oxford last year (in the name of research for the Cheeky Guide to Oxford), we can put your mind at ease that the only difference between the supposedly decadent and glamorous Oxbridge balls and other university balls, is that the Oxbridge tickets are frighteningly expensive (well over £100) and the dress code for women is much, much frumpier.

Student balls will always be decidedly tacky affairs, but if approached with; a sense of fun, a sense of irony, and the sense to make the most of the bar, you will have a terrific time.

DRESSING FOR THE BALL
MEN

You're not going to wow the ladies (or gentlemen) in your interview suit from when you were sixteen. And it's no use trying to get away with a "comedy" outfit, (e.g. wearing a black plastic bin bag and going around telling everyone you're Osama Bin Liner). Generally speaking, and with few exceptions, acceptable male dress breaks down into the following categories:

The Classic

Tuxedo, white shirt with wing collar, black cummerbund/ waistcoat, black bow tie, black patent leather shoes. If you want to be a bit racy, you could try a floral waistcoat or cummerbund, but who wants to look like Simon Callow in Four Weddings and a Funeral? Another slight take on this could be the Viva Las Vegas-style frilly shirt. Unless you're Jimi Hendrix or Doctor Who you'll need a lot of charisma to pull this off though.

The Bogart/Bond

'Of all the balls on all of the campuses, she had to walk into this one'. Look cool as you order your vodka martini in a white dinner jacket, white Oxford collar shirt, black dress trousers, black patent leather shoes, black bow tie, slicked back hair and cigarette dangling off your lip. Look ever-so-slightly less cool as you spill red wine down your jacket. Oh well, if you're playing Bond/ Marlowe for the evening you can always pretend you've been shot.

The Celt

Black dinner jacket, black tie, white wing collar shirt, kilt, Sporran and Dirk, hairy legs, no underpants, tartan socks with holdy-uppy things, black or brown shoes (not trainers). Always a big hit with women this one as they seem endlessly fascinated by kilts and what lies under them, so if you're hung like a donkey, this could work to your advantage. The Scots, however, tend to get a bit tetchy if any old bloke from Essex starts dressing up in their national attire so if challenged, claim some vague Celtic blood runs in the family, even if it is only the leaky haemorrhoids of your gran's old Scottie dog.

WOMEN

There are two basic clothing options for women:

The Frilly Taffeta Nightmare

It's a bad colour and designed by an embittered wedding cake designer on a magic mushroom trip. It's all balloony and ruffled and has a thousand things that can get caught on corners (the ruffles serve as catchers and display areas for any passing vomit). Worn to balls at Oxbridge colleges, York, Durham, Bath and Edinburgh, these horrors still seem to be favoured by those ladies whose chins are weak and blood is blue.

THE FRILLY Taffeta NIGHTMARE

1980's HAIRDO, HELD TOGETHER WITH THREE CANS OF HAIRSPRAY

"PUFFBALL" SLEEVES

ILL-FITTING BODICE

THROWING UP INTO HER GRANDMOTHERS ANTIQUE SILK HANDBAG

SKIRT OF SCARLET O'HARA PROPORTIONS

DANGEROUSLY SMOULDERING MARLBORO

DRAGGING DRUNKEN STIFF ALONG WITH HER AS SHE DASHES FOR THE LOO

Something Slinky / Nice

We at Cheeky do not presume to teach you taste. By owning this book you have already shown that. But simple, stylish, understated and sexy dresses are always going to be a winner. You don't have to be Elizabeth Hurley in some safety-pinned handkerchiefs; just choose something tasteful and refined. Or you could just say 'the hell with it' and show some cleavage. That works every time.

PRANKS

Practical jokes, pranks and collecting police cones are, of course, an age-old university tradition, particularly amongst first years in halls of residence. On no other occasion in your life will you have the time to carry out such devious and petty acts, so if you are bored and of a juvenile disposition, why not try out some of these unsavoury antics on your neighbours…

- **CLING FILM OVER THE TOILET SEAT** (made all the more satisfying by also removing the bathroom light bulb)
- **CRESS SEEDS IN THE CARPET** (needs a little planning but extremely satisfying if you can pull it off. While your neighbour is away for a couple of weeks over Xmas/ Easter, plant the seeds in his/her carpet, soak them in water, and wait with delight for their room to transform into a garden)
- **OXO CUBE IN THE SHOWER HEAD** (steal into your neighbours room, remove the shower head and deftly place an oxo cube in there. You'll know when they're next having a shower by the screams).
- **THE BEDROOM IN THE PARK** (laboriously shifting the entire contents of a friend/ neighbour's bedroom to the grassy bit outside the Student Union/ D Block/ the local park, is a tried and tested classic, particularly favoured on birthdays and during post-exam periods. Try not to pick a day when it might rain or you'll really piss them off)
- **THE BEDROOM ON THE CEILING** (a similar theme to the one above but this one involves a lot of nails, glue and sellotape)
- **THE BEDROOM WRAPPED IN NEWSPAPER** (you can continue this theme on your own now)
- **THE DOG-TURD SANDWICH** (this particularly revolting prank, is to be reserved only for someone for whom you have a personal vendetta. To execute, collect a fresh dog-turd and wrap it up carefully in a piece of paper so that it's hidden. Ensuring your intended victim is going to be at home, leave the turd sandwich on their doorstep, set it alight, knock on the door and run to a safe hideaway. If you haven't guessed what happens next, let's just say that the natural impulse is to stamp…)

Floorwars

With the right ingredients of isolation, boredom, and misanthropy, it is all to easy to find yourself, by the second term, re-enacting the final scenes of 'Lord of the Flies' in your halls of residence. By February/ March the corridors of every student hall in the country have the potential to turn into a battleground, with water-fights, the letting off of fire-extinguishers, towel fights, mock battles and even mud-wrestling becoming an everyday occurrence. On the whole this is all fairly harmless fun, but should you find yourself brandishing a noose and spearheading an angry lynch mob against the inhabitants of the 4th floor, or keeping prisoners tied up in your wardrobe, it's probably time to take stock of your situation.

THE SHAME-FACED CONFESSIONS OF A COVENTRY GRADUTE

"I have to confess, much of my first year (which I spectacularly failed), was occupied with many of the pursuits mentioned above. I lived on the 9th floor of a huge ugly tower block, 4 miles out of Coventry, which fell foul to the 'Lord of the Flies Syndrome' after a bus strike in the first term left all 300 of us isolated (we were too lazy to walk or cycle) and with too much time on our hands.

Not surprisingly then, that by term two, alliances and apartheid had already been instigated between different floors, and battles were in full swing. Floor wars were fought regularly; firstly just with water in squeezy bottles, then as time passed, we moved into biological warfare as more insidious concoctions were developed that permanently stained floors, walls and carpets, and made our hair and teeth fall out. In fact, the enforced separatism eventually became so intense that we ended up far too paranoid to leave our rooms to go to lectures, lest we return to discover our entire bedroom contents super-glued into an enormous sculpture of Hitler.

Perhaps the single greatest act of terrorism we ever committed was against the hall stud; Mike. Mike was smug, drove a TR7 and spent an inordinate amount of time admiring himself in the mirror. But more importantly he lived on Floor Seven, the floor for losers.

So, having foolishly returned home for a weekend in Nottingham to visit his sick mother, he left his room open to all the vultures and pranksters, who naturally took full advantage of this.

Over an entire day, 8 people working flat out, successfully removed the screws from every conceivable object in the room. Every cabinet, every table, every door, every wardrobe, every chair was left delicately hanging, like props in a Charlie Chaplin film, while the screws were hidden in the butter dish. Next we took out all the light-bulbs and fuses, which naturally called for the cling-film to be used in the toilet. Meanwhile, Mike's air-vent was diligently dismantled and two eggs broken and left in there. But perhaps the cruellest act was performed by an art student called Tom, who brought a small Phillips screwdriver with him and proceeded to take apart Mike's vast tape collection. Every one of Mike's two hundred tapes was dismantled, and the reel of tape turned upside down and replaced in the plastic holder. Only after Mike had got his electricity back on the following day, would he discover that his entire tape collection now played backwards.

I still think of him sometimes, returning on that fateful Sunday night to utter anarchy and chaos, stumbling around in his room with cupboards and tables collapsing around him, doors falling on his head and his bedroom reeking of rotten eggs. I often feel pangs of guilt too, and wish I could find some way of saying sorry, but then I remember- the bastard lived on Floor 7."

ANONYMOUS

CONE HEADS

It's a cliché we know (and the favoured topic of countless stand up comedians) but the truth is that nothing will mark you out as a student so clearly as the presence of a traffic cone somewhere in your house. The practice of bringing back a cone as a trophy at the end of a drunken night out is one that has been in existence since time immemorial.

Nobody knows why going to university fills one with an irresistible desire to steal road-safety devices, but it does. Perhaps it's a badge of courage – the student equivalent of the mounted tiger's head proudly displayed on a retired colonel's wall.

FUN TRICKS TO PLAY WITH YOUR TRAFFIC CONE

'PEG-LEG PETE'   'COD-PIECE'   'HARRY POTTER'

PETTY LARCENY GAME

Naturally, as with most status symbols, there is much competition amongst students as to who can bag the greatest number of useless, pointless objects on drunken midnight sorties. If yours is the kind of household that enjoys nothing better than a treasure-hunt style challenge, allow each member of the household one week to collect as many of the following items listed below, and the one with the most points at the end of the 7 days is exempt from washing up for the rest of the year....

* shopping trolley (to be left quietly rusting in the front garden)
  10 points ☐

* A road-sign e.g. 'Keep Left'
  25 points ☐

* A slightly cheekier sign that might be mistaken for a double entendre, i.e. 'No Entry', 'Danger – Escaped Gas', 'Do Not Pull', 'Beware of the beavers'
  20 points ☐

* A shop dummy
  30 points ☐

* A full-size cardboard cutout of a celebrity (e.g. Pierce Brosnan as Bond)
  10 points ☐

* A pub ashtray advertising a beer they no longer make ie. Skol lager, or Barbican. 5 points each with a maximum of 25 points ☐

* A banner headline nicked from outside a newsagents at four in morning that can be construed in either a humorous or surreal fashion – *"Chelsea manager pulls off star player"*
  10 points ☐

THE SINGULAR CUSTOMS
AND TRADITIONS OF OXBRIDGE

OXFORD

England's oldest university boasts a cocktail of ludicrous traditions and ceremonies, many of which date back for many centuries. From the compulsory wearing of formal wear for the first evening dinner, to the clock at Christchurch being permanently 5 minutes slow, this is a city that is proud of its customs. No matter how silly. Here are just a few:

1. Sconcing

An old tradition still occasionally practised at the college's daily formal dinners, whereby if a student (or don for that matter) challenges another to drink a yard of ale (2 and a half pints) they must accept the challenge. Should the participant fail to complete the challenge disgrace will swiftly follow, giving him* little choice but to leave college immediately and join the Foreign Legion.

2. The Mallard Feast

At the beginning of every new century, tradition decrees that after dinner on All Souls Day (14th January), Fellows and Masters from All Souls' College grab sticks and torches and go wandering around the college grounds and rooftops pretending to search for the ghost of a mallard duck. Lord Mallard, who carries a long stick and wears a plastic beak around his mouth heads the search, then, after giving up the ghost, everybody celebrates and sings the Mallard Song. The 'logic' for it all seems to stem from the story that when the college foundations were being laid, a mallard was found in one of the ditches. It still however, begs the question 'why?' and also 'why don't they all go looking for earthworms, millipedes and moles as well?'

For anyone interested in attending, the next Mallard Feast takes take place on January 14th 2101.

3. The Wearing of Carnations

If you happen to be in Oxford the middle of June, don't be surprised to see the students wearing pink, white or red carnations; this will tell you they're in the middle of exams. They wear white for their first exam, pink for the middle and red for their last. Keep an eye out especially for those with red carnations. Tradition decrees that after their last exam has finished, friends and strangers alike are now at liberty to pelt them with eggs and flour and empty tins of baked beans over their heads as a way of saying well done.

*Being an old tradition, it's strictly for the men, but rare exceptions have been made for St Hilda's all-women rugby club

4. Feuds
There are many long-standing feuds between a great number of Oxford colleges, none more intense though than that of Balliol and Trinity. Balliol College even has a society dedicated to the upkeep of mischief against its neighbouring Trinity. The Harry Lime Society, as it is known, is infamous for having applied lime-coloured paint to a great number of the sacred cows of Trinity College, including their boathouse, the roof of the chapel and the college porter.

CAMBRIDGE
Many traditions at this esteemed institution revolve around the river Cam, and, as you can guess, involve a fair amount of falling in, jumping in and seeing how much of it you can drink. Not a pleasant thought, but the river is today a stream of ambrosia compared to its sorry state little more than 100 years ago. There is a story that when Queen Victoria first visited the City and asked the Master of Trinity why there was so much paper floating in the Cam, he replied that they were notices telling people not to bathe in the river, which in effect they were – it was actually used toilet paper.

1.Bridge-hopping
Certain bridges along the Cam are low enough to be climbed up on from the punt, and advanced punters with certificates in heroic athleticism have been known to attempt a bridge-hop. The bridge is approached at low speed and the pole laid down in the punt. The punter then vaults up onto the bridge, runs across and climbs down the other side to alight upon the punt before it drifts past and takes up the pole again. Hard to imagine this being done with any semblance of grace, but it's still a neat trick. If this feat is witnessed by a Dean of any college you are automatically awarded an Oceanography degree.

2. Nightclimbing
Unique to Cambridge, this is a curious undergraduate hobby, which has been furtively pursued for over a century and possibly much longer. It basically involves scaling any grand and venerated building available, and is done either under cover of darkness or very early in the morning so as to avoid having one's collar felt. It is thought to have developed from student climbers' frustration at the dearth of good climbing sites in the local area.

A number of guidebooks exist on the subject, including 'Cambridge Nightclimbing' by 'Hederatus' (available, bizarrely, in the University Library). Hederatus and his friend Brian climbed just about every large building in central Cambridge whilst apparently consuming astonishing amounts of curry and cigarettes, and were responsible for a famous 'Piece in Vietnam' [sic] banner strung between the two spires of King's Chapel. They were finally sent down after being discovered on the roof of the Senate House.

Despite its aura of adventure and romance, please be aware that nightclimbing is not a traditional Cambridge activity that casual visitors may take part in. Proper nightclimbers are highly specialised reckless lunatics, and unless you possess a Captain Scarlet-esque invulnerability to death, it would be wiser to stay on the pavement.

A Cheeky Tale

Cambridge at one time had an over-zealous Climbing Club keen on pranks. Once, they hung a huge flag from a metal pole sticking up from a high wall in a very inaccessible place. The authorities, rather than being intelligent and asking the climbing club to remove it, began to build scaffolding to get it down. Day by day, it reached higher, coming closer and closer to the offending object. Finally, it was almost there, with only a few more hours of work needed. The next day dawned, and to the authorities' vexation, the object had moved to the next pole over, rendering the scaffolding useless.

MUSIC

To some students there can be no other subject more emotive and divisive than that of music. Dare to belittle the latest offerings by DJ Shabby in front of some Anorak, call Stravinsky 'unlistenable rubbish' before a music undergrad, or make a snide comment about Meatloaf in the presence of a Physics student, and you may well find yourself embroiled in a huge argument/ lawsuit/ bloodbath. Music obsessives are usually best left to mix with their own kind where they can sit po-faced in the corner of the uni bar fervently bickering over which is the worst Blur album.

Regardless of your level of passion for music, it will, unquestioningly play a huge role in your life at uni, from the dance-floor favourites and the songs that you will remember friends by, to the ones you will play over and over again whilst at home late at night, writing essays and studying. In years to come you will treasure these records as much as any photos or other relics of your time at university, as they will, we hope, bring back fond memories.

CULTURE

FIFTY CLASSIC STUDENT ALBUMS OF YESTERYEAR

Below we have selected a cross-section of bedroom/ dance floor favourites from the last four decades, beginning with those heady days of the Sixties, when vinyl was king and a band would (literally) write a song on Monday and have it in the shops by Friday, to the floppy-quiffed janglings of the Eighties Indie scene, right through to the cool, knowing sounds of the Nineties.

If you're an open-minded, music-lover, you really should have no excuses for not owning, or at least giving a listen to these albums. There are forty years of classic pop history represented here and with the exception of pompous Prog-Rock noodlers 'Yes', each still comes highly recommended.

THE 1960S
Beach Boys – Pet Sounds
Beatles – Revolver
Beatles – Sgt. Peppers
Rolling Stones – Let it Bleed
Van Morrison – Astral Weeks
Jefferson Airplane – Surrealistic Pillow
Jimi Hendrix – Electric Ladyland
Simon and Garfunkel – Parsley, Sage, Rosemary and Thyme
Jimi Hendrix – Electric Ladyland
Bob Dylan – Blonde on Blonde
The Who – Tommy
Leonard Cohen – Songs from a Room

THE 1970S
Pink Floyd – The Dark Side of the Moon
Joni Mitchell – Blue
Marvin Gaye – What's Going On?
Canned Heat- Canned Heat
Led Zep – Four
Queen – A Night at the Opera
Fleetwood Mac – Rumours
Neil Young -After the Goldrush
The Jam – Setting Sons
The Clash – The Clash
Yes – Fragile
Stevie Wonder – Songs in the Key of Life
Bowie – Hunky Dory

THE 1980s

The Cure – Pornography
Cocteau Twins – Victorialand
Human League – Dare
Pixies – Dolittle
The The -Infected
Michael Jackson – Thriller
Smiths – The Queen is Dead
Stone Roses – Stone Roses
Duran Duran – Rio
Talking Heads – Little Creatures
Wonderstuff – The 8-legged
groove machine
U2 – The Joshua Tree

1990s

Primal Scream – Screamadelica
Prodigy – Fat of the Land
Pulp – Different Class
Blur – Parklife
Chemical Brothers – Exit Planet Dust
Air – Moon Safari
Nirvana – Nevermind
Oasis – What's the Story?
Fatboyslim – You've Come a Long Way Baby
Verve – Urban Hymns
Radiohead – OK Computer
Portishead – Dumb
DJ Shadow – Entroducing

So, how many have you heard?*

Less than 15 Very poor. Music is the food of love after all, and at the moment you've only got one dish on the menu. It's time to educate your palate with a more varied finger-buffet of toothsome classics.

15-30 Not bad cheeky-chops. You have taken the road less travelled but at the last minute veered off at the crossroads of timidity. Time to hitch a lift on the articulated lorry of eclecticism, and take a front-row seat next to the lorry driver of diversity.

Over 30 Congratulations! You have bent over the kitchen table of completism, spread your infinitely receptive buttocks of experimentation, and willingly received the musical love-baton of enlightenment. Good on you.

*This exercise is to be repeated annually

TELEVISION

With the exception of the long-term unemployed, insomniacs and the mentally ill, you are still more likely to watch daytime and early morning programmes than any other social group. Hard-hitting cop shows, trail-blazing dramas about incest and tough documentaries on inner-city turmoil may well pass you by, but children's cartoons, afternoon quiz shows, old episodes of 'Hawaii 5-0', Ricki Lake clones, Channel 5 erotic dramas, and, of course, 'Banzai', may well make up your staple TV diet. It's odd though, that advertisers have never realised that 75 percent of the people watching, say, 'Watercolour Challenge' are under 21 and that, rather than stair-lifts and pension plans, they should be trying to sell trainers, mobile phones, and Ibiza holidays.

UNIVERSITY-THEMED TV SHOWS
THE YOUNG ONES

Cult 80s British TV comedy set in a student house. From the pitfalls of fridge-sharing to the arrival of a vampire through the post, this show (co-written by Ben Elton, Rik Mayall and Lise Mayer) bristles with surreal and anarchic comedy. As the show developed, so did its four main characters, and the brutal humour of their petty conflicts often echoed those of a typical nuclear family. Hippy Neil is the downtrodden mother figure, while Rick (with his tantrums and Marxist politics) and Vivien (the aggressive simpleton) play the squabbling teenage daughter and son. Peppered with appearances from live bands (from Motörhead to Madness) and crammed with incidental but wonderfully bizarre sketches and animations, The Young Ones did for the sitcom what The Simpsons did for cartoons.

Though it only ran for two series, the show made overnight heroes of Rik Mayall, Ade Edmonson and Nigel Planer, paved the way for the likes of Bottom, Black Adder and South Park and was, of course, a huge hit with students. Track it down on video and invite your mates round for a six-hour binge of retro comedy that you won't forget.

UNIVERSITY CHALLENGE

University Challenge has a long and illustrious history. It originally ran on ITV from 1962 – 87, hosted by the golden-haired sexpot, Bamber Gascoigne, and invariably featured pompous scarf-sporting undergraduates, with pudding haircuts and rosy cheeks, answering questions about the likes of Mozart and Chaucer. Yet it proved to be something of a national institution and at its peak had 12 million viewers! Not bad for a poncy, intellectual game-show. Famous contestants have included David Mellor, Clive James, and Stephen Fry (who went down in the show's history for answering every question correctly!).

It was axed in 1987, when viewing figures had shrunk to a paltry 1 million but was resurrected on BBC2 in 1994, under the stewardship of Jeremy Paxman.

Paxman brought his sneering persona to bear on the programme, giving it a somewhat harder edge; his – *'Oh for heaven's sake Pembroke, come on!'* catchphrase making the show ideal for those who like to see others suffer. (Newnham College's dismal no-scoring failure was another 'highpoint').

Brilliantly parodied in one of the episodes of 'The Young Ones', 'Bamber Gascoigne' (played by Griff Rhys Jones) knowingly proclaims, *'the posh kids are going to win – they always do'.*

MOVIES

Watching a classic movie with a bunch of friends can be an evening of near-perfection, especially if you can also persuade one of them to feed you pizza whilst massaging your feet at the same time. But how can you guarantee the quality of the choice of film? For every good movie in the local video store, the next 50 are awful (try watching the latest rubbish from Kevin Costner, Mel Gibson or Sylvester Stallone and you'll soon get the idea).

Below, therefore, we present the current top fifty favourite student films* to help you in your search for that perfect home movie experience.

With the list however, definitely having a bias towards gangster flicks, blockbusters, sci-fi and comedy (with Tarantino, Scorcese and Coppola favouring particularly well) it simply remains our duty to remind you that notable absentees (Hitchcock, Billy Wilder, Nicholas Roeg, Roman Polanski, Fellini, Godard etc) equally deserve the love and attention of any true movie buff.

2001: A SPACE ODYSSEY
AMERICAN BEAUTY
ANNIE HALL (WOODY ALLEN)
APOCALYPSE NOW
BEING JOHN MALKOVICH
BIG BLUE (THE)
BLADE RUNNER
BLUE VELVET
BOOGIE NIGHTS
BREAKFAST AT TIFFANY'S
CLERKS
CLUELESS
DAZED AND CONFUSED
DEER HUNTER (THE)
DIRTY DANCING
DUMBO
ENTER THE DRAGON
FARGO
FIGHT CLUB
GET CARTER
GODFATHER TRILOGY
GOLDFINGER
GOODFELLAS
GRADUATE (THE)
GREASE
INDIANA JONES TRILOGY

JUNGLE BOOK (THE)
LEON
MATRIX (THE)
MIDNIGHT EXPRESS
MONTY PYTHON'S LIFE OF BRIAN
ONE FLEW OVER THE CUCKOO'S-NEST
PIANO (THE)
PULP FICTION
RAGING BULL
RESERVOIR DOGS
SATURDAY NIGHT FEVER
SCARFACE
SEVEN
SHAWSHANK REDEMPTION (THE)
SILENCE OF THE LAMBS (THE)
SLEEPER
STAR WARS TRILOGY
TAXI DRIVER
THERE'S SOMETHING ABOUT-MARY
THIS IS SPINAL TAP
TOY STORY 1 AND 2
TRAINSPOTTING
USUAL SUSPECTS (THE)
WITHNAIL AND I

*Compiled from questionnaires to over 1,000 students

UNIVERSITY THEMED MOVIES

ANIMAL HOUSE

(Dir. John Landis, 1978)

Eighties gross-out comedy, indirectly responsible for Porky's, American Pie, Something About Mary etc. The Animal House of the title is Delta House, the worst fraternity on campus, whose members indulge in an orgy of booze, drugs, pranks, sex and toga parties lead by Bluto Blutovski (John Belushi at the peak of his powers). Recently voted the best comedy film ever by American audiences.

CHARIOTS OF FIRE

(Dir. David Puttnam, 1981)

This multi-Oscar winning film is an all-boys-together eulogy to sporting spirit and quintessential Englishness. Based on the true story of the 1936 British Olympics team and set around the colleges of Oxbridge; Nigel Havers, Sir John Geilgud and Ben Cross excel at being decent and struggling manfully. Vangelis' soundtrack also works wonders. Who else could prevent us openly laughing at men in Damart underwear running in slow-motion through the surf? It's all very lovely and lyrical, and the College-based scenes are beautiful. Ideal to watch if you're planning to study at one of Britain's great bastions of privilege, and want to see how to drag a teddy bear around and wear a cravat.

DAZED AND CONFUSED

(Dir. Richard Linklater, 1993)

It's the early Seventies, and 'School's out for summer!' Richard Linklater's follow-up to Slackers is another excellent student-orientated piece, dealing nostalgically with that strange interim, the summer after leaving school and before attending college. Witness the character who left high-school ten years ago but still lives for the homecoming university students – a comic yet tragic figure, epitomising the eternal drop-out, caught forever in a Beach Boys Endless Summer. The soundtrack is excellent, featuring Alice Cooper, Kiss, Iggy Pop and other Glam Rock heroes.

Marina and Holly from 'Me Without You'

ME WITHOUT YOU

(Dir. Sandra Goldbacher 2001)
Following childhood friends Marina and Holly through teenage years and beyond, this rather lacklustre tale of jealousy and heartache suffers a bit from 'I love the Seventies/ Eighties' syndrome with so much emphasis on perfectly placed songs/ band posters and kitsch furniture, that the plot suffers profusely. The film's strength comes mid-way when the girls move to Brighton to study at Sussex University, and amidst lectures on Barthes and other usual suspects, they both start to have a fling with their tutor (Kyle McLachlan) who plays the role of Dr Love down to a tee, complete with V-neck sweater, mane of hair, a coke habit, and the classic chat-up line 'let's discuss this over tea at my place.' From hereon however, the film gets increasingly tedious over the theme of Holly's unrequited love for Marina's brother Nad, and by the end you may well be chomping at the bit for it to finish.

LAUREL AND HARDY'S 'A CHUMP AT OXFORD'

(Dir. Alfred Goulding, 1940)
Having inadvertently foiled a bank robbery, the hapless duo are rewarded with a chance to gain a proper education at Oxford. On their arrival, the students take every opportunity to lampoon them, until a blow on the head to Stan reveals him to be an English aristocrat who had been suffering amnesia. An endearing classic from the Laurel and Hardy vaults, with plenty of clichéd English catchphrases like 'well done old bean' and 'he's jolly well asking for a punch on the nose'. Look out for a cameo from the very young master of horror, Peter Cushing.

PORNOGRAPHY

Up until the late-Eighties and early Nineties, the pornography debate amongst students definitely erred on the side of 'oh dear me no'. Radical Feminism in the Sixties and Seventies, followed by the 'Politically Correct' Eighties ensured that the kind of male student who enjoyed an evening in bed with a copy of Razzle would have kept it a very dark secret, lest he wanted his genitals confiscated and mounted for display on the Women's Room wall. Those brave enough to publicly declare any interest in photographed nakedness were invariably gay men and engineering students (granted special dispensation on the grounds that they were unlikely to ever see the real thing). And of course back then, pornography for women was still in its infancy, comprising little more than crude diagrams of men's genitalia, accompanied by captions like 'goodness me!' or 'ooh, that's very nice.'

Although it's still true today that putting up a poster of a motorbike ridden by a lady wearing nothing but cowboy boots is an effective form of contraception, things have by and large changed a great deal. In the last ten years, the 'New Lad' culture, spearheaded by the likes of Loaded magazine, TFI Friday, and 'Ibiza Uncovered', brought voyeurism and titillation into vogue, offering a nation of horny young men the opportunity to stroll into WHSmith every month to ogle at Danni Minogue's tits in over 50 different dwarf porn-mags* such as Front, FHM, Maxim etc

Add to this the fact that cult porn flicks such as 'Deep Throat' can now be purchased in Virgin and HMV, and it would seem that pornography has finally infiltrated the mainstream.

*So called because its 'young' readers are unable to reach the real stuff on the top shelf

Or has it? One could argue that 'lifestyle' magazines such as Men Only and FHM are little more than a tarted up version of page 3, while the re-release of 'Deep Throat' et al have been largely a waste of time, owing to the fact that they've had all the 'good bits' chopped out, leaving just the plot!

Perhaps the real revolution has come quietly and steadily in the form of a small, but ever-growing market of pornography for women. While countless male students have settled for second best, women it seems are beginning to reach for the real thing. No crappy style magazines with centre pull-outs of Robbie Williams in a pair of Y-fronts. Just pictures of naked men, and lots of big willies.

So, where does that leave you? Is it all right to drag your bursting suitcase of porn to the university dorm? While we're not at liberty to pass judgement, what we can say is this; if it doesn't involve animals or corpses, printed or filmed erotica may not make male or female students into the social outcasts it once would have done. Fact is, you'll probably end up getting it nicked by most of the people in your house/ corridor, regardless of their gender.

Cover of a genuine American porn mag!

UNIVERSITY-THEMED NOVELS

THE SECRET HISTORY
DONNA TARTT

A group of Classics' students at an exclusive New England university are driven to re-discover the euphoric states of the ancient Dionysian rituals they have learned so much about. They ultimately succeed, but with tragic results. Utterly compelling – part thriller, part Generation X satire, and part comedy – it is probably the only novel to successfully blend horror with Greek scholarship. Read it and you will be chomping at the bit, waiting for Tartt's next masterpiece. And from experience, this is the perfect holiday read.

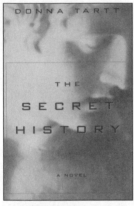

LUCKY JIM
KINGSLEY AMIS

This Fifties comic novel focuses around the life of Jim Dixon, a struggling young historian who hates everything about the establishment around him, and also seems prone to a disastrous love life. Very funny snapshot of Fifties intellectual pretensions and social snobbery, it is regarded as one of the first and finest contributions to the

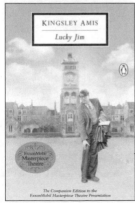

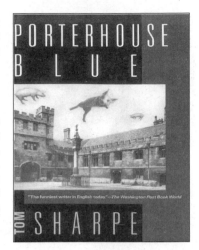

'angry young man' canon (the most famous being John Osborne's 'Look Back in Anger'). The film starring Ian Carmichael isn't half bad either.

THE HISTORY MAN
MALCOLM BRADBURY
Seventies satire on radicalism, charting the adventures of yet another history lecturer; Howard Kirk; a monstrous, bearded, manipulative, cheese-cloth-shirt-wearing, sexually predatory left-wing fascist. With the exception of the cheesecloth, this portrait remains, alas, just as relevant today.

BRIDESHEAD REVISITED
EVELYN WAUGH
Much-loved, partly Oxford-based novel describing the platonic, near-homosexual friendship of two students, Charles Ryder and Lord Sebastian Flyte. The latter, a seemingly vacuous dandy, who derives most of his humour from his teddy bear Aloysius, is in fact a troubled alcoholic, victim of his dysfunctional aristocratic family the Marchmains and their uneasy espousal of Catholicism. About as far removed from modern university life as you can get, (even at Oxford,) it is, nonetheless nostalgic, warm, and something of a departure for the more usually acerbic Waugh.

ZULEIKA DOBSON
MAX BEERBOHM
Ghosts, weird portents and magical phenomena abound in this wonderful, 1911 black comic fantasy. The eponymous heroine is an Oxford college warden's granddaughter, so beautiful and heartless that she causes the entire male student population to commit suicide during the 'Eights' boat race. Elegant, playful, and deliciously ruthless, it is currently, and unaccountably, out of print, but definitely worth the schlep round the second-hand bookshops.

PORTERHOUSE BLUE
TOM SHARPE
A bawdy, outlandish and beautifully constructed farce, involving all the familiar Sharpe ingredients (inflated condoms, improbable death, sexual obsession, and institutional hypocrisy). Zipser, a fresher tragically obsessed with his fat middle-aged room-cleaner, unwittingly becomes fuel for the new warden's campaign to modernise the college. But the 'forces of conservatism', in the form of the head porter, Scullion, are determined to preserve the college's archaic traditions – at any price. A ribald and rich satire on all the excess of 'High Table', it doesn't take a don to work out that Peterhouse at Cambridge is its intended target.

FIVE BOOKS YOU SHOULD NEVER BE CAUGHT WITH ON YOUR SHELF
1) 'Mein Kampf' A.Hitler
2) 'The Penguin Book of Racist Jokes'
3) 'Learning to fly' Victoria Beckham
4) 'The New English Bible'
5) 'Young Conservative's Manifesto' (Or the Labour one for that matter)

It's surprising how little this list has changed in the last ten or even twenty years, as the same old faces seem to pop up on posters found in student living rooms and bedroom walls, but then you might easily disagree, wondering why Samantha from 'Sex and the City' doesn't even get a look in. Nevertheless, this top eleven was carefully compiled after years of research, soul-searching and endless questionnaires. Oh all right, we just asked the bloke who sells the posters every year at Freshers' Fair. It might be an interesting exercise to make your own and see how it changes at the end of every year…

1. CHE GUEVARA
Highlights: *Making berets fashionable, and bringing about revolution in Cuba.*
The number one poster boy and one-time heroic symbol for all budding revolutionaries, this Argentinian freedom-fighter (i.e. terrorist) is now little more than a meaningless icon, along the same lines as the bloke with the moustache on packets of 'Pringles'. Ask anyone with a Che Guevara T-shirt exactly what he stood for and they'll say something like 'Y'know, revolution. Fighting the government, and that. Smash the state!' before running away. In actual fact, Che is probably the world's most celebrated student activist – he was studying medicine when he joined Fidel Castro to start the revolution in Cuba, although this might just have been a Rag-week prank.

2. BRUCE LEE
Highlights: *Enter the Dragon, The Way of the Dragon, Carry on Dragonning*
Mould-breaking martial arts star and first Hong Kong chop-socky merchant to break Hollywood; indeed the first Asian superstar in the West. Also something of a civil rights campaigner, he died very young and under mysterious circumstances. Theories range from a 'body vibration' mystical killer martial arts experiment gone wrong to a CIA hit. Responsible for the pub-conspiracy-theory *'He was so fit, right, that his body just exploded. That's right – exploded.'*

CULTURE

3. OSCAR WILDE

Highlights: *The Picture of Dorian Grey, Salome, The Selfish Giant, Importance of Being Earnest, generally being a witty bastard.*

Eccentric genius, essayist, poet, playwright, and all-round velvet pantalooned dandy. Wilde's homosexuality (in particular his relationship with Lord Alfred Douglas) brought his foppish lifestyle to an end forever, landing him 3 years in chokey, a harrowing account of which can be found in 'The Ballad of Reading Gaol'. After being released he had a stab at a comeback, but died a pauper in Paris. His last words were, reputedly *'Either that wallpaper goes, or I do.'* Years ahead of his time, Wilde paved the way for such future iconoclastic dandies as Quentin Crisp, Stephen Fry (who even played him in the film 'Wilde') and Jarvis Cocker.

4. JOHN LENNON

Highlights: *Strawberry Fields, Tomorrow Never Knows, the good bit in A Day in the Life, Bagism.*

Still a huge icon the world over, Lennon, to many people represents revolution, surrealism, pacifism and a great sense of mischief. True, he could often be something of a paradox (a millionaire who asked us to 'imagine no possessions'? A pacifist who gave donations to terrorists?), perhaps it is due to his tragic death at the hands of a psychotic fan in 1980 that Lennon has been so favourably remembered by history, but he has somehow always held incredible popularity with the masses.

His marriage to Yoko Ono has, however, always been problematic for many Beatles fans, as she was widely resented for splitting up the Beatles (although not as widely-resented as she was for singing). Nevertheless, she did encourage him to spend a week in bed with a bag over his head for peace, which surely makes up for it.

5. BUDDHA

Highlights: *finding enlightenment and making fat cool.*

Since the Sixties, interest in Eastern religions has been on the increase in the UK, with Buddhism in particular growing from strength to strength, while Christianity has all but fallen by the wayside.

With no God to believe in, no boring church services in cold damp buildings, and no antiquated attitudes towards sexuality, Buddhism has proved to be a comfortable starting point for the fledgling spiritual seekers, offering a chance for self-realisation through meditation, chanting and eating lots of pies.

Buddha statues are now a common feature in student bedrooms and mantle pieces, with Buddha recently voted 'Religious figurine most likely to be used as a drugs stash.' Well, would you rather store your illicit goodies in a big fat laughing man or a man nailed to a wooden cross?

Anyone remember the episode of the Simpsons where someone asks Bart the old Zen Koan ' what is the sound of one man clapping?' and he works out the answer?*

6. MADONNA

Highlights: *Material Girl, In Bed With, Drowned World Tour, Live Internet broadcast of London gig for Music.*

Eighties plastic pop star who went on to become bigger than the original Madonna by taking her clothes off a lot more than Christ's mum ever did. Famous for being the most ambitious person on the planet, a clever, strategic shagger and not letting her not-particularly good voice get in the way of having one of the most spectacular music careers of all time. She has, though, never managed to succeed as an actress; try watching 'Shanghai Suprise' or 'Body Of Evidence' if you want to see acting so wooden that you feel like giving it a coat of Ronseal.

7. SEAN CONNERY AS JAMES BOND

Highlights: *Goldfinger Dr No, From Russia with Love, Thunderball.*

Violent, misogynistic murderer, or, a suave, sophisticated British secret agent? It all depends on your point of view. Connery was by far the coolest Bond, and the best-dressed (despite having to wear a hair-piece). The first four Bond films of the Sixties remain compulsive Xmas and Easter viewing, bringing out a yearning in young men the world over to lead a lifestyle that includes secret assignments in Rio, skiing down mountains whilst dodging machine-gun fire, quipping 'how shocking' after electrocuting their adversaries in the bath, and going to bed with a woman called Miss Goodfanny that they picked up at the casino.

*We can't do the answer justice in words so we'll leave it for you to find out for yourself. Besides, do you think we're going to give away the answer to a 2,000-year-old conundrum just like that?

8. SALVADOR DALI

Highlights: *Dali Museum in Spain, his moustache, melting clocks, tigers, pomegranates, legs.*
Spanish surrealist, painter, pervert, and egomaniac . Second only to Madonna as one of the last century's most remorseless self-publicists and mythologisers. That postcard of his wacky, gurning mug can still be found blu-tacked to the wall in countless student households. Most famous for his melting clocks, flaming giraffes, and ants coming out of people's hands. Famously sent his own dad a bag of his spunk with a note saying 'now we're quits'.

9. BUFFY

Highlights: *keeping America free from vampires, demons, and ghosts. And saving the world. (A lot.)*
Definitely a post-feminist icon for the 21st century, Buffy proves that you can kick seven shades of shit out of a bloodsucker while still looking pretty and keeping your lipgloss nice and shiny. Girls want to be her, and boys want to be beaten up by her. Joss Whedon has managed to create a gutsy, feisty heroine who isn't irritating or self-righteous.

10. DAVID BECKHAM

Highlights: *Greece, 93rd Minute*
Goldenballed husband of Posh and idiot savant football genius. It is possible to study him and his missus at degree level, although the shaven-headed numbskull would probably manage to flunk even this. His low I.Q. and tiny little boy's voice aside, he is much loved. Beckham has managed to combine great footballing skills with a touchy-feely parenting side that appeals to the ladies, and daring fashion sense (most footballers, let's face it, dress like Delboy). Let's try not to think of the Marks and Spencer boys range.

BECKHAM JOKE:

Why does Posh Spice blow in David Beckham's ear?
To give him a refill.

11. HOMER SIMPSON

Highlights: going to space, driving Springfield's first monorail, averting nuclear disaster (by accident), getting to the top of the charts with the B-Sharps, earning his own entry in Webster's Dictionary, inventing the 'Flaming Homer' (nicked by Moe)

Homer J. Simpson is the eternal everyman – with his laziness, stupidity, love of doughnuts, poor parenting skills, anger at authority, and credulous belief in everything the TV tells him, Homer is someone we can all identify with. Essentially a thoughtless man struggling to be good, he is redeemed only by his (sorely tested in the case of Bart) love for his family.

As Homer says while sitting an exam – *'Okay brain, I don't like you, and you don't like me. So let's just get through this, and then I can get back to killing you with beer.'* Does that ring any bells with anyone?

HOW WELL DO YOU KNOW YOUR ICONS?

To needlessly pad out this book we've listed eleven little-known 'facts' about the icons above. E-mail the correct answers to us and win a top night out, all expenses paid, at the Harry Ramsden's chip shop in Brighton. The correct solutions can be found on page 373, unless you're serious about the free fish and chips, in which case you have to promise not to peek.

1) Was in court for sexual harassment after peeling a 'Gummi Bear' off a woman's bottom.
2) Posed covered in blood for the Sunday papers.
3) Suffered terrible body odour.
4) Ritually set fire to a full-sized stuffed giraffe every year.
5) When asked by American customs if he had anything to declare announced 'nothing but my genius.'
6) Publicly embarrassed Warren Beatty.
7) This person's full name inadvertently includes the name of a famous sex-shop.
8) Wore a wig and dentures right from the beginning of his career.
9) Reputedly a very nice chap.
10) Pissed on a nun for fun. Also subject of a film that alluded to a homosexual affair with his manager.
11) His films had to be slowed down so his moves could be seen by the human eye.

DON'T SUFFER IN SILENCE

Feeling uncultured? Don't know your Dylan Thomas from your Bob Dylan? Fallen for an English Lit student and don't want to be found out that the only thing you've ever read is the Beano?

Of course there's no quick solution to turning from Liam Gallagher to Melvyn Bragg but we can recommend the 'Introducing' series of books as a good starting point. From topics ranging from Plato and Einstein to Post-Modernism, these are an easy read, use cartoons and illustrations to help clarify the information, and what's more, you can read one cover to cover in about two hours. And, if you can find any that cover some of the subjects featured in your course – all the better.

TRAVEL

Money worries aside, your student days are a perfect time for seeing the world. While in only a few years time you could be weighed down by a full-time job, a crippling student loan to repay and twelve children to feed, right now you have three gloriously care-free months every summer to play with; ideal for a long jaunt overseas.

Adventuring abroad can be a wondrous cure for the fustiness of mind brought on by months spent in libraries hunched over books and engaging in complex intellectual theorising. Although what you actually do abroad may well be pretty much what you would do at uni (drinking, dancing and copping off with someone) there's something about distant lands and climes, in which so many aspects of life are different – the weather, the culture, the architecture, the art, the language, the toilets – turning your travels into a profoundly rich and spiritual experience. Even if you do spend half your time sleeping in Eastern European Railway stations, eating nothing but cheese sandwiches and wearing the same clothes you started your travels in five weeks previously, these experiences will broaden your horizons and form memories you will treasure for the rest of your life.

Of course, money is bound to be an issue, but don't worry, there are various low-budget ways to visit other countries and even some opportunities to make money out of your travels including; working holidays, teaching English abroad and 'development and relief work'. Furthermore, many offers and opportunities are only open to students (including special visa arrangements) and discounts are available the whole world over at the production of a student card, from the record shops of San Francisco to the brothels of Bangkok. Bear in mind too that your parents might be surprisingly supportive of your desire to travel. Many hold that some travelling is essential to an all-round education – and they're right. But if mum and dad won't stump up the cash, your overdraft is fit to bursting and your only option is to spend the entire summer working, ask yourself this – would you rather spend 12 weeks at the cement factory back home in Swindon, or as a holiday rep in the South of France?

Globe-trotting Elton John-style doesn't come cheap. As tempting as it might seem, it's wise to avoid attempting to travel on an ultra-low budget (i.e. simply turning up in some foreign city with just enough money to get drunk and eat burgers for a day) and hope it'll somehow turn into a jolly adventure. You will most likely spend all your daylight hours recovering from hellish nights in which you are repeatedly thrown out of parks and doorways by unsympathetic policeman with big truncheons and poor communication skills.

As in Zen, however, there is a middle path. There are countless opportunities for working holidays abroad, and some organisations will even pay for your flight or travel costs up front, on the agreement that it will come out of your total earnings, still leaving you with enough cash leftover to do a month's sight-seeing at the end. Many other less formally organised opportunities exist too, like picking grapes in Italy, farming work in Spain, panning for gold in Belgium and so on. Most of these will usually involve large or small gangs of other students and travellers from diverse places for you to befriend, learn the true spirit of multiculturalism and international co-operation, and get off with.

CAMP AMERICA

Several organisations provide access to this popular way for students to visit the States for a working vacation. Thousands of camps take place all over America every summer, offering children from ages 8 – 14 activity-intensive holidays in the country. For this they need 'camp counsellors' to be available for at least nine weeks, generally from early/mid June to mid-August, and to supervise and take part in an almost endless list of camp activities, i.e. canoeing, sailing, rock-climbing, archery, circus skills, overnight camping trips, all manner of artistic pursuits, music entertainments and theatre, story-telling, scientific experiments, football and baseball and of course, fighting off the hideously deformed psychopath who will be lurking in nearby woods having recently escaped from a Seventies horror B-movie. Camp Counsellor is a role for those who have an interest in working with children (like prospective teachers) and a genuine liking for them, and Summer Camp organisations particularly like it if you have some sports or arts ability you can share. There are also many openings for those with experience of working with the mentally or physically disabled, or anyone who's ever shared a room with a Physics student. There are also places available in specific summer camps, which are themed in certain specialist areas:

- **Camp Obesity:** Spend a summer trying to stop fat kids flicking each other with twisted towels in the shower.

- **Camp Alienated Goth:** learn how to bring together monosyllabic spotty nerds in "spontaneous" group hugs and supervising Death Metal CD-smashing sessions.

If, for some reason you'd rather not spend a summer constantly surrounded by over-excited kids, you can still visit summer camps on the same basic deal as a cleaning and maintenance operative doing work in the kitchens and suchlike.

The major organisations (see links) offering Summer Camp placements provide a total service which includes outward flight to North America and return flight (chosen by you), plus bus on arrival, accommodation and transport to camp the following morning.

www.bunac.org.uk
www.campamerica.co.uk

INTERNSHIPS & WORKING HOLIDAYS FOR STUDENTS

A whole host of programs are available to students (including ex-students who were students within the last year), as well as work and travel opportunities for non-students. This can include internships in the USA, Australia, New Zealand, or Canada, where you find work related to your qualifications and career plans. Special visa arrangements exist to allow students to visit and work for periods up to a year in other countries. Also available are placements teaching English in countries like China, Japan, Thailand and Wales.

www.councilexchanges.org.uk
Work, travel, teach and learn abroad on cultural exchange programmes

www.aiesec.org
Facilitates international exchanges of students and recent graduates in paid traineeships or as volunteers for a non-profit organisation

www.iaeste.org
Vocation-based exchanges in member countries working in fields related to the student's disciplines or study

www.payaway.co.uk (recommended)
Friendly non-industry travel website packed with links aimed at young Brits 'keen to take the best chance of prolonged travel before 40+ solid years of slaving for the boss drains the life from them'.

www.ccusa.com

CAMPSITE COURIERS

The tourism industry generates thousands of jobs, and companies are constantly on the lookout for young people to work on a seasonal, temporary basis. A major source of jobs are the many continental campsites, big and small, which employ people in a variety of tasks. The season starts and ends with 'montage and demontage' i.e. putting up tents and taking them down, but the main source of jobs is the need for 'couriers'. From an outsider's perspective, couriers seem to do little more than walk around with a clipboard, show off their tan, get drunk with you in the evenings, and politely let you know that your farting is keeping others awake at night. But the job description generally involves stuff like greeting arrivals, cleaning tents and caravans, dealing with any problems such as illness/ theft/ espionage, arranging parties and events, entertaining children, and regularly removing the congealed wads of hair and dead skin that accumulate under the shower plug-holes. For this you will get between £90 – £110 per week, including accommodation (a tent or caravan) and meals.

HOLIDAY REPS

A slightly more upmarket field is working as a holiday company rep at beachclub hotels during the summer across the Mediterranean as nightclub managers, clerical staff, receptionists, sport and activities instructors, cooks, bar staff, and the like. The salary varies from between £40 and £160 per week depending on your skills. Again food and accommodation are usually included, as well as travel expenses, health insurance, use of facilities and lots of partying. A knowledge of crap Eighties songs and how to dance to them is essential.

SKI RESORTS

Winter tourism also generates a lot of work, and there are many seasonal vacancies at ski resorts. The most common posts are for 'Floaters'; general handymen involved in repair work, cleaning and possibly some driving; 'Plongeurs; kitchen work and table waiting, and Chalet Girls/Boys & Couples where you will live with holidaymakers in the chalet. The blurb says you are there to 'ensure the guests have a wonderful holiday,' but in practise this means general skivvying; such as doing their cooking, cleaning and laundry, making the beds and having sex with them. How much fun this is depends a lot on the nature of the guests, but most chalet-workers manage, and if you do get stuck with a bunch of miserable snotty gits who complain you've lost their favourite socks and won't eat your pasta dish for the seventh night in a row, you can always find insidious ways of getting your revenge (see pranks in 'Traditions').

www.payaway.co.uk/dirtourism.htm
A multitude of links to companies employing students for seasonal tourism and holiday rep jobs
www.clubmed.com
Has links to recruitment pages
www.skirecruit.com
Working holidays in ski resorts
www.skistaff.co.uk
Yet more working holidays in ski resorts

VSO – VOLUNTARY SERVICES OVERSEAS
www.vso.org.uk

If taking your empty wine bottles down to the bottle bank every week and buying eco-friendly shampoo isn't enough to salve your social conscience over the state of the world, then talk to these people. VSO is an international development charity that works in third world countries with volunteers of all ages, enabling anyone to share their skills and experience with local communities in the developing world. VSO aren't messing around, and want teachers, health professionals, IT specialists, business, management and finance professionals, social and community workers and technical and media people, and they can provide courses in essential teaching skills for people who want to volunteer but don't have a specialist skill to offer. The basic package is a two-year placement (with flights paid for you) and a comfortable subsistence wage while you're abroad. On your return you'll receive a lump sum of approx £1500 to aid the resumption to normal life and work, with which you'll be able to immediately rush out and do all the things you've missed for the last 24 months, such as eating marmite sandwiches, fish and chips and drinking warm beer.

PASSPORTS

OK, it's rather obvious that you'll need one to go abroad, but if you don't possess one, bear in mind they cost £28 and should be applied for weeks in advance of your travels. It is possible to get a passport at the last minute, but this will cause you untold stress and will probably involve driving to a remote village in Cornwall to collect it.

For applications: 0870 521 0410/ www.ukpa.gov.uk

BACKPACKS

Choose one carefully, it will be your home for the duration of your trip, and if it's uncomfortable, or too heavy and bulky you may grow to hate it with a passion. Most backpacks come with internal frames, and while these may look neater and less bulky, the purpose of an external frame is to keep the backpack away from your back and thus avoid excessive sweatiness and chafing on long hikes.

However many neat pockets and super-sneaky extra compartments a pack has, you will still have to leave behind at least half the things you want to take; including your laptop. Backpacking is all about efficient packing and minimalism, and if you take too much stuff you'll either end up throwing some of it away, or one day you'll collapse in utter exhaustion on the side of the road leaving your companions no option but to put you out of your misery by shooting you.

Some backpacks come with a detachable smaller pack, which can be very useful for day trips out (if the hostel or hotel provides lockers to keep your main pack safe).

HOSTELS

There are essentially two types of Youth Hostels in the world today; the independent and the official. **The Independent hostels** (www.hostels.com) tend to be a little more lively than their official counterpart, but a little messier. **The International Youth Hostel Association** (www.yha.org.uk) has hostels all over the world, and these can range from the very cheap to the relatively plush. The Hostels of Europe website (www.hostelseurope.com) gives a rough price guide for European hostels per night as below:

> A – under 10 Euros (£3.50p)
> B – 10 -15 Euros (£6.20p)
> C – 15 – 20 Euros (£10)
> D – 20 – 25 Euros (£13)
> E – 25 + (£16)

As above, some accommodation is very cheap, but can be as basic as a large room full of cushions and mats with everyone sleeping where they like – this can be charmingly rugged and informal, or make you feel like you've stepped into a scene from Midnight Express. Most hostels also have a shared cooking area with pots and pans etc for preparing your own meals.

It's a very good idea to book at least your first few nights stay before you leave the UK to ease you into the game – you can do this through various websites (see Hostels of Europe above). There are also lists of recommended hostels in major cities throughout the world. Finding a hostel is usually not a big problem unless there's some kind of festival or big public event going on and everywhere is full. Seasoned backpackers sometimes earn extra pocket money by hanging round railway and airport terminuses handing out leaflets advertising specific hostels to new visitors, and often the problem on arrival is not so much finding somewhere to stay, as getting the hell away from the swarming gangs of hostel touts thrusting leaflets at you and giving you the hard sell.

MEETING OTHER TRAVELLERS

The shared experience of being far from home forges a common bond between travellers, and friendships can be formed very quickly and without the usual social malarkey, which involves repeatedly bumping into each other at dinner parties, making hours of small talk, swapping favourite films and comparing childhood traumas. On arrival at a hostel in an unknown city, in an unfamiliar country, on an unexplored continent it is not unusual to find yourself six hours later completely pissed and playing charades with a gang of backpackers from all four corners of the world, whose only other common feature is that none of them have changed their underwear for at least four days.

Obviously a certain amount of common sense applies, but this camaraderie can be reassuring and also very useful. Other travellers can provide local knowledge and top tips about where to stay, and where to visit or find temporary work, as well as dispensing general travellers' wisdom and telling exciting tales of extraordinary places you may never see for yourself.

TRAVELOGUES

The advent of the Internet has enhanced the whole concept of keeping a travel journal, and there are internet booths and cafés all over the world, sometimes in the unlikeliest places such as Hull. By creating a mailing list (for example at www.yahoogroups.com and elsewhere) and subscribing friends and family to it, you can email your news to all and sundry in one fell swoop, thus keeping everyone agog with excitement and interest in your latest adventures. Some sites provide free online Travelogue facilities to which you can add installments then automatically send the URL of the latest update to the email addresses of everyone in a pre-defined list. These online travelogues also allow you to upload images using the digital cameras and scanners (available in some internet cafés,) so everyone at home can see how tanned and happy you are. It's also a good opportunity to reveal the tattoo you had done in term two, giving your parents a few weeks to come to terms with it before you return home for a good flogging.

Online Travelogues:

www.travel-experiences.com
www.trekshare.com

Finding Yourself

As you can't really lose yourself, this metaphorical maxim has always seemed a trifle nonsensical. And even if you could, the sensible thing to do would be to look in the last place you saw yourself (in the manner of someone looking for their car keys) not to go aimlessly wandering across the globe, as that would suggest your self has secretly emigrated, which would be silly.

If you do truly believe that you've lost yourself, be comforted that you've probably only wandered off for a bit because you were bored or lonely, and chances are, come suppertime you'll sheepishly re-appear in the doorway before tucking straight into the Spaghetti Bolognese you made yourself earlier.

TRAVEL

SOME BIG TICKETS
INTER-RAIL

An Inter-Rail pass is a magic ticket, not wholly unlike one of Willy Wonka's, that runs for a month and lets you go anywhere in Europe within pre-defined zones of your choice. Prices range from roughly £150 to £250 per month (if you're under 26), depending on how far you want to go.

For an intense whistle-stop tour of the highlights of Europe, trains are the very thing: none of the queasy bum-numbing torture of long bus trips, or the claustrophobic terror of hurtling through the stratosphere in a long metal tube. Instead, you just sit back at leisure and watch Europe unfold before you, occasionally stopping to explore the really good bits. There are no limitations on how many journeys you can make with an Inter-Rail ticket, and if you are some kind of crazed train fetishist, you could conceivably spend the entire month on trains reading Harry Potter, listening to your MP3 player, eating buffet food, and solving unlikely murder mysteries involving monocle-sporting colonels, rich widows and illegitimate offspring.

www.raileurope.co.uk/railpass/prices
www.railpassdirect.co.uk
www.raileurope.co.uk

ROUND-THE-WORLD FLIGHTS

If you feel that Europe is a little too predictable and might fail to satisfy your craving for a wild experience, then a Round-the-World flight is the very thing to stiffen your travel-nipples. Prices can range from between £600 – £1500 (a combined Xmas and birthday present from understanding parents?) depending on the route taken and the number of stops involved, and most tickets run for a year (although this can be extended or worked around if you have the money). The exact route you follow is up to you – there are estimated to be up to 25,000 possible variations – But as a rule it must be decided before the ticket is bought. Some airline alliance groups do allow you to make changes while you are travelling, but charge an admin fee of approx £50.

Most travel companies supplying RTW flights will recommend you include at least one independent overland journey between airports – known as a 'surface sector'. This will add colour to your journey and has the advantage of not being included as a 'hop' on your ticket. Classic overland routes include:

Bangkok to Singapore
Cairo to Istanbul
Moscow to Beijing (Trans-Siberian Express)
Torquay to Weston-Super-Mare (National Express)

The actual dates that you choose to go between destinations are very flexible: you can pencil in some approximate dates when you buy the ticket, but can change these on-the-fly if, for example, you are kidnapped by Guatemalan bandits but escape and spend three weeks in the jungle living on maggots and tree toads, or alternatively, you find you have accidentally lost a fortnight immersed in the sordid depravity of the fleshpots of Bangkok.

STUDENT FRIENDLY TRAVEL AGENTS & OTHER USEFUL LINKS

www.bridgetheworld.com
One-stop travel shop offering services from discounted flights and adventure travel to tailor-made & long-haul holidays.

www.campustravel.co.uk
Independent travel site for students and young travellers with routes, special deals and advice.

www.cheapflights.com
Includes Round-the-World flights section.

www.clubmed.com
Big Mediterranean holiday provider with recruitment links

www.ctstravel.com

www.freedomtrek.com
All-in-one student travel site.

www.gonomad.com
Alternative travel site with info on unique lodgings and alternative transportation.

www.only1travel.co.uk/

www.roundtheworldflights.com
Includes online push-button route planner with approximate prices, options, events, activities, tours, resources and work, study and volunteer opportunities.

www.statravel.co.uk/
One of the biggest and most popular student travel agencies with probably more branches in the UK than any other. Often your best first port of call to compare and contrast with other offers.

www.studenttravels.com
Work and study opportunities, travel guides, travel writing and top tips.

www.studenttrips.co.uk
Not a web for free drugs but a student and youth travel guide that includes links, offers and advice, plus a Gap Year Out section.

www.trailfinders.co.uk
One for the backpackers, this offers everything from overland tours to visa and immunisation services.

www.travelcuts.co.uk
Excellent prices for things like rail passes and adventure tours.

www.thetravellerslounge.co.uk
Round-the-world travel guide featuring route-planner.

www.airline-network.co.uk

www.easyjet.com
Based in Luton, Easyjet offers very reasonable fares to the continent as long as you book well in advance

www.ryanair.com
Home of the more or less free flights, get to many places in Europe for 30p, but as above, flights need to be booked well in advance.

www.britishairways.com
The 'Worlds Favourite Airline' now offers discounted fares that actually seem to be a better deal that the 'low fares' carriers.

Ruins at Chichen Itza, Mexico

THE CHOICE IS YOURS

Fish and Chips in Cleethorpes

LEAVING

"Sociology degrees. Please take one."

PERENNIAL GRAFITTI INSCRIBED ABOVE TOILET-ROLL
DISPENSERS IN UNIVERSITY TOILETS

ON DISCOVERING YOUR DEGREE IS WORTHLESS

It is your graduation day; you have had your photo taken with hundreds of people (none of whom you'll ever see again) and in the last three hours sat through a tedious ceremony somewhat akin to a church service where the vicar has decided to shake hands with every single person in the congregation. But as you step up to the Vice Chancellor to shake his hand and he presents you with an elaborate scroll and as your proud parents beam from the crowd below, your bosom swells with pride. Here it is in your grasp at long last, the culmination of three or four years hard graft. But has the struggle really been worth it? Is the piece of paper you hold – surrounded by impressive-looking heraldic designs and the Latin motto 'scroteo corpus mentus scratchus' (Do not wash the armadillo) – really any use to you in the world of employment?

Clearly, there are certain subjects that automatically lead to specific careers. Law students go on to become solicitors, Medical students may become doctors and Art students are always guaranteed work at McDonald's. And while some degrees may only qualify you for teaching (e.g. Classics) a good number will leave you high and dry in the jobs market. (Any Media Studies graduate who imagines that there are boards up in the Jobcentre advertising for Blue Peter presenters is going to be sorely disappointed.)

Part of the problem is that with more and more people going to university, having letters after your name isn't as impressive as it once was. So what do you do? After all, this piece of paper has not only cost you three years of hard work, but also a very great deal of money.

Firstly, don't despair. No degree, no matter how esoteric, is entirely worthless. The disciplines you have mastered (i.e. being able to write an intelligible sentence, meet deadlines, conduct your own research etc) can be applied to any number of careers, however seemingly unrelated. Secondly, the time you spent not doing your degree was probably more beneficial than all the hours spent beavering away in the library, and your extra-curricular activities can often bear fruit – Rowan Atkinson didn't study being funny at University any more than Tony Blair studied being Prime Minister (of course, some might argue that it shows).

Last but not least, remember that at the end of the day, it doesn't really matter if you do tear up your Chemistry Degree and decide to become a goat-farmer, scuba-diver or transvestite pub-singer. Your years at university might have left you with a considerable debt, but if in the process you've realized what you actually do want to do, then it's money well spent. Much of the point of going to uni is that it gives you time to consider your options, gives you a flavour of different kinds of life, and the chance to dabble in what really interests you. And with a little imagination you can turn all this to your advantage in the workplace. Saying all that, if you do end up leaving with a degree in Philosophy, mine's a Big Mac.

RECONCILING YOUR PARENTS TO YOUR LOUSY RESULTS

A friend who shall remain nameless (but Shihab is pretty close) got a Third in his finals. As his parents were middle-aged immigrants from Bangladesh and not really au fait with the working of British universities, he merely told them that a Third was the highest possibly degree, followed by 2:2, 2:1, and, finally, a First. They believed this, and spent graduation day smiling pityingly at his friends who had received 2:1s and Firsts. Indeed they believe it to this day, and have his certificate proudly framed on their wall. If they ever find out the truth they'll probably kill him.

Though you might be unable to pull the wool over your parents' eyes with that particular scam, there is still an art to preparing mum and dad for your (potentially) disappointing results, so it may be a good idea to adopt one of the following strategies...

1. THE PRINCE HAL*

By the end of your first year at uni, convince your parents that you have turned into little more than a drunken, bone-idle good for nothing who is destined never to make anything of him/herself in life. Let them think that you have skipped all your lectures, failed to write your essays and have only been kept on at university as a case study into idiocy for a PhD Psychology graduate.

On no account say anything like, *'Ah yeah, it's easy. A first should be a doddle if I can be bothered to do a bit of work in the third year.'* In short, prepare your parents for the worst. Thus – when you do get your 2:2 they'll be positively relieved that you managed to pass at all. (And if you can convince them that, in your final year, you've matured into a half-decent human being you might get them to pay off some of your loan as well).

2. SCARFACE

Tell your folks endless grisly stories of students who have been driven over the edge by working too hard. Describe the brilliant maths scholar who got a First, but ended up having a nervous breakdown, a huge cocaine problem and converting to Hare Krishna. Tell the tale of Carl Vincent, the third year film student who went mad while studying 'The Shining' and garrotted every member of the Dungeons and Dragons Society with an A4 metal folder. Suggest that your third class honours degree was the price you paid for keeping your sanity.

3. HONEST JOE

As a last resort – tell all. Confess that you spent most of your time hanging around the bar, discussing the esoteric references in 'Buffy' with your mates, but you made some good friends, met people from all walks of life and have even learned to juggle. And who needs a degree anyway? Shakespeare didn't have one, and he was a clever man; neither did Einstein, or even Liam Gallagher (OK, bad example). But after your university experiences, tell them that you're finally ready to stand on your own two feet and face the world – but could you just borrow fifty quid to see you through the week?

*If you're not au fait with Henry the 4th Pt 1, the young Prince Hal acts like an idle buffoon throughout his teens, to his father's disappointment. But when eventually Hal becomes king he decides to act a bit more responsible and grown up, sending his father into such raptures over his son's 'transformation' that he buys him a Ferrari.

GRADUATION DAY

Make no bones about it – graduation is an ordeal. Sitting on a hard chair for three hours listening to a bunch of dignitaries in garish robes drone on is nobody's idea of a good time, but miss it, and chances are, you will forever carry the guilt and regret of a footballer who's scored three own goals in the World Cup Final.

The first thing you need for the graduation ceremony is a cap and gown, for which your university will normally offer a hire service. On no account should you buy them, unless there's absolutely no alternative (as the only way to recuperate the expense will be to spend the rest of your life going to every fancy dress party you are ever invited to as a Dickensian schoolmaster). You will also require a nice, smart suit or dress and a nifty pair of shoes, as going 'au naturel' underneath the gown is still frowned upon. Of course, you don't have to dress up – each year throws up a small minority who take great pride in turning up to the ceremony in jeans, sandals and Slipknot T-shirts as a form of rebellion. We don't recommend this – not only is it more naff than wearing the gowns themselves, but you will shame your poor parents and have to spend the rest of your life explaining yourself whenever anyone sees your graduation photo.

Finally, you will need something to keep yourself occupied during the ceremony's endless role-call of names, the three volumes of 'Lord of the Rings' should do the trick, or a Gameboy.

After the ceremony, everyone will rush into the foyer of the soulless complex which has been venue to the great occasion. This is where the fun of the day really starts. Your mum and dad, pole-axed by delight at seeing their dear one's day of glory, will wish to make small-talk with all your associates. Now you have to act quickly. At all costs steer them clear of anyone you've slept with in the last twelve months, anyone who has provided you with drugs on a regular basis (and is such a space cadet that they're likely to offer your parents ganja at a 'really competitive price') and anyone who absolutely cannot stop swearing for more than 45 seconds, even in the company of the Queen.

Instead, mingle with your more presentable alumni, hugging, kissing, and exchanging phone numbers, swearing that you'll keep in touch for the rest of your life, while your parents take umpteen snapshots of you with them, and their parents of them with you. The fact that you will never contact or have anything to do with these people ever again, should not in any way dampen the high-spirits of the occasion.

At long last you will have to face the horror of the official photograph in which, despite your best endeavours, you will definitely look like a grinning imbecile. This touching memento of your salad days will set your folks back twenty-odd quid and remain on their living room wall for the rest of eternity, embarrassing you whenever you take anyone to the family home. If you don't believe how bad these photos can be, then take a look at this guy on the right.

After the whole tortuous shebang is over, all that remains is for your parents (if you haven't by then already bankrupted them) to treat you to a nice meal at some up-market restaurant, and that's it. All done and dusted. Time for the real world now. The world of mortgages, income tax, water-rates, alimony, pensions, conferences, child-rearing, nervous breakdowns, redundancy, shift-work, divorce, credit card bills, Ikea catalogues, babysitters, thickening waistlines, early nights, early mornings, commuting, rush-hour, season-tickets, M.O.T.s, double-glazing, and back-trouble. You see, it really was the happiest time of your life.

NB. Quite the worst thing that can happen at graduation is for your parents to buy the video of the ceremony. Worse than the photo, which can at least be turned to the wall, this three hour long extravaganza could be played back to every hapless friend or lover you happen to introduce to your parents to for the next hundred years. Curiously though, there will come a time when you, with no prompting, will actually want to see this video yourself, but only when you are old, grey, wizened and bent, and wish to remind yourself of the days when your hair was blond and your tits didn't sag.

At 72 years old, Bob Grayson (above), is currently the UK's oldest student

HOW TO STAY AT UNIVERSITY FOREVER

If you decide that you really can't face life in the real world, and money is no object, you may choose to remain within the hallowed walls of academe for as long as you possibly can. The simplest way of doing this is by running the gamut of post-graduate courses, viz an MA, and PhD, before going on to become a probationary lecturer, a lecturer, and then finally, a professor. By these means you can cleverly avoid having to deal with anything pertaining to normal life. You will die happy at the age of 80, surrounded by unmarked essays and obscure tomes without once having had to endure the vagaries of everyday existence, such as sitting through a board meeting, lifting a heavy object or having to develop acceptable social skills.

Unfortunately, this path does require a modicum of application and academic ability. The MA (a one to two year full-time course specialising in a chosen field) can be quite hard graft, usually requiring something like a 20,000 word dissertation on whatever nonsense you've been studying. And to cap it all, if you don't get a 2:1 or First, it's very unlikely you'll get any funding for it.

The MA paves the way for the dreaded PhD, which can last anything from four to forty years, leaving you, at the end, burned out, depressed and overqualified, yet lacking the necessary work experience for any job other than lecturing.*

But don't be discouraged; there remain certain methods by which you can prolong your time at university by a good few years, thereby extending the holiday period and at the same time warding off the dreaded spectre of work and responsibility. These are delineated below.

1. THE STOP-START APPROACH

Year 1. First year of course
Year 2. Intermit – backpacking in India to 'find yourself'
Year 3. Complete second year
Year 4. Do sabbatical year as member of S.U.
Year 5. Intermit (again) – kibbutz in Israel
Year 6. Finals

2. THE COURSE SWAPPING/EXCHANGE YEAR GAMBIT

Year 1. Study first year of course in Engineering
Year 2. Change to Modern Language course – study first year
Year 3. Exchange year
Year 4. Switch to different Modern Language course (somewhere hotter, and with better surfing opportunities)
Year 5. Exchange year
Year 6. Switch to Business Studies
Year 7. Complete Second year
Year 8. Business placement at I.C.I.
Year 9. Switch back to Engineering, retaking your first year
Year 11. Finish degree
Year 12. Retire

3. MOVE TO BRIGHTON

By far and away the coolest city in the UK, Brighton offers the biggest Arts festival in England, a large gay community, a thriving student/ club scene and, of course, a beach. Home of Fatboyslim, Skint Records, half the cast of Eastenders and errr.....Chris Eubank, this is a young, vibrant, party town where people visit for a weekend and end up never returning home. So, if you're unsure as to what you want to do after leaving but know you want to get away from Cardiff/ Southampton/ Stoke-on-Trent etc, then Brighton is a perfect place to lay your hat for a year or two, meet some good people, get an easy job and work out what to do next. And we can even recommend a great guide book.

*OK, a bit of a generalisation

DON'T SUFFER IN SILENCE

While it's true to say many students know exactly what their career will be upon graduating, it's equally true to point out that plenty more are none the wiser as to what it is they want to do with themselves at the end of their third year than they were at the start of their first. If you fall into the second category, don't panic. Leaf through the employment sections of broadsheets to look for inspiration; visit the jobs fairs and 'milk rounds' recruitment shin-digs that your university should lay on; talk to as many different people as possible, and most importantly, visit your Occupational Advisory Service. Most universities have them, and they are an invaluable counselling and resource centre for the terminally directionless.

Alternatively, why not take a 'year out' after graduating? Go travelling, work abroad, try VSO – seeing a bit more of the world can do wonders to help you discover your true talents. Failing all that, if you think you've got what it takes to write a Cheeky Guide and don't mind working for less than the minimum wage, drop us an e-mail…

ANSWERS PAGE

Tv Nostalgia Quiz (page 15)

1) 'I love it when a plan comes together.' and Boy George
2) That naughty witch 'Amy'.
3) We've no way of knowing whether you can actually whistle the theme, unless you record it and e-mail it to us as an m-peg. But please don't. But we can reliably inform you that the voices were provided by Tim Brooke-Taylor, Bill Oddie and Graham Garden of the Goodies.
4) He hasn't got any legs!
5) Peter Davison
6) Cut-Throat Jake. Pugwash was alleged to mean blowjob in French.
7) Hysteriocal blindness
8) the Rocky Horror Picture Show
9) Seventies sit-com 'Terry and June' links them. Terry did Penfold's voice, while June Whitfield played Edina's mum.
10) 'By the power of Greyskull'
11) Matthew Broderick
12) Buster Rhymes
13) 'God bless Hookey Street'. Which offered: no income tax, no V.A.T., no money back, no guarantee.
14) Spitting
15) a)
16) Hilly and Queeg
17) Despite resembling a female version of Fungus the Bogeyman, she was supposed to be the most desirable woman in the Galaxy.
18) Tex Mex
19) Helicopter
20) That's Trev on the left…..no hang on, that's Simon. No, no it's Trev on the right…….or is it?

Student Icons Quiz

1) Homer Simpson
2) David Beckham
3) Che Guevara
4) Dali
5) Oscar Wilde
6) Madonna
7) Buffy Ann Summers
8) Sean Connery
9) Buddha
10) John Lennon
11) Bruce Lee

Other Cheeky Titles

Thoroughly researched and packed with anecdotes and humour, the Cheeky Guide to Oxford will take you on a rollercoaster ride through this world-famous city. Featuring the usual Cheeky trademarks, the book provides information on the city's famous music scene, its vast array of drinking establishments, restaurants, shops, museums and shoddy selection of nightclubs. Peppered with cartoons and illustrations by local artists, this guide really does give an insider's perspective on Oxford and even includes information on famous movie locations and a spotters guide to local celebrities and eccentrics.

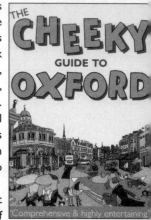

"Comprehensive & highly entertaining"

Of course Oxford wouldn't be the same without the students, and the Cheeky Guide includes an A-Z of the many ridiculous University traditions, from tortoise races to hitting Marks and Spencers with sticks, as well as providing detailed information, fruity stories and map to some of the city's most celebrated colleges. Whether you're staying in Oxford for a weekend, three years or a lifetime, this book is a must.

The Cheeky Guide to Brighton will take you on a factual but comic journey to the many corners of this celebrated town, taking in its famous nightlife, gay scene and exotic shops, as well as lesser-known features such as llama-trekking and where to contact the dead. Expect a wealth of funny stories and bizarre characters, as the book dishes out such essential information as where to eat the best fish and chips, where to spot your favourite celebrity, and what to do in an emergency, should you find yourself at Brighton Marina.

"Captures the spirit of Brighton perfectly" – Skint Records

This second edition comes with over 500 new entries, more cartoons and photos, four new chapters, (including the much-awaited section on local eccentrics) and even a free 'scratch and sniff' guide to the best local restaurants.

Coming Soon from Cheeky Guides

The **Cheeky Guide** to **Love**

The **Cheeky Guide** to **Brighton** (third edition)

The **Cheeky Guide** to **Oxford** (second edition)

The **Cheeky Guide** to **Sex**

+ four more titles in 2003

INDEX

Y

Z